Measuring National Well-being 2017

CD containing supplementary articles and reference tables relating to:

Chapter 2 - Personal well-being in the UK - Tables

Chapter 4 - International Comparisons, 2017 - Tables

Chapter 5 - Economic Well-being - Tables

Chapter 7 - Life in the UK 2017 - Tables

Chapter 8 - Young People's Well-being: 2017 - Tables

Chapter 9 - Effects of taxes and benefits on UK household income: financial year ending 2016 - Tables

Chapter 10 - Social capital in the UK: May 2017 - Tables

Supplementary article 1 and tables - UK Environmental Accounts, 2017

Supplementary article 2 and tables- Persistent poverty in the UK and EU: 2015

Measuring National Well-being 2017

In replacement of 'Social Trends'

The data displayed in this document was correct at the time of downloading 13/12/17

Source: Office of National Statistics reproduced under the Open Government Licence V3.0

Measures of National Well-being

Monitors and reports how the UK is doing by producing accepted and trusted measures for the different areas of life that matter most to the UK public.

For more information, or to provide feedback on the dashboard please contact: qualityoflife@ons.gsi.gov.uk

The dashboard provides a visual overview of the data and can be explored by the areas of life (domains) or by the direction of change. It supports the Measuring National Well-being programme which provides a more detailed look at life in the UK

We assess change over a short term (1 year) and long term (3 year) basis. Change is assessed over a 1 year basis in the dashboard below, however trend information can be found below in the graphs for each indicator.

The latest update provides a broadly positive picture of life in the UK, with the majority of indicators either improving or staying the same over the 1 year period. Areas of life that are improving include: satisfaction with our lives, jobs, health and leisure time. One area deteriorated over the 1 year – waste from households that is recycled.

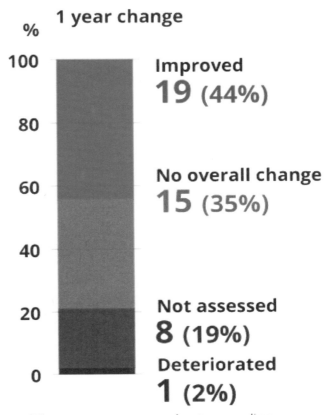

% 1 year change

100

80

Improved
19 (44%)

60

No overall change
15 (35%)

40

20

Not assessed
8 (19%)

0

Deteriorated
1 (2%)

*Figures may not sum due to rounding

All indicators (43)   ▲ Positive Change (19)   ▼ Negative Change (1)   ◆ No Change (15)   ▬ Not assessed (8)

Personal Well-being

Includes individual's feelings of satisfaction with life, whether they feel the things they do in their life are worthwhile and their positive and negative emotions.

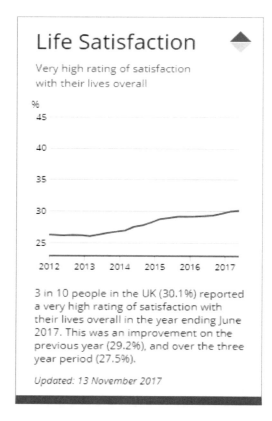

Life Satisfaction

Very high rating of satisfaction with their lives overall

3 in 10 people in the UK (30.1%) reported a very high rating of satisfaction with their lives overall in the year ending June 2017. This was an improvement on the previous year (29.2%), and over the three year period (27.5%).

Updated: 13 November 2017

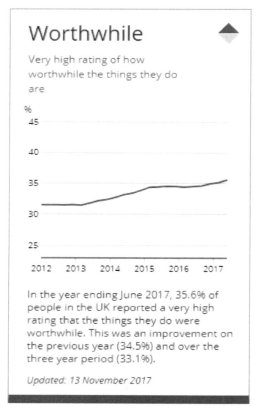

Worthwhile

Very high rating of how worthwhile the things they do are

In the year ending June 2017, 35.6% of people in the UK reported a very high rating that the things they do were worthwhile. This was an improvement on the previous year (34.5%) and over the three year period (33.1%).

Updated: 13 November 2017

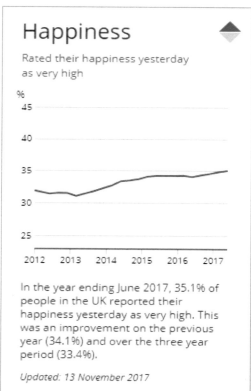

Happiness

Rated their happiness yesterday as very high

In the year ending June 2017, 35.1% of people in the UK reported their happiness yesterday as very high. This was an improvement on the previous year (34.1%) and over the three year period (33.4%).

Updated: 13 November 2017

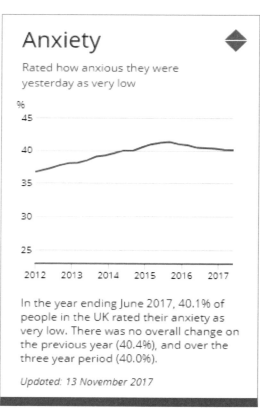

Anxiety

Rated how anxious they were yesterday as very low

In the year ending June 2017, 40.1% of people in the UK rated their anxiety as very low. There was no overall change on the previous year (40.4%), and over the three year period (40.0%).

Updated: 13 November 2017

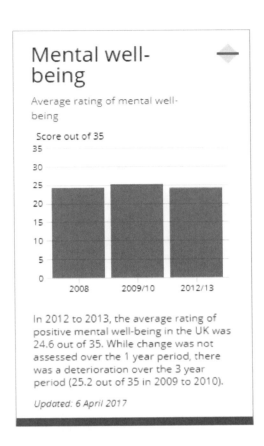

Mental well-being

Average rating of mental well-being

Score out of 35

In 2012 to 2013, the average rating of positive mental well-being in the UK was 24.6 out of 35. While change was not assessed over the 1 year period, there was a deterioration over the 3 year period (25.2 out of 35 in 2009 to 2010).

Updated: 6 April 2017

Our Relationships

Positive relationships have one of the biggest impacts on our quality of life and happiness. This domain includes satisfaction with personal relationships and feelings of loneliness.

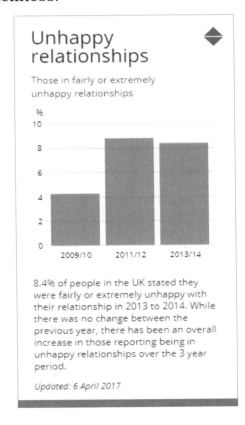

Unhappy relationships

Those in fairly or extremely unhappy relationships

%

8.4% of people in the UK stated they were fairly or extremely unhappy with their relationship in 2013 to 2014. While there was no change between the previous year, there has been an overall increase in those reporting being in unhappy relationships over the 3 year period.

Updated: 6 April 2017

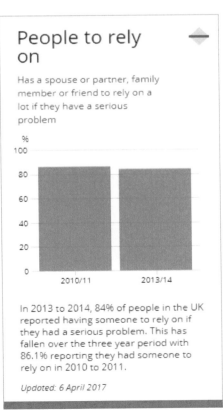

People to rely on

Has a spouse or partner, family member or friend to rely on a lot if they have a serious problem

%

In 2013 to 2014, 84% of people in the UK reported having someone to rely on if they had a serious problem. This has fallen over the three year period with 86.1% reporting they had someone to rely on in 2010 to 2011.

Updated: 6 April 2017

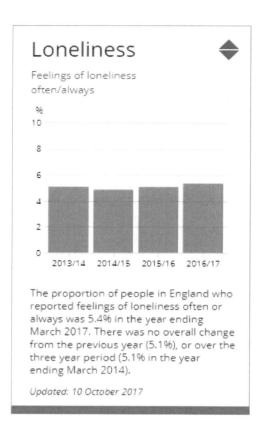

Loneliness

Feelings of loneliness often/always

The proportion of people in England who reported feelings of loneliness often or always was 5.4% in the year ending March 2017. There was no overall change from the previous year (5.1%), or over the three year period (5.1% in the year ending March 2014).

Updated: 10 October 2017

Health

An individual's health is recognised as an important component of their well-being. This domain contains both subjective and objective measures of physical and mental health.

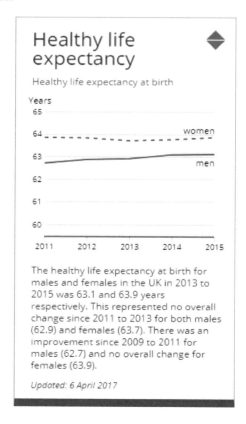

Healthy life expectancy

Healthy life expectancy at birth

The healthy life expectancy at birth for males and females in the UK in 2013 to 2015 was 63.1 and 63.9 years respectively. This represented no overall change since 2011 to 2013 for both males (62.9) and females (63.7). There was an improvement since 2009 to 2011 for males (62.7) and no overall change for females (63.9).

Updated: 6 April 2017

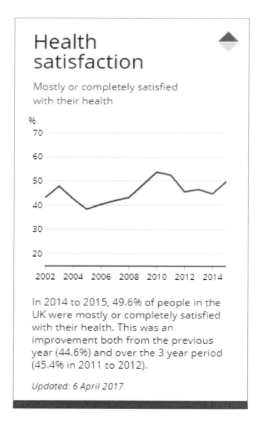

Health satisfaction

Mostly or completely satisfied with their health

In 2014 to 2015, 49.6% of people in the UK were mostly or completely satisfied with their health. This was an improvement both from the previous year (44.6%) and over the 3 year period (45.4% in 2011 to 2012).

Updated: 6 April 2017

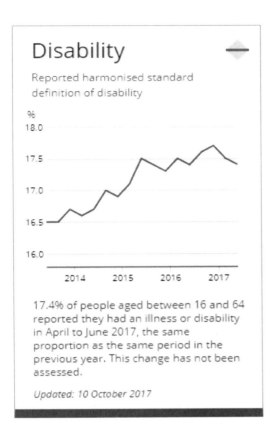

Disability

Reported harmonised standard definition of disability

17.4% of people aged between 16 and 64 reported they had an illness or disability in April to June 2017, the same proportion as the same period in the previous year. This change has not been assessed.

Updated: 10 October 2017

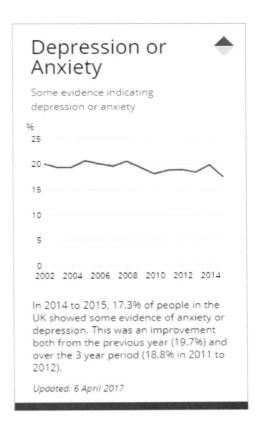

Depression or Anxiety

Some evidence indicating depression or anxiety

In 2014 to 2015, 17.3% of people in the UK showed some evidence of anxiety or depression. This was an improvement both from the previous year (19.7%) and over the 3 year period (18.8% in 2011 to 2012).

Updated: 6 April 2017

What we do

Includes work and leisure activities and the balance between them.

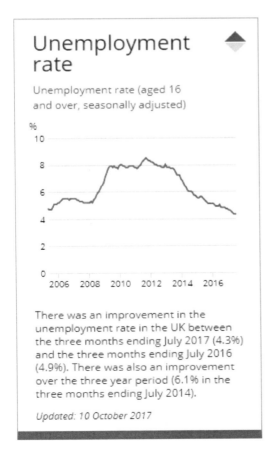

Unemployment rate

Unemployment rate (aged 16 and over, seasonally adjusted)

There was an improvement in the unemployment rate in the UK between the three months ending July 2017 (4.3%) and the three months ending July 2016 (4.9%). There was also an improvement over the three year period (6.1% in the three months ending July 2014).

Updated: 10 October 2017

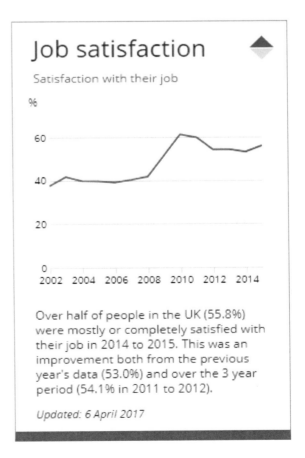

Job satisfaction

Satisfaction with their job

Over half of people in the UK (55.8%) were mostly or completely satisfied with their job in 2014 to 2015. This was an improvement both from the previous year's data (53.0%) and over the 3 year period (54.1% in 2011 to 2012).

Updated: 6 April 2017

Satisfaction with leisure time

Satisfaction with their amount of leisure time

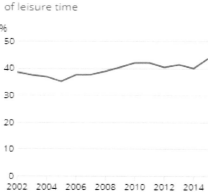

The proportion of people in the UK who were mostly or completely satisfied with their amount of leisure time was 43.7% in 2014 to 2015, a improvement from the previous year (40.0%) and over the 3 year period (40.4% in 2011 to 2012).

Updated: 6 April 2017

Volunteering

Volunteered more than once in the last 12 months

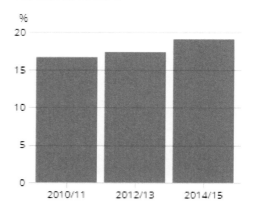

Almost 1 in 5 people in the UK (19.1%) reported that they had participated in some kind of volunteering more than once in the last year in 2014 to 2015. This was an improvement from the previous year (17.4%) from 2010 to 2011 (16.7%).

Updated: 6 April 2017

Art and culture participation

Engaged with/participated in arts or cultural activity at least 3 times a year

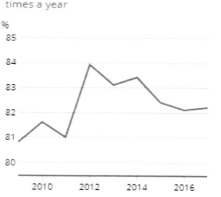

In the year ending March 2017, just over 8 in 10 people in England (82.2%) had participated in an arts or cultural activity at least three times in the past year. This has remained unchanged on both the one year and three year basis (82.1% and 83.4% respectively).

Updated: 10 October 2017

Sports participation

Adult participation in 30 mins of moderate intensity sport once per week

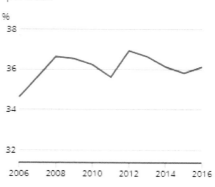

In the year ending September 2016, 36.1% of people in England participated in 30 minutes of moderate intensity sport, once per week. While there was no overall change since the previous year (35.8%) there was a deterioration over the 3 year period (36.6% in the year ending September 2013).

Updated: 6 April 2017

Where we live

Reflects an individual's dwelling, their local environment and the type of community in which they live. Measures include having a safe, clean and pleasant environment, access to facilities and being part of a cohesive community.

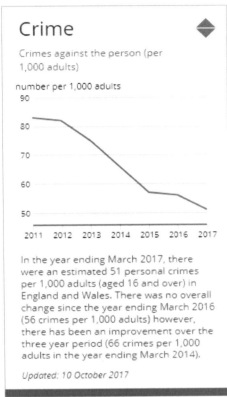

Crime

Crimes against the person (per 1,000 adults)

In the year ending March 2017, there were an estimated 51 personal crimes per 1,000 adults (aged 16 and over) in England and Wales. There was no overall change since the year ending March 2016 (56 crimes per 1,000 adults) however, there has been an improvement over the three year period (66 crimes per 1,000 adults in the year ending March 2014).

Updated: 10 October 2017

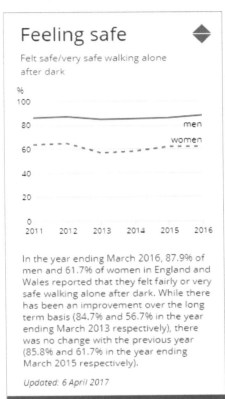

Feeling safe

Felt safe/very safe walking alone after dark

In the year ending March 2016, 87.9% of men and 61.7% of women in England and Wales reported that they felt fairly or very safe walking alone after dark. While there has been an improvement over the long term basis (84.7% and 56.7% in the year ending March 2013 respectively), there was no change with the previous year (85.8% and 61.7% in the year ending March 2015 respectively).

Updated: 6 April 2017

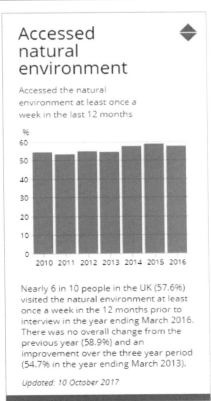

Accessed natural environment

Accessed the natural environment at least once a week in the last 12 months

Nearly 6 in 10 people in the UK (57.6%) visited the natural environment at least once a week in the 12 months prior to interview in the year ending March 2016. There was no overall change from the previous year (58.9%) and an improvement over the three year period (54.7% in the year ending March 2013).

Updated: 10 October 2017

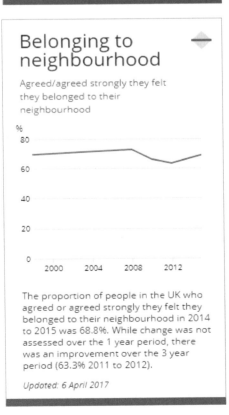

Belonging to neighbourhood

Agreed/agreed strongly they felt they belonged to their neighbourhood

The proportion of people in the UK who agreed or agreed strongly they felt they belonged to their neighbourhood in 2014 to 2015 was 68.8%. While change was not assessed over the 1 year period, there was an improvement over the 3 year period (63.3% 2011 to 2012).

Updated: 6 April 2017

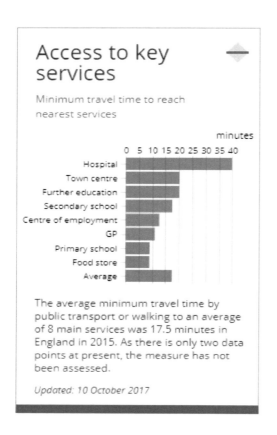

Access to key services

Minimum travel time to reach nearest services

minutes

The average minimum travel time by public transport or walking to an average of 8 main services was 17.5 minutes in England in 2015. As there is only two data points at present, the measure has not been assessed.

Updated: 10 October 2017

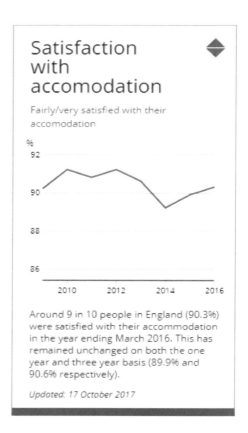

Satisfaction with accomodation

Fairly/very satisfied with their accomodation

Around 9 in 10 people in England (90.3%) were satisfied with their accommodation in the year ending March 2016. This has remained unchanged on both the one year and three year basis (89.9% and 90.6% respectively).

Updated: 17 October 2017

Personal Finance

Includes household income and wealth, its distribution and stability.

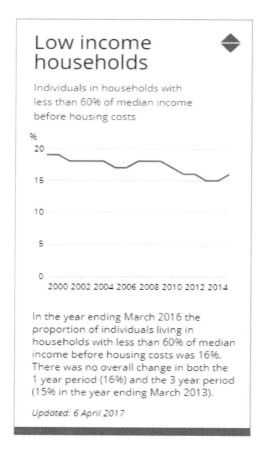

Low income households

Individuals in households with less than 60% of median income before housing costs

In the year ending March 2016 the proportion of individuals living in households with less than 60% of median income before housing costs was 16%. There was no overall change in both the 1 year period (16%) and the 3 year period (15% in the year ending March 2013).

Updated: 6 April 2017

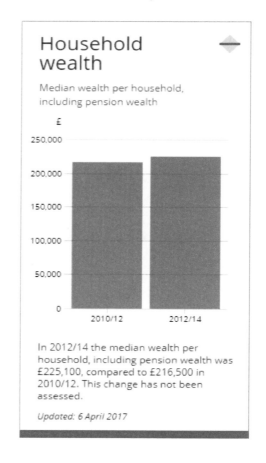

Household wealth

Median wealth per household, including pension wealth

In 2012/14 the median wealth per household, including pension wealth was £225,100, compared to £216,500 in 2010/12. This change has not been assessed.

Updated: 6 April 2017

Household income

Real median houshold income

£ per year (2015/16 prices)

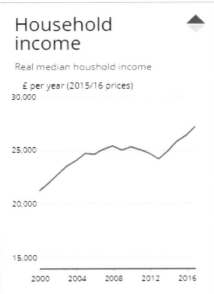

Real median household income was £26,332 in the UK in the year ending March 2016, an improvement over the one year period (£25,768) and over the three year period (£24,137). Data for year ending March 2017 have been included in the chart, but is a provisional estimate and has not been used for the assessment of change.

Updated: 10 October 2017

Satisfied with household income

Mostly or completely satisfied with the income of their household

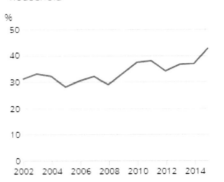

In 2014 to 2015, 42.8% of people in the UK were mostly or completely satisfied with the income of their household. This was an improvement both from the previous year's data (36.8%) and over the 3 year period (34.0% in 2011 to 2012).

Updated: 6 April 2017

Difficulty managing financially

Report finding it quite or very difficult to get by financially

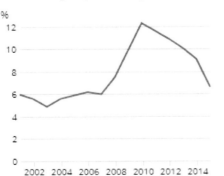

In 2014 to 2015, 6.6% of people in the UK were reporting finding it quite or very difficult to get by financially. This was an improvement both from the previous year's data (9.1%) and over the 3 year period (10.9% in 2011 to 2012).

Updated: 6 April 2017

Economy

Provides an important contextual domain for national well-being and includes measures of inflation and public sector debt.

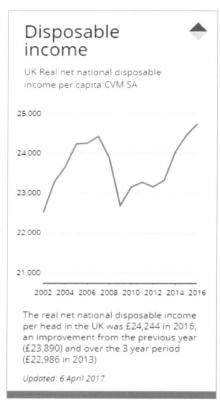

Disposable income

UK Real net national disposable income per capita CVM SA

The real net national disposable income per head in the UK was £24,244 in 2016, an improvement from the previous year (£23,890) and over the 3 year period (£22,986 in 2013)

Updated: 6 April 2017

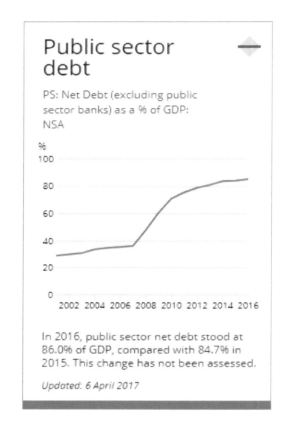

Public sector debt

PS: Net Debt (excluding public sector banks) as a % of GDP: NSA

In 2016, public sector net debt stood at 86.0% of GDP, compared with 84.7% in 2015. This change has not been assessed.

Updated: 6 April 2017

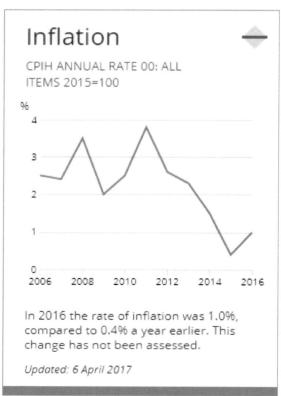

Inflation

CPIH ANNUAL RATE 00: ALL ITEMS 2015=100

In 2016 the rate of inflation was 1.0%, compared to 0.4% a year earlier. This change has not been assessed.

Updated: 6 April 2017

Education and Skills

Includes aspects of education and the stock of human capital in the labour market with some more information about levels of educational achievement and skills.

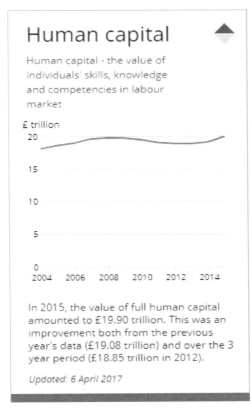

Human capital

Human capital - the value of individuals' skills, knowledge and competencies in labour market

£ trillion

In 2015, the value of full human capital amounted to £19.90 trillion. This was an improvement both from the previous year's data (£19.08 trillion) and over the 3 year period (£18.85 trillion in 2012).

Updated: 6 April 2017

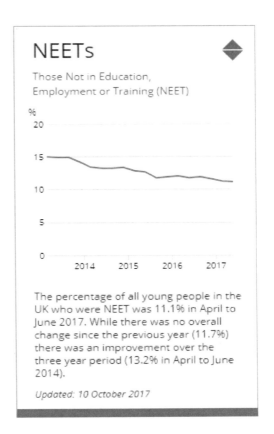

NEETs

Those Not in Education, Employment or Training (NEET)

%

The percentage of all young people in the UK who were NEET was 11.1% in April to June 2017. While there was no overall change since the previous year (11.7%) there was an improvement over the three year period (13.2% in April to June 2014).

Updated: 10 October 2017

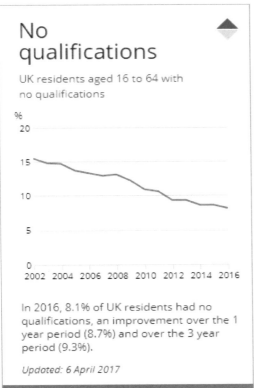

No qualifications

UK residents aged 16 to 64 with no qualifications

%

In 2016, 8.1% of UK residents had no qualifications, an improvement over the 1 year period (8.7%) and over the 3 year period (9.3%).

Updated: 6 April 2017

Governance

Includes democracy and trust in institutions

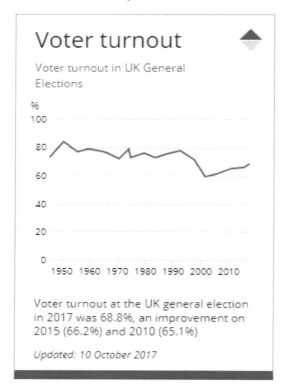

Voter turnout

Voter turnout in UK General Elections

%

Voter turnout at the UK general election in 2017 was 68.8%, an improvement on 2015 (66.2%) and 2010 (65.1%)

Updated: 10 October 2017

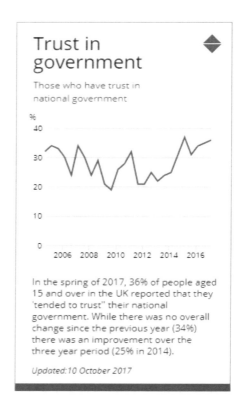

Trust in government

Those who have trust in national government

%

In the spring of 2017, 36% of people aged 15 and over in the UK reported that they 'tended to trust" their national government. While there was no overall change since the previous year (34%) there was an improvement over the three year period (25% in 2014).

Updated:10 October 2017

Environment

Reflects areas such as climate change, the natural environment and the effects our activities have on the global environment.

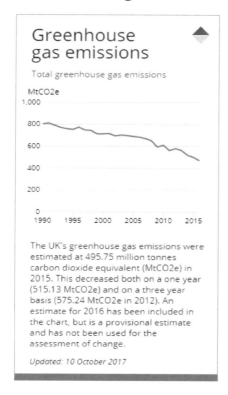

Greenhouse gas emissions

Total greenhouse gas emissions

MtCO2e

The UK's greenhouse gas emissions were estimated at 495.75 million tonnes carbon dioxide equivalent (MtCO2e) in 2015. This decreased both on a one year (515.13 MtCO2e) and on a three year basis (575.24 MtCO2e in 2012). An estimate for 2016 has been included in the chart, but is a provisional estimate and has not been used for the assessment of change.

Updated: 10 October 2017

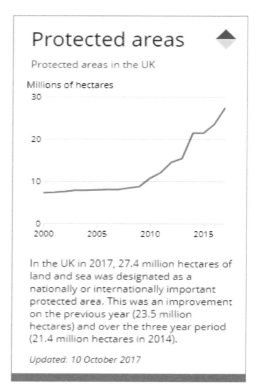

Protected areas

Protected areas in the UK

Millions of hectares

In the UK in 2017, 27.4 million hectares of land and sea was designated as a nationally or internationally important protected area. This was an improvement on the previous year (23.5 million hectares) and over the three year period (21.4 million hectares in 2014).

Updated: 10 October 2017

Renewable energy

Energy consumed within the UK from renewable sources

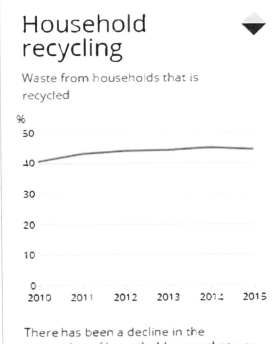

8.9% of energy consumption came from renewable sources in 2016. This has improved over both the short term (8.2% in 2015) and the long term (5.7% in 2013).

Updated: 10 October 2017

Household recycling

Waste from households that is recycled

There has been a decline in the proportion of household waste that was recycled between 2014 and 2015 (44.9% and 44.3% respectively).

Updated: 6 April 2017

Statistical bulletin

Personal well-being in the UK: Oct 2015 to Sept 2016

Estimates of life satisfaction, whether you feel the things you do in life are worthwhile, happiness and anxiety in the UK and for constituent countries for the period October 2015 to September 2016.

| Contact:
Eleanor Rees
QualityOfLife@ons.gsi.gov.uk
+44 (0)1633 651631 | Release date:
13 January 2017 | Next release:
To be announced |

Table of contents

1 . Main points

Average ratings of anxiety increased slightly between the years ending September 2015 and 2016.

Average life satisfaction, worthwhile and happiness ratings were unchanged between the years ending September 2015 and 2016.

Wales was the only country to have higher anxiety ratings than the UK average.

2 . Statistician's quote

"At a time when economic measures are generally improving, this is not necessarily reflected in how people tell us they are feeling about their lives. Whilst it is too early to say why anxiety ratings have increased slightly and why life satisfaction, happiness and worthwhile ratings have levelled off in the past 12 months, we know from our previous research that factors impacting most on people's personal well-being include health, work situation and relationship status. Publishing this data quarterly, rather than annually, means we can monitor these trends more closely."

Matthew Steel, Office for National Statistics.

3 . How we measure personal well-being

Since 2011, we have asked personal well-being questions to adults in the UK, to better understand how they feel about their lives. This release presents headline results for the year ending September 2016, together with how things have changed over the last 5 years.

The 4 personal well-being questions are:

- overall, how satisfied are you with your life nowadays?

- overall, to what extent do you feel the things you do in your life are worthwhile?

- overall, how happy did you feel yesterday?

- overall, how anxious did you feel yesterday?

People are asked to respond on a scale of 0 to 10, where 0 is "not at all" and 10 is "completely". We produce estimates of the mean ratings for all 4 personal well-being questions, as well as their distributions, using the thresholds.

4 . Things you need to know about this release

For the first time we are presenting annual estimates of personal well-being on a rolling quarterly basis. These estimates provide a timelier picture of how the UK population are feeling and allows us to monitor how well-being is changing in the UK more frequently.

16

The annual reporting period for this release includes only 3 months worth of data for the period after the EU referendum. The first release to include data solely for the period after the referendum and therefore enabling pre- and post-referendum comparisons, will be July 2016 to June 2017, and will be published in autumn 2017.

We are able to compare with the same period last year (October 2014 to September 2015) to identify any changes that may have occurred. However, we are not able to reliably compare with the preceding period (July 2015 to June 2016) as they include overlapping time periods which contain the same data.

We welcome feedback on these changes. Please contact the Quality of Life team (QualityOfLife@ons.gsi.gov.uk) with any comments or suggestions, including your views on improvements we might make.

5 . Self-reported anxiety rises

The average (mean) ratings across the 4 measures of personal well-being in the year ending September 2016 were:

- 7.7 out of 10 for life satisfaction

- 7.8 out of 10 for feeling that what you do in life is worthwhile

- 7.5 out of 10 for happiness yesterday

- 2.9 out of 10 for anxiety yesterday

Average ratings of anxiety increased when comparing the years ending September 2015 and 2016 (Figure 1b). Over the same period, ratings of life satisfaction, feeling that things done in life are worthwhile and happiness were unchanged (Figure 1a).

Despite the recent increase in anxiety, average ratings remained lower compared with the years ending September 2012 and 2013. Although we have not seen year-on-year improvements in life satisfaction, worthwhile or happiness, average ratings remain at their highest level since we began collecting the data in 2011.

Figure 1a: Average life satisfaction, worthwhile and happiness ratings, year ending March 2012 to year ending September 2016

United Kingdom

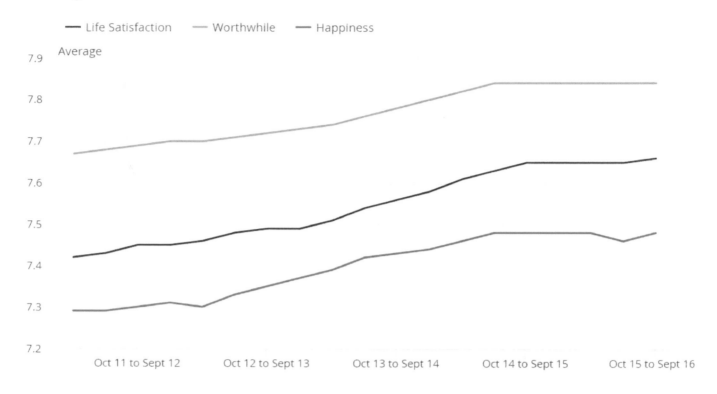

Source: Annual Population Survey, Office for National Statistics

Notes:

1. Chart axis does not start at 0.

2. Year ending March 2012 was the first year of data collection.

Figure 1b: Average anxiety ratings, year ending March 2012 to year ending September 2016

United Kingdom

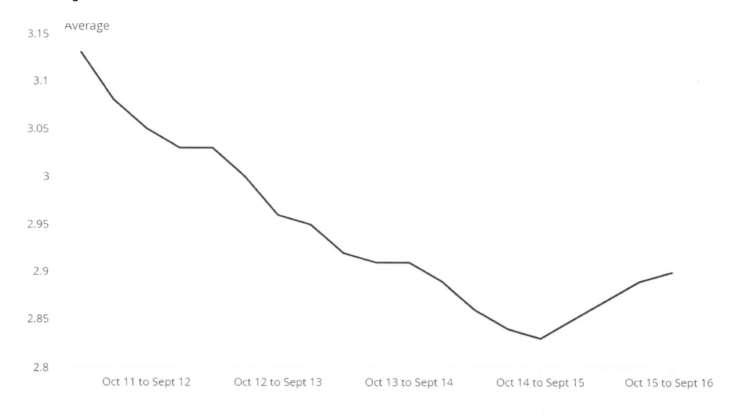

Source: Annual Population Survey, Office for National Statistics

Notes:

1. Chart axis does not start at 0.

2. Year ending March 2012 was the first year of data collection.

To better understand the increase in anxiety in the UK, Figure 2 shows the change in reported anxiety between the years ending September 2015 and September 2016. There has been both a reduction in those reporting very low anxiety and an increase in those reporting high anxiety.

Figure 2: Proportions reporting very low, low, medium and high, years ending September 2015 and September 2016

United Kingdom

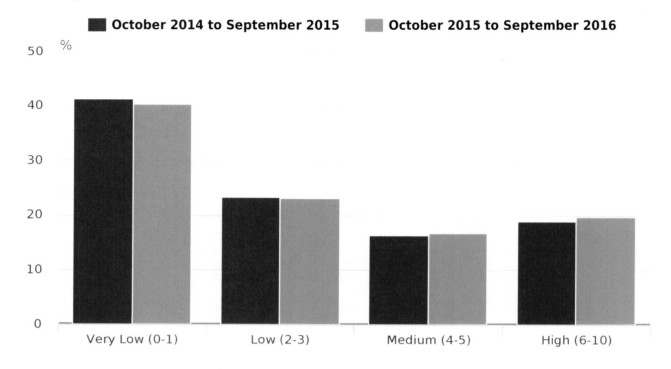

Source: Annual Population Survey, Office for National Statistics

6 . Personal well-being ratings continue to be highest in Northern Ireland

Northern Ireland continues to have the highest personal well-being ratings when compared with the other constituent countries of the UK (Figure 3).

Ratings of life satisfaction, worthwhile and happiness in Northern Ireland are higher than those in England, Wales, Scotland and the UK average.

Wales has higher anxiety than the UK average. Conversely, Northern Ireland has lower anxiety than the UK average.

Figure 3: Difference in anxiety ratings compared with UK average ratings, year ending September 2016

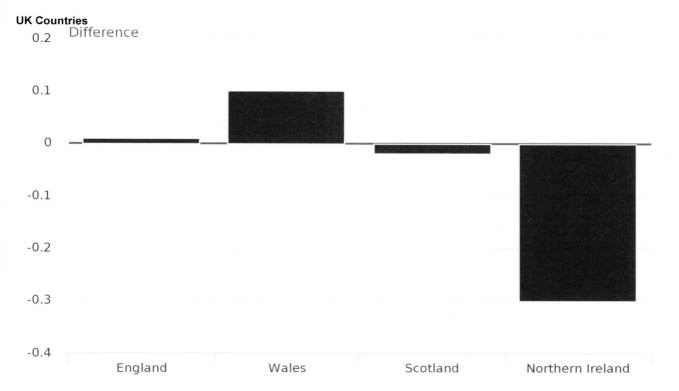

Source: Annual Population Survey, Office for National Statistics

It is also important to consider how personal well-being ratings have changed for each country across the years; we have been collecting the data to see whether there is a differing picture (Figure 4).

Figure 4: Average life satisfaction ratings, years ending March 2012 to September 2016

UK countries

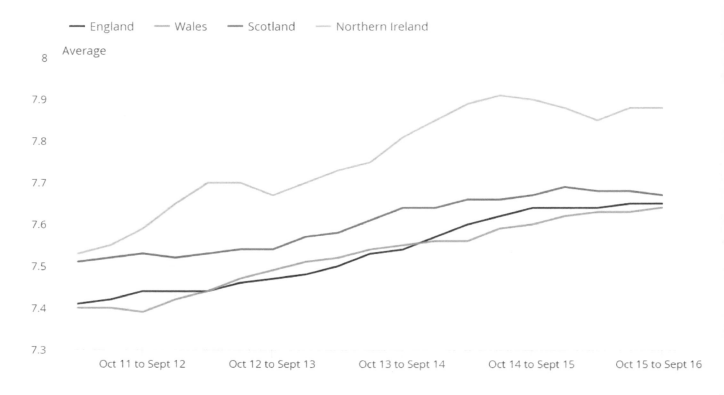

Source: Annual Population Survey, Office for National Statistics

Notes:

1. Chart axis does not start at 0.

2. Year ending March 2012 was the first year of data collection.

In England and in Wales there were no year-on-year improvements between the years ending September 2015 and September 2016 for life satisfaction, worthwhile and happiness. However, there was an increase in anxiety between these 2 time periods.

Scotland and Northern Ireland have not seen a significant change in any of the well-being measures between the years ending September 2015 and September 2016.

7 . What may explain these results

In previous research we identified people's self-reported health as the most important factor associated with personal well-being, followed by their work situation and relationship status.

During the year ending September 2016, the unemployment rate has continued to fall and GDP per head has increased. There has been a mixed picture in health outcomes for the period 2013 to 2015. Life expectancy has continued to increase for both males and females. However, both the proportion of life spent disability-free and the proportion of life spent in good health have fallen between 2009 to 2011 and 2013 to 2015, for both males and females.

It is possible the lack of improvement in 3 of the 4 personal well-being measures and increase in anxiety in this period compared with this period last year could be associated with the uncertainties surrounding governance, the economy and global security. For example, the latest period covered by these data included campaigning for the EU referendum, as well as 3 months post-EU referendum. In addition there was severe flooding across parts of the UK and numerous terror attacks around the world.

These results may also be reflecting people's thoughts and feelings about the future, where an Ipsos Mori poll in February 2016 showed that 54% of people believed that today's youth would have a worse quality of life than their parent's generation. This was up from 35% in 2011 and 12% in 2003.

8 . Links to related statistics

Personal well-being in the UK: 2015 to 2016

Personal well-being in the UK: local authority update, 2015 to 2016

Measuring national well-being in the UK, domains and measures: Sept 2016

Measuring National Well-being: At what age is Personal Well-being the highest?

Measuring National Well-being, What matters most to Personal Well-being?

Economic Well-being: Quarter 3 July to September 2016

Social capital across the UK: 2011 to 2012

Health State Expectancies, UK: 2013 to 2015

9 . Quality and methodology

1. The <u>Personal Well-being in the UK Quality and Methodology Information document</u> contains important information on:

   - the strengths and limitations of the data

   - the quality of the output: including the accuracy of the data and how it compares with related data

   - uses and users

   - how the output was created

2. Labelling of thresholds

Table 1: Labelling of threshold

Life satisfaction, worthwhile and happiness scores		Anxiety scores	
Response on an 11 point scale	Label	Response on an 11 point scale	Label
0 – 4	Low	0 – 1	Very low
5 – 6	Medium	2 – 3	Low
7 – 8	High	4 – 5	Medium
9 – 10	Very high	6 – 10	High

Source: Office for National Statistics

3. All the differences noted in the text are statistically significant. The statistical significance of differences are approximate because they are determined on the basis of non-overlapping confidence intervals. This method provides a conservative estimate of statistical significance, which may result in estimates that are statistically significantly different to one another being assessed as not.

Contact details for this statistical bulletin

Eleanor Rees

QualityOfLife@ons.gsi.gov.uk

Telephone: +44 (0)1633 651631

Statistical bulletin

Personal well-being in the UK: Jan to Dec 2016

Estimates of personal well-being for UK and countries of the UK for the year ending December 2016.

Contact:
Eleanor Rees
QualityOfLife@ons.gsi.gov.uk
+44 (0)1633 651631

Release date:
21 April 2017

Next release:
To be announced

Table of contents

1 . Main points

- No change in personal well-being ratings for the UK overall between years ending December 2015 and 2016.

- Anxiety ratings increased slightly in England but fell in Northern Ireland between years ending December 2015 and 2016.

2 . Statistician's quote

"Today's figures show there are no changes in personal well–being ratings at a UK level. However, average ratings of life satisfaction, feeling things done in life are worthwhile and happiness remain at their highest since we began collecting this data in 2011. There is a different picture at a country level, with self–reported anxiety improving in Northern Ireland but getting slightly worse in England over the past year.

"Whilst it is too early to say why this is, we know from our prior research that factors impacting on people's well–being include a person's sense of choice and contentment with their situation, along with health, job status and relationship status."

Matthew Steel, Office for National Statistics

3 . How we measure personal well-being

Since 2011, we have asked personal well-being questions to adults aged 16 and over in the UK, to better understand how they feel about their lives. This release presents headline results for the year ending December 2016, together with how things have changed over the last 5 years.

The four personal well-being questions are:

- overall, how satisfied are you with your life nowadays?

- overall, to what extent do you feel the things you do in your life are worthwhile?

- overall, how happy did you feel yesterday?

- overall, how anxious did you feel yesterday?

People are asked to respond on a scale of 0 to 10, where 0 is "not at all" and 10 is "completely". We produce estimates of the mean ratings for all four personal well-being questions, as well as their distributions, using thresholds.

4 . Things you need to know about this release

Annual estimates of personal well-being have been presented on a rolling quarterly basis since January 2017. These estimates provide a timelier picture of how the UK population are feeling and allow us to monitor how well-being is changing in the UK more frequently.

The annual reporting period for this release includes 6 months worth of data before and 6 months worth of data after the EU referendum. The first release to include data solely for the period after the referendum, and therefore enabling pre- and post-referendum comparisons, will be July 2016 to June 2017, which will be published in autumn 2017.

We are able to compare with the same period last year (January 2015 to December 2015) to identify any changes that may have occurred. However, we are not able to reliably compare with the preceding period (October 2015 to September 2016) as they include overlapping time periods that contain the same data.

We are always looking for ways to improve our releases and make them more useful and helpful. Please contact the Quality of Life team via email at QualityOfLife@ons.gsi.gov.uk with any comments or suggestions, including your views on improvements we might make.

5 . No change in personal well-being ratings for the UK overall

The average (mean) ratings across the four measures of personal well-being in the year ending December 2016 were:

- 7.7 out of 10 for life satisfaction

- 7.9 out of 10 for feeling that what you do in life is worthwhile

- 7.5 out of 10 for happiness yesterday

- 2.9 out of 10 for anxiety yesterday

When comparing the years ending December 2015 and December 2016, there has been no statistically significant change in any of the four personal well-being measures for the UK overall, as shown in Figures 1a and 1b. Despite this, average ratings of life satisfaction, worthwhile and happiness remain at their highest level since we began collecting the data in 2011. Average anxiety ratings are also lower compared with the years ending December 2012 and 2013.

Figure 1a: Average life satisfaction, worthwhile and happiness ratings, year ending March 2012 to year ending December 2016

UK

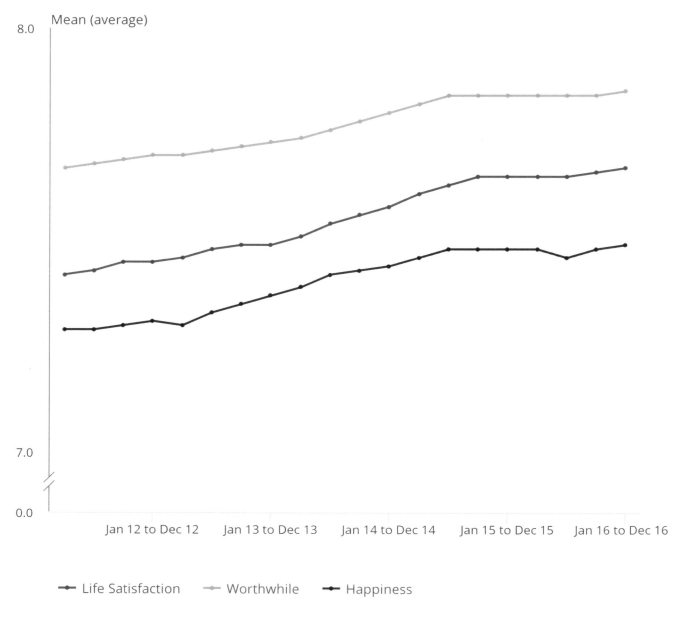

Figure 1a: Average life satisfaction, worthwhile and happiness ratings, year ending March 2012 to year ending December 2016

UK

Source: Office for National Statistics, Annual Population Survey (APS)

Source: Office for National Statistics, Annual Population Survey (APS)

Notes:

1. Chart axis does not start at 0.

2. Year ending March 2012 was the first year of data collection.

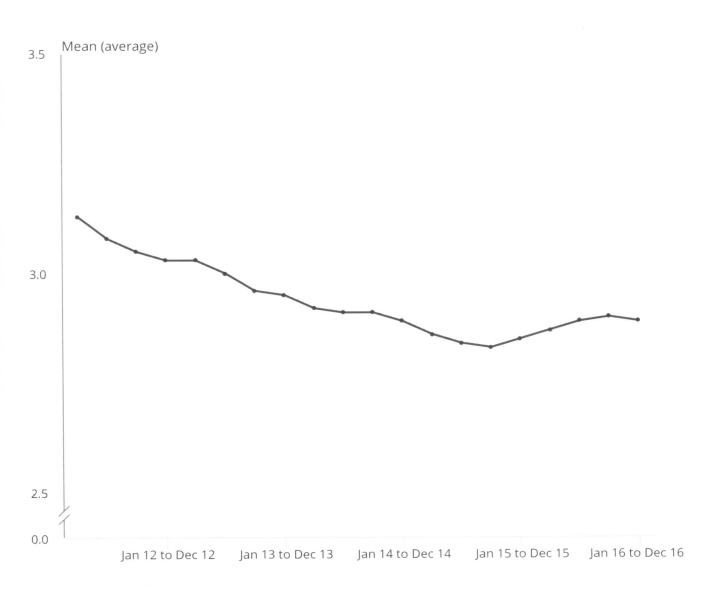

Figure 1b: Average anxiety ratings, year ending March 2012 to year ending December 2016

UK

Source: Office for National Statistics, Annual Population Survey (APS)

Source: Office for National Statistics, Annual Population Survey (APS)

Notes:

1. Chart axis does not start at 0.

2. Year ending March 2012 was the first year of data collection.

It is important to consider how personal well-being ratings have changed for each country across the 5 years we have been collecting the data to see whether there is a differing picture.

6 . Anxiety ratings increased in England but fell in Northern Ireland

In the year ending December 2016, Northern Ireland continues to report the highest life satisfaction, worthwhile and happiness ratings, and the lowest anxiety ratings, when compared to the other constituent countries of the UK.

Considering change over time between the years ending December 2015 and 2016, average (mean) ratings of anxiety have increased slightly in England, as shown in Figure 2. This rise has been driven by a small decline in those reporting their anxiety yesterday as very low (0 or 1 out of 10). Over the same time period, average (mean) ratings of anxiety fell in Northern Ireland, whilst ratings remained unchanged in Wales and Scotland.

Ratings of life satisfaction, worthwhile and happiness remained unchanged between years ending December 2015 and 2016 for each country of the UK.

Figure 2: Average anxiety ratings, year ending December 2012 to year ending December 2016

UK countries

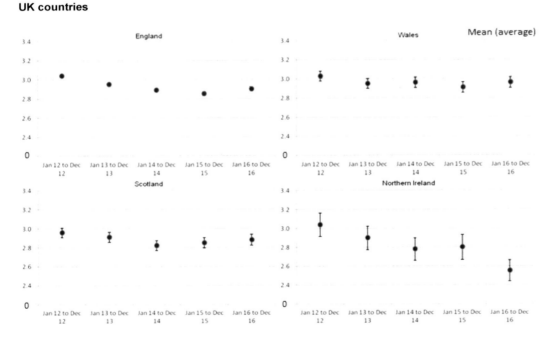

7 . What may explain these results?

Despite no change in personal well-being ratings at a UK level, breaking analysis down to country level has revealed some interesting differences in how adults report feeling about their lives.

When assessing people's feelings and opinions it is important that we understand the context of the time. The latest period covered by these data include a period of political uncertainty, not least campaigning for the EU referendum, as well as 6 months post-EU referendum. Also, during this period, a number of terrorist attacks were experienced across the world.

Along with health, job status and relationship status, a person's sense of choice and contentment with their situation is also important to personal well-being. Over time changes and differences between areas could be related to uncertainties felt about events at the time.

These results may also be reflecting people's mixed thoughts and feelings about the future and how this may have an impact on their lives. A survey conducted by Ipsos Mori, in December 2016 asked respondents the question "And looking ahead to 2017, do you think it will be a good year or a bad year for each of the following?"

- 72% thought that 2017 would be good for their family

- 45% thought that 2017 would be good for the UK

We also monitor and report how the UK is doing against a set of measures on the different areas of life that matter most to the UK. The latest data can be explored in our well-being dashboard.

Asking how people feel about their lives also helps us to see whether, and how, changes such as an increase in reported anxiety, are linked to other changes in society, for example, an increase in symptoms of mental or physical ill health. It also highlights the importance of looking at who reports higher anxiety and why, and whether some groups are disproportionately affected. This is something we will look at in greater depth in our next release of findings from the 3-year combined dataset, to be published on 9 May 2017.

8 . Links to related statistics

Personal well-being in the UK: Oct 2015 to Sept 2016
Personal well-being in the UK: 2015 to 2016
Personal well-being in the UK: local authority update, 2015 to 2016
Measuring national well-being in the UK, domains and measures: April 2017
Measuring National Well-being: At what age is Personal Well-being the highest?
Measuring National Well-being, What matters most to Personal Well-being?
Economic Well-being: Quarter 4, Oct to Dec 2016
Social capital across the UK: 2011 to 2012
Health State Expectancies, UK: 2013 to 2015

9 . Quality and methodology

1. The Personal Well-being in the UK Quality and Methodology Information document contains important information on:

   - the strengths and limitations of the data

   - the quality of the output: including the accuracy of the data and how it compares with related data

   - uses and users

   - how the output was created

2. **Table 1: Labelling of thresholds**

Life satisfaction, worthwhile and happiness scores		Anxiety scores	
Response on an 11 point scale	**Label**	**Response on an 11 point scale**	**Label**
0 – 4	Low	0 – 1	Very low
5 – 6	Medium	2 – 3	Low
7 – 8	High	4 – 5	Medium
9 – 10	Very high	6 – 10	High

Source: Office for National Statistics

3. All the differences noted in the text are statistically significant. The statistical significance of differences are approximate because they are determined on the basis of non-overlapping confidence intervals.

4. Comparisons have been based on unrounded data.

Contact details for this statistical bulletin

Eleanor Rees

QualityOfLife@ons.gsi.gov.uk

Telephone: +44 (0)1633 651631

Office for
National Statistics

Statistical bulletin

Personal well-being and sexual identity in the UK: 2013 to 2015

Personal well-being estimates by age, disability, relationship status, ethnicity, religion, sex and sexual identity using the Annual Population Survey three year combined dataset.

Contact:
Eleanor Rees
QualityOfLife@ons.gsi.gov.uk
+44 (0)1633 651631

Release date:
9 May 2017

Next release:
To be announced

Table of contents

1 . Main finding

Those who identify as gay or lesbian, or bisexual report lower well-being than the UK average for all personal well-being measures. This difference is largest for feelings of anxiety.

2 . Things you need to know about this release

This release examines how personal well-being ratings vary dependent on a person's sexual identity. Sexual identity is one part of the umbrella concept of sexual orientation, a recognised protected characteristic under the Equality Act (2010). Sexual identity does not necessarily reflect sexual attraction or sexual behaviour – these are separate concepts, which we currently do not measure.

For information on the measurement of personal well-being and sexual identity please see the Quality and methodology section of this release.

The Equality Act (2010) lists the following as protected characteristics, and our accompanying dataset provides personal well-being statistics broken down by 7 of these:

- age

- disability

- gender reassignment (data not available in this release)

- marriage and civil partnership

- pregnancy and maternity (data not available in this release)

- race

- religion or belief

- sex

- sexual orientation

Personal well-being statistics are designated as National Statistics, having been assessed against the Code of Practice for Official Statistics in accordance with the Statistics and Registration Service Act 2007. However, sexual identity estimates have not been assessed in this way and should therefore be treated as Experimental Statistics. Whilst this publication has been badged as a National Statistic, you should apply caution in interpreting estimates of sexual identity in this release.

These are estimates from the Annual Population Survey (APS) 3-year dataset. This dataset allows for more granular analysis of personal well-being, however, currently it does not allow for over time comparisons. For more timely estimates and comparisons over time, please see the rolling annual estimates of personal well-being.

This is the first time that the 3-year dataset has been created on a calendar year basis (January to December). The previous two have been created on a financial year basis (April to March).

We welcome feedback on these changes. Please contact the Quality of Life team (QualityOfLife@ons.gsi.gov.uk) with any comments or suggestions, including your views on improvements we might make.

3 . Average ratings highest for those identifying as heterosexual or straight

Figure 1 presents average personal well-being ratings broken down by self-reported sexual identity. Those who identify as heterosexual or straight tended to report the highest average levels of well-being across all four measures of personal well-being.

Figure 1: Personal well-being by self-reported sexual identity, 3 years ending December 2015

UK

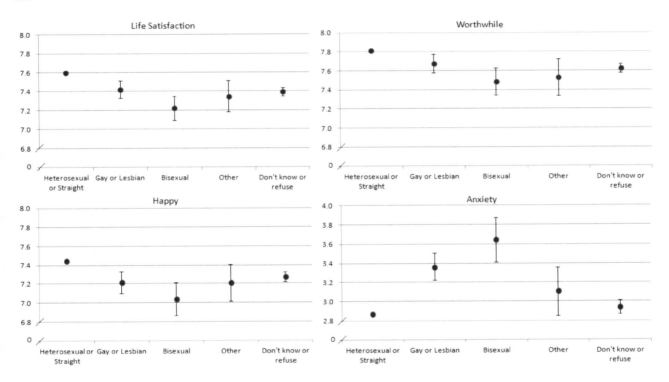

Figure 2 illustrates how average personal well-being ratings by self-reported sexual identity compare with the UK average rating. Those who identify themselves as gay or lesbian, or bisexual report lower well-being than the UK average for all personal well-being questions. Those who identify themselves as "other" or "do not know or refuse" report lower life satisfaction, worthwhile and happiness than the UK average.

Figure 2: Difference in personal well-being ratings by self-reported sexual identity compared with UK average, 3 years ending December 2015

UK

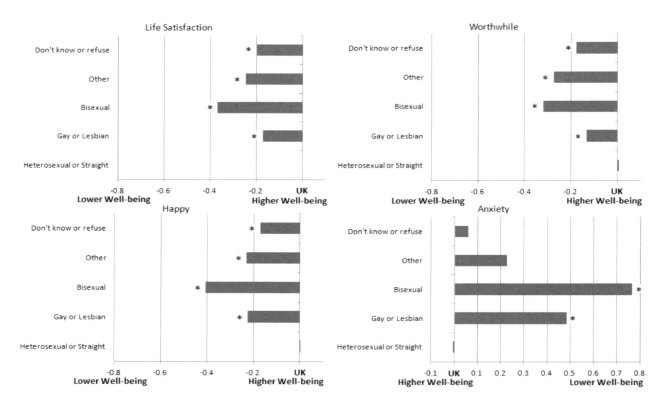

4 . Differences between sexual identities largest for anxiety

The largest differences in personal well-being between self-reported sexual identities, for both means and thresholds, were seen in anxiety. The largest difference was seen for those reporting high anxiety (those answering 6 to 10 out of 10).

Three in every ten people (30.1%) who identify themselves as bisexual reported their anxiety as high (answering 6 to 10 out of 10). This compares with two in every ten people (19.5%) who identify themselves as heterosexual or straight (see Figure 3).

Figure 3: Percentage reporting low life satisfaction, worthwhile and happiness, and high anxiety by self-reported sexual identity, 3 years ending December 2015

UK

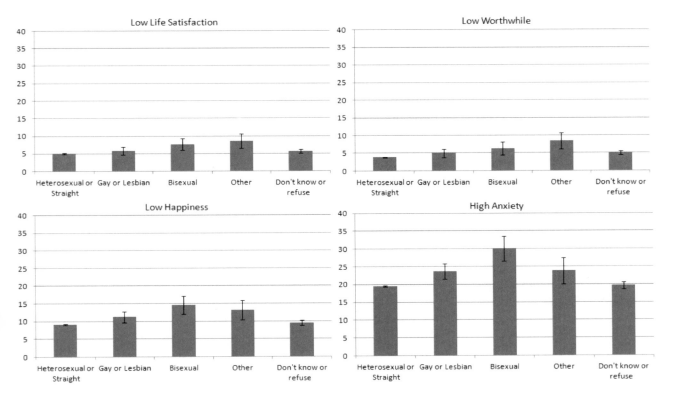

5 . What factors may explain these results?

Previous research has identified that general health, employment and relationship status have the largest association with personal well-being. Relating to this, potential factors influencing the results presented in this release could include health outcomes, discrimination in access to services (including health services) and in the workplace (Albuquerque etc al., 2014; Welsh government, 2014; Hudson-Sharp and Metcalf, 2016; Stonewall 2013; Stonewall).

It must also be recognised that these estimates do not account for other potential factors which may influence well-being ratings. The release Sexual Identity, UK: 2015 showed that you are more likely to report identifying as lesbian, gay or bisexual if you live in London and previous research has shown that personal well-being is generally lower in London.

This is the first time that we have produced estimates of personal well-being by sexual identity. This analysis provides initial insight looking at personal well-being and sexual identity, we hope to build upon this work going forwards.

6 . Links to related statistics

Personal well-being in the UK: 2015 to 2016

Personal well-being in the UK: local authority update, 2015 to 2016

Measuring national well-being: Life in the UK, Apr 2017

7 . Quality and methodology

1. The <u>Personal Well-being in the UK Quality and Methodology Information</u> document and <u>Sexual identity Quality and Methodology Information</u> document contain important information on:

   - the strengths and limitations of the data

   - the quality of the output: including the accuracy of the data and how it compares with related data

   - uses and users

   - how the output was created

2. How we measure personal well-being

   Since 2011, we have asked personal well-being questions to adults in the UK, to better understand how they feel about their lives. This release presents estimates of personal well-being for the 3 years ending December 2015.

   The four personal well-being questions are:

   - overall, how satisfied are you with your life nowadays?

   - overall, to what extent do you feel the things you do in your life are worthwhile?

   - overall, how happy did you feel yesterday?

   - overall, how anxious did you feel yesterday?

   People are asked to respond on a scale of 0 to 10, where 0 is "not at all" and 10 is "completely". We produce estimates of the mean ratings for all four personal well-being questions, as well as their distributions, <u>using the thresholds</u>.

   For more information on personal well-being please see the Personal Well-being user guide.

3. **Table 1: Labelling of thresholds**

Life satisfaction, worthwhile and happiness scores		Anxiety scores	
Response on an 11 point scale	Label	Response on an 11 point scale	Label
0 to 4	Low	0 to 1	Very low
5 to 6	Medium	2 to 3	Low
7 to 8	High	4 to 5	Medium
9 to 10	Very high	6 to 10	High

Source: Office for National Statistics

4. All the differences noted in the text are statistically significant. The statistical significance of differences are approximate because they are determined on the basis of non-overlapping confidence intervals. This method provides a conservative estimate of statistical significance, which may result in estimates that are statistically significantly different to one another being assessed as not.

5. The results are not the outcome of regression analysis, trying to hold all other characteristics (for example, age) equal. Results therefore do not tell us how important self-reported sexual identity matters to well-being ratings compared against other factors.

6. This analysis is based on the Annual Population Survey 3-year dataset covering the period January 2013 to December 2015. This dataset covers the population over the age of 16 living in private households and contains around 300,000 unique responses to the personal well-being questions.

7. The sexual identity question is asked of respondents aged 16 years and over; it is not asked by proxy. Proxy interviews are defined as those where answers are supplied by a third party, who is usually a member of the respondent's household.

   The sexual identity question is asked in both face-to-face and telephone interviews, at first personal contact. During the face-to-face interviews, adults were asked: "Which of the options on this show card best describes how you think of yourself?" For telephone interviews, a slightly different way of collecting the information was used: "I will now read out a list of terms people sometimes use to describe how they think of themselves". The list is read out to respondents twice. On the second reading, the respondent has to say "stop" when an appropriate term they identified with is read out. In both modes, the order in which the terms appeared, or are read out, is unique for each household's respondent to ensure confidentiality. The "Other" option on the question is included to address the fact that not all people will consider they fall in the first three categories, that is, heterosexual or straight, gay or lesbian, or bisexual.

8. Why is this release not LGBT?

   T stands for Transgender or Trans, which are umbrella terms used to refer to people whose Gender Identity differs from what is typically associated with their assigned sex at birth.

   Although gender and sexual identity are related, the focus of this publication is Sexual Identity not Gender Identity. Your Gender Identity is how you identify and present yourself at a point in time, your Sexual Identity is a subjective view of yourself which may change over time, in different contexts and may differ from sexual attraction and behaviour.

Contact details for this statistical bulletin

Eleanor Rees

QualityOfLife@ons.gsi.gov.uk

Telephone: +44 (0)1633 651631

Office for
National Statistics

Statistical bulletin

Personal well-being in the UK: April 2016 to March 2017

Estimates of life satisfaction, whether you feel the things you do in life are worthwhile, happiness and anxiety at the UK, country, regional and local authority level.

Contact:
David Tabor
QualityOfLife@ons.gsi.gov.uk
+44 (0) 1633 455871

Release date:
26 September 2017

Next release:
To be announced

Table of contents

1 . Main points

- We continue to see small year-on-year improvements in average life satisfaction ratings.

- There has been a slight increase in average happiness ratings over this period. This comes after ratings leveled off between the years ending March 2015 and 2016. Earlier years saw regular increases.

- For both anxiety and feelings that the things we do in life are worthwhile, ratings continue to remain level. These measures last saw small improvements between the years ending March 2014 and 2015.

- People in Northern Ireland continue to give higher average ratings across each of the personal well-being measures, when compared with the other UK countries.

- This publication also presents estimates of personal well-being for UK local authorities between the years ending March 2012 and 2017.

2 . Statistician's comment

"Today's figures may surprise some, showing a small increase in both reported happiness and life satisfaction during a period that has seen political change and uncertainty. It's worth noting that employment rates rose during the period covered by this report, and other ONS analysis showed people perceiving an improvement in their own financial situations and in the overall economy. These are factors we believe may account for some people's increased sense of personal well-being."

Matthew Steel – Office for National Statistics

3 . Average life satisfaction and happiness ratings reach highest levels since 2011

The average (mean) ratings across the four measures of personal well-being in the year ending March 2017 were:

- 7.7 out of 10 for life satisfaction

- 7.9 out of 10 for feeling that what you do in life is worthwhile

- 7.5 out of 10 for happiness yesterday

- 2.9 out of 10 for anxiety yesterday

Comparing the years ending March 2016 and 2017, there have been statistically significant improvements in average ratings of life satisfaction and happiness for the UK overall. There was no change in average ratings of anxiety and the sense that things done in life are worthwhile.

Figures 1a and 1b display the changes in personal well-being between the years ending March 2012 and 2017. Average ratings of life satisfaction and happiness were at their highest levels in the year ending March 2017 since we began measuring personal well-being in 2011. Despite no statistically significant change in average worthwhile ratings between the years ending March 2016 and 2017, levels remain at their joint highest since 2011. For anxiety, average ratings reached a low in the year ending September 2015 but subsequently rose. They have since levelled off and were unchanged between the years ending March 2016 and 2017 and remain lower compared with the years ending March 2012 and 2013.

Figure 1a: Average life satisfaction, worthwhile and happiness ratings, year ending March 2012 to year ending March 2017

UK

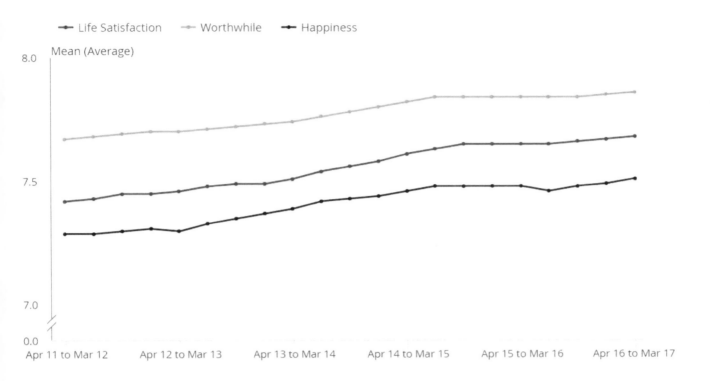

Source: Annual Population Survey, Office for National Statistics

Notes:

1. Chart axis does not start at 0.

Figure 1b: Average anxiety ratings, year ending March 2012 to year ending March 2017

UK

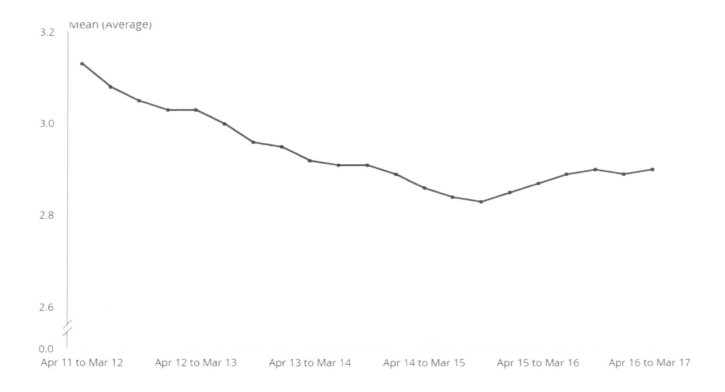

Source: Annual Population Survey, Office for National Statistics

Notes:

1. Chart axis does not start at 0.

4 . More people report very high levels of life satisfaction and worthwhile ratings

Between the years ending March 2016 and 2017, there has been a statistically significant increase in the proportion of people reporting very high levels of life satisfaction and feeling that things done in life are worthwhile, as shown in figures 2a and 2b.

There were no changes in the proportion of people who reported their ratings of life satisfaction, worthwhile or happiness as low. This indicates that increases in mean life satisfaction are being driven by more people reporting the highest levels of well-being, rather than a decrease in those reporting the lowest levels of well-being.

Figure 2a: Proportion of respondents reporting very high ratings of life satisfaction - year ending March 2012 to year ending March 2017

UK

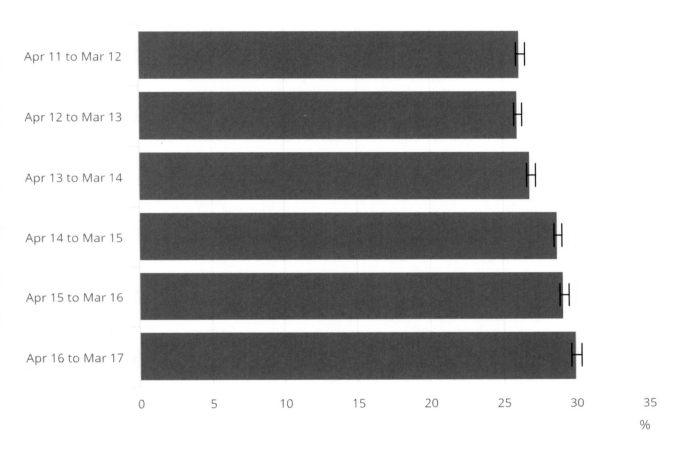

Figure 2a: Proportion of respondents reporting very high ratings of life satisfaction - year ending March 2012 to year ending March 2017

UK

Source: Annual Population Survey, Office for National Statistics

Source: Annual Population Survey, Office for National Statistics

Notes:

1. Very high life satisfaction is defined as those reporting 9 or 10 out of 10.

Figure 2b: Proportion of respondents reporting very high ratings of worthwhile - year ending March 2012 to year ending March 2017

UK

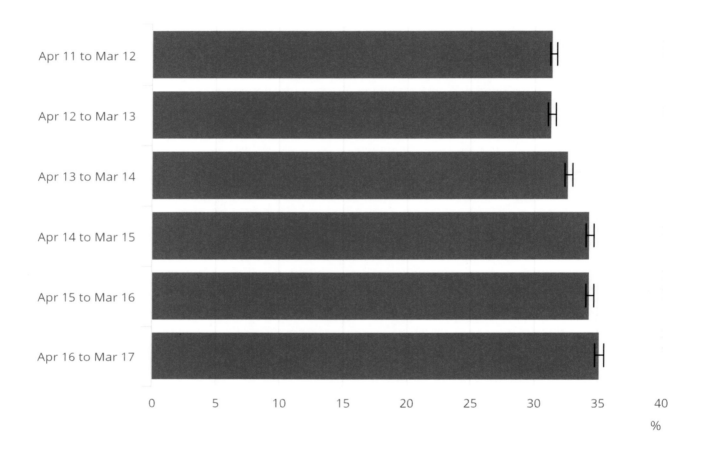

Figure 2b: Proportion of respondents reporting very high ratings of worthwhile - year ending March 2012 to year ending March 2017

UK

Source: Annual Population Survey, Office for National Statistics

Source: Annual Population Survey, Office for National Statistics

Notes:

1. Very high worthwhile is defined as those reporting 9 or 10 out of 10.

Figure 2c: Proportion of respondents reporting very high ratings of happiness - year ending March 2012 to year ending March 2017

UK

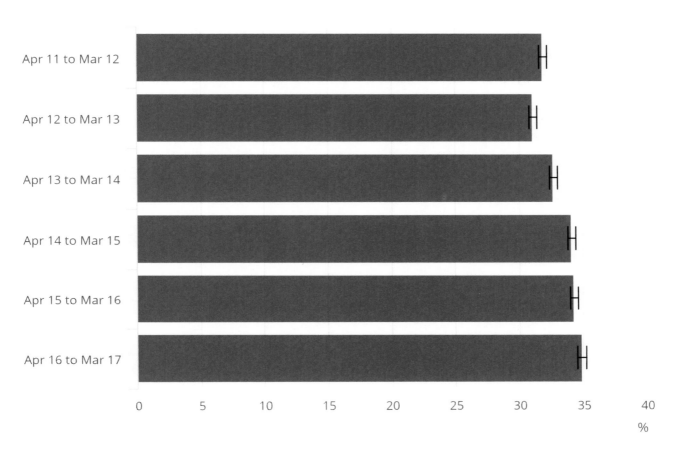

Figure 2c: Proportion of respondents reporting very high ratings of happiness - year ending March 2012 to year ending March 2017

UK

Source: Annual Population Survey, Office for National Statistics

Source: Annual Population Survey, Office for National Statistics

Notes:

1. Very high happiness is defined as those reporting 9 or 10 out of 10.

Figure 2d: Proportion of respondents reporting very low ratings of anxiety - year ending March 2012 to year ending March 2017

UK

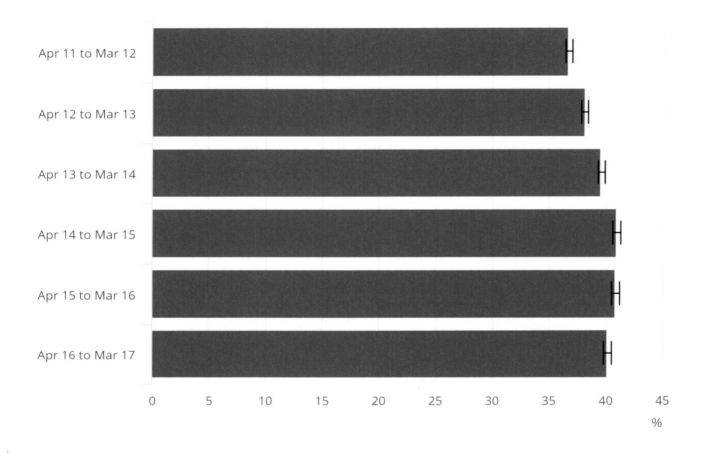

Figure 2d: Proportion of respondents reporting very low ratings of anxiety - year ending March 2012 to year ending March 2017

UK

Source: Annual Population Survey, Office for National Statistics

Source: Annual Population Survey, Office for National Statistics

Notes:

1. Very low anxiety is defined as those reporting 0 or 1 out of 10.

5 . People in Northern Ireland report the highest personal well-being

At a country level, average (mean) ratings of life satisfaction and happiness have increased slightly in England between the years ending March 2016 and 2017. There were no other changes in any aspect of well-being for the rest of the countries in the UK over this period.

In the year ending March 2017, people in Northern Ireland continue to report the highest average life satisfaction, worthwhile and happiness ratings, and the lowest anxiety ratings, when compared with the other constituent countries of the UK.

6 . What may explain these results?

Considering some of the changes discussed previously, it is important to reflect on factors that could be influencing them. Research shows that a number of factors influence our quality of life and well-being. Employment or job satisfaction, our health, the quality of our relationships and our personal financial security are just some of the aspects of our lives shown to have an effect. Over time, changes and differences between areas could be related to these factors.

Over the year that this publication covers, various situations of uncertainty, not least in political terms have unfolded in the UK. For example, the UK public voted on the EU referendum and there was a new prime minister appointed. Considering this, it is interesting to see that the latest figures covered by Economic Well-being (Office for National Statistics): show that, "between Quarter 4 2016 and Quarter 1 2017, consumers reported perceived improvements in their own financial situation and the general economic situation over the last year".

In addition to this, the UK employment rate is at its highest since comparable records began in 1971. The unemployment rate is at its joint lowest since 1975.

Taking this into account, some of the events mentioned previously may not have caused any sudden changes. If we consider the public's own perceptions and experiences over the last year, there was perhaps relatively little change in terms of day-to-day experiences, which may explain why employment and economic well-being remain high.

In line with this, Ipsos MORI's Political Monitor asked the UK population: "Now that Britain has voted to leave the EU, to what extent do you think it will be better or worse for your own standard of living, or will it make no difference?" Of the population, 40% reported in March 2017 that it will make no difference, which is up from 24% in October 2016.

Our next release, which will be published later this year, will be the first that will include a year's worth of data post-EU referendum; thus, allowing direct comparisons pre- and post-EU referendum. The dataset associated with this release will also include the general election.

We are always looking for ways to improve our releases and make them more useful and helpful. Please contact the Quality of Life team via email at QualityOfLife@ons.gsi.gov.uk with any comments or suggestions, including your views on improvements we might make.

7 . How do people rate their personal well-being in your area?

The interactive tools in this section provide the opportunity to compare average ratings of personal well-being across UK local authorities. The most appropriate comparisons are progress over time within the same local authority, or across local authorities that share a similar demographic composition to one another. Simply ranking local authorities by their numerical scores can be misleading.

The What Works Centre for Wellbeing have also recently published a local well-being indicators set and guidelines. These provide a helpful starting point for looking at issues that contribute to well-being in local areas.

The Personal Well-Being Explorer, which can be found at https://www.ons.gov.uk/peoplepopulationandcommunity/wellbeing/bulletins/measuringnationalwellbeing/april2016tomarch2017 allows you to view changes to personal well-being ratings across time and to compare the scores for different local authorities. The following four pages contain illustrations of the Explorer where we have randomly chosen one local area from each of the four home nations, and have compared these against each other and on a time-series basis from year ending March 2012 to year ending March 2017.

Personal well-being Explorer, year ending March 2012 to year ending March 2017

| Life Satisfaction | Worthwhile | Happiness | Anxiety |

Start typing some area names, or click the lines to select up to 6 areas

Orkney Islands ✖   Harlow ✖   Belfast ✖   Pembrokeshire / Sir Benfro ✖

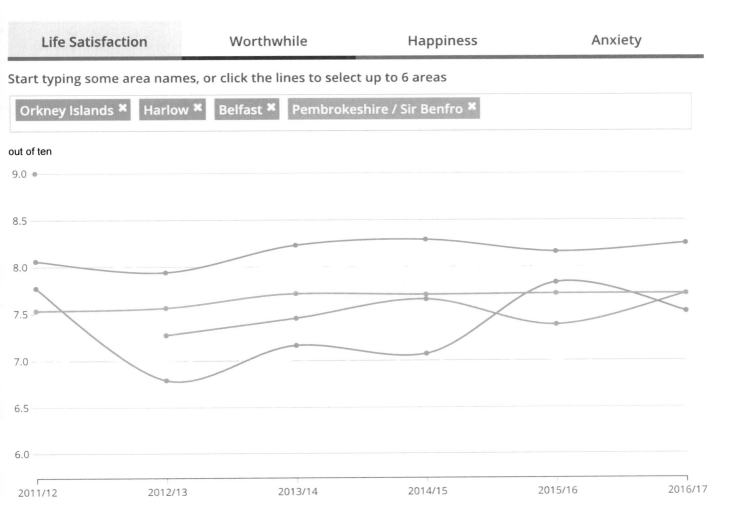

Source: Annual Population Survey, ONS

Note:
1. Data are weighted mean averages.

2. 2011/12 was the first period this data was collected.

3. Northern Ireland data are unavailable for 2011/12.

Personal well-being Explorer, year ending March 2012 to year ending March 2017

| Life Satisfaction | Worthwhile | Happiness | Anxiety |

Start typing some area names, or click the lines to select up to 6 areas

Orkney Islands ✖   Harlow ✖   Belfast ✖   Pembrokeshire / Sir Benfro ✖

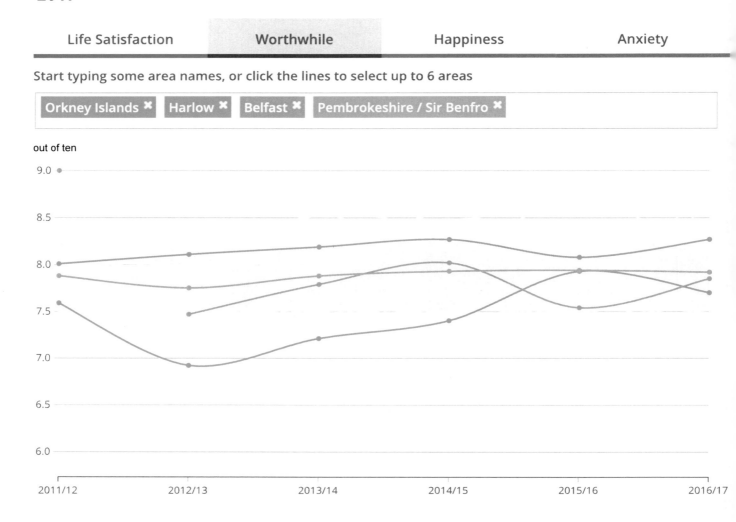

out of ten

Source: Annual Population Survey, ONS

Note:
1. Data are weighted mean averages.

2. 2011/12 was the first period this data was collected.

3. Northern Ireland data are unavailable for 2011/12.

Personal well-being Explorer, year ending March 2012 to year ending March 2017

| Life Satisfaction | Worthwhile | Happiness | Anxiety |

Start typing some area names, or click the lines to select up to 6 areas

Orkney Islands **✕**   Harlow **✕**   Belfast **✕**   Pembrokeshire / Sir Benfro **✕**

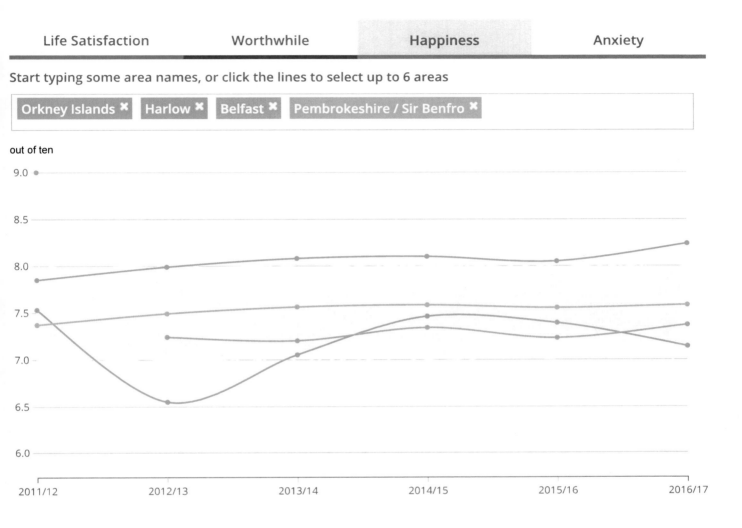

out of ten

Source: Annual Population Survey, ONS

Note:
1. Data are weighted mean averages.

2. 2011/12 was the first period this data was collected.

3. Northern Ireland data are unavailable for 2011/12.

Personal well-being Explorer, year ending March 2012 to year ending March 2017

Life Satisfaction   Worthwhile   Happiness   Anxiety

Start typing some area names, or click the lines to select up to 6 areas

Orkney Islands ✖ Harlow ✖ Belfast ✖ Pembrokeshire / Sir Benfro ✖

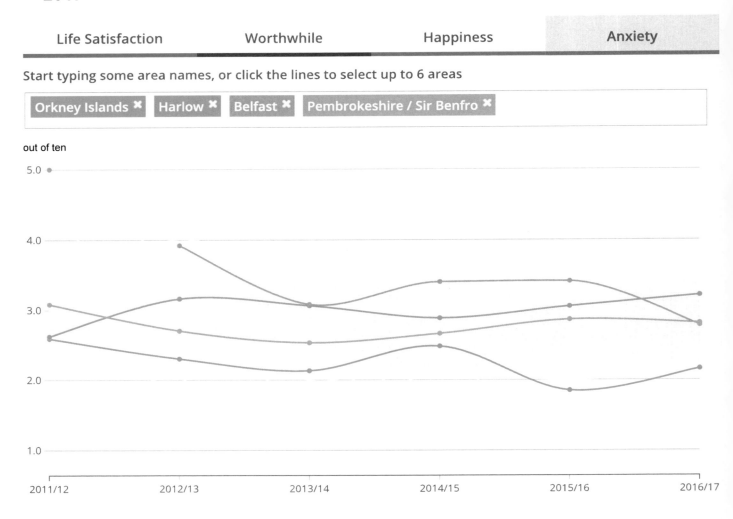

Source: Annual Population Survey, ONS

Note:
1. Data are weighted mean averages.

2. 2011/12 was the first period this data was collected.

3. Northern Ireland data are unavailable for 2011/12.

Comparisons between areas should be done so with caution as these estimates are provided from a sample survey. Confidence intervals should be taken into account when assessing differences.

Personal well-being interactive maps, year ending March 2012 to year ending March 2017

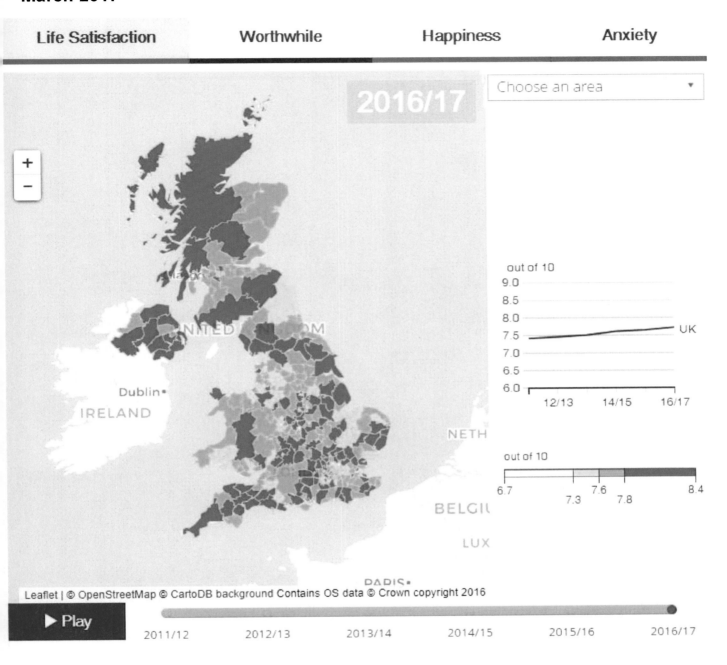

Source: Annual Population Survey, ONS

Note:

1. Data are weighted mean averages.

2. 2011/12 was the first period this data was collected.

3. Northern Ireland data are unavailable for 2011/12.

Personal well-being interactive maps, year ending March 2012 to year ending March 2017

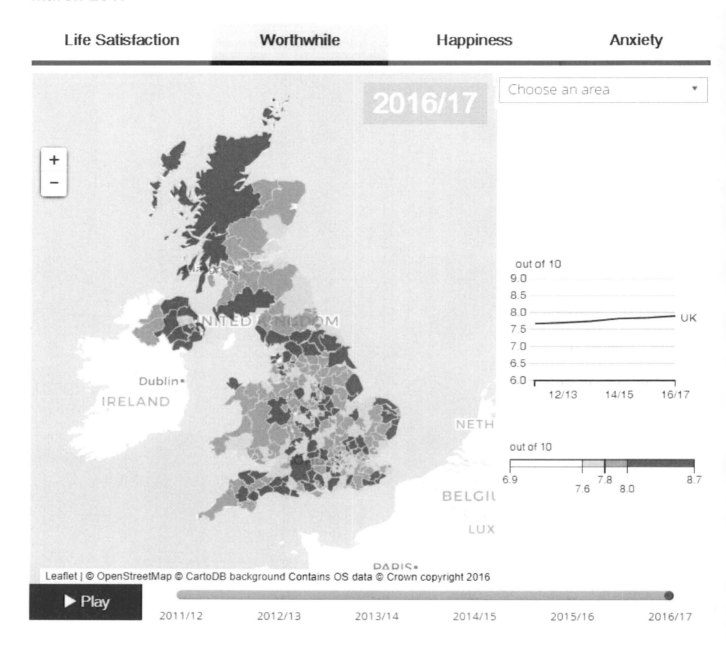

Source: Annual Population Survey, ONS

Note:
1. Data are weighted mean averages.

2. 2011/12 was the first period this data was collected.

3. Northern Ireland data are unavailable for 2011/12.

Personal well-being interactive maps, year ending March 2012 to year ending March 2017

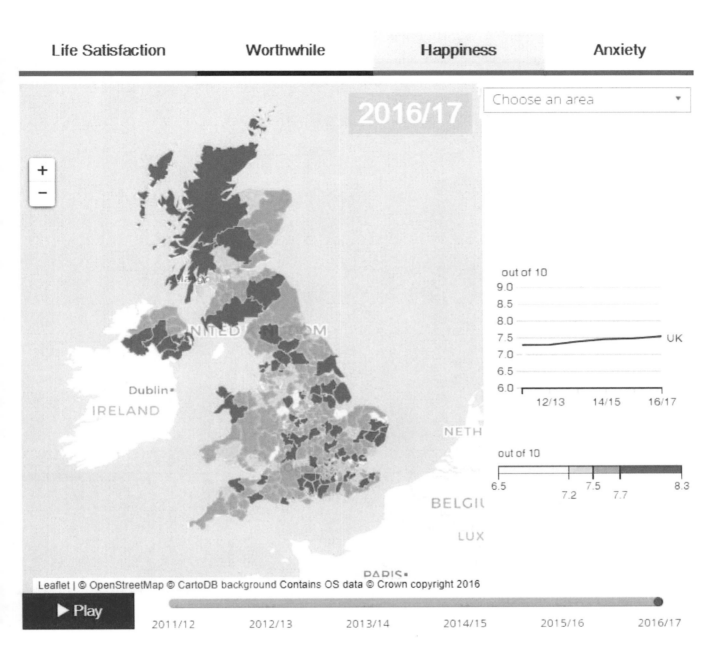

Source: Annual Population Survey, ONS

Note:
1. Data are weighted mean averages.

2. 2011/12 was the first period this data was collected.

3. Northern Ireland data are unavailable for 2011/12.

Personal well-being interactive maps, year ending March 2012 to year ending March 2017

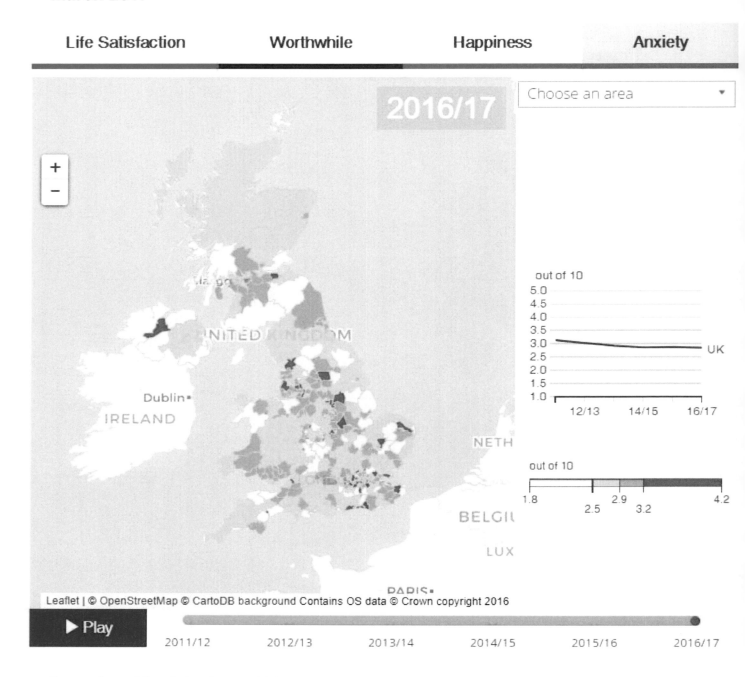

| Life Satisfaction | Worthwhile | Happiness | Anxiety |

Source: Annual Population Survey, ONS

Note:
1. Data are weighted mean averages.

2. 2011/12 was the first period this data was collected.

3. Northern Ireland data are unavailable for 2011/12.

Comparisons between areas should be done so with caution as these estimates are provided from a sample survey. Confidence intervals should be taken into account when assessing differences.

8 . Links to related statistics

Recent Office for National Statistics (ONS) publications related to well-being:

Personal well-being in the UK: Jan 2016 to Dec 2016

Measuring national well-being in the UK, domains and measures: April 2017

Measuring National Well-being: At what age is Personal Well-being the highest?

Measuring National Well-being, What matters most to Personal Well-being?

Economic Well-being: Quarter 1, Jan to Mar 2017

Social capital in the UK: May 2017

9 . Quality and methodology

1. The Personal Well-being in the UK Quality and Methodology Information report contains important information on:

   - the strengths and limitations of the data

   - the quality of the output: including the accuracy of the data and how it compares with related data

   - uses and users

   - how the output was created

2. How we measure personal well-being

   Since 2011, we have asked personal well-being questions to adults aged 16 and over in the UK, to better understand how they feel about their lives. This release presents headline results for the financial year ending 2017, along with changes over the last six years. It provides data at a national level and at a local authority level.

   The four personal well-being questions are:

   - overall, how satisfied are you with your life nowadays?

   - overall, to what extent do you feel the things you do in your life are worthwhile?

   - overall, how happy did you feel yesterday?

   - overall, how anxious did you feel yesterday?

People are asked to respond on a scale of 0 to 10, where 0 is "not at all" and 10 is "completely". We produce estimates of the mean ratings for all four personal well-being questions, as well as their distributions, using thresholds.

For more information on personal well-being please see the personal well-being user guide.

3. **Table 1: Labelling of thresholds**

Life satisfaction, worthwhile and happiness scores		Anxiety scores	
Response on an 11 point scale	Label	Response on an 11 point scale	Label
0 – 4	Low	0 – 1	Very low
5 – 6	Medium	2 – 3	Low
7 – 8	High	4 – 5	Medium
9 – 10	Very high	6 – 10	High

Source: Office for National Statistics

4. The statistical significance of differences noted within the release are approximate because they are determined on the basis of non-overlapping confidence intervals.

5. Comparisons have been based on unrounded data.

6. We are able to compare with the same period last year (April 2015 to March 2016) to identify any changes that may have occurred. However, we are not able to reliably compare with the preceding period (January 2016 to December 2016) as they include overlapping time periods that contain the same data.

7. Personal well-being data is now included within the main Annual Population Survey (APS) dataset rather than released as a separate dataset. As part of this transition, personal well-being estimates now go through the regular APS re-weighting timetable. For the series published in this release the estimates for the years ending March 2013 through to 2017 have been weighted to 2015 mid-year population estimates (MYPEs). For more information see Impact of transition to Annual Population Survey dataset. (Please note that this was incorrectly referred to as 2017 MYPEs but corrected 24 October 2017)

Contact details for this statistical bulletin

David Tabor

QualityOfLife@ons.gsi.gov.uk

Telephone: +44 (0)1633 455871

Statistical bulletin

Personal well-being in the UK: July 2016 to June 2017

Estimates of personal well-being for the UK and countries of the UK for the year ending June 2017.

Contact:
David Tabor, Lauren Stockley
QualityOfLife@ons.gsi.gov.uk
+44 (0) 1633 455871

Release date:
7 November 2017

Next release:
To be announced

Table of contents

1 . Main points

- Average ratings of life satisfaction, feeling that the things we do in life are worthwhile and happiness have increased slightly in the UK between the years ending June 2016 and 2017.

- There was no change in average anxiety ratings in the UK between the years ending June 2016 and 2017.

- Improvements in life satisfaction, worthwhile and happiness ratings in the UK were driven by England, the only country where average ratings across these measures improved.

- People in Northern Ireland report the highest levels of personal well-being, when compared with the UK average.

- This publication is the first to present a full year of personal well-being data since the EU referendum.

2 . Statistician's comment

"Today's figures, the first to be based on a full year of data since the EU referendum, show small increases in how people in the UK rate their life satisfaction, happiness and feelings that the things they do in life are worthwhile. The improvements were driven by England - the only country where quality of life ratings got better over the last year."

Matthew Steel – Office for National Statistics

3 . Average life satisfaction, worthwhile and happiness ratings reach highest levels since 2011

The average (mean) ratings across the four measures of personal well-being in the year ending June 2017 were:

- 7.7 out of 10 for life satisfaction

- 7.9 out of 10 for feeling that what you do in life is worthwhile

- 7.5 out of 10 for happiness yesterday

- 2.9 out of 10 for anxiety yesterday

Between the years ending June 2016 and 2017, there have been statistically significant improvements in average ratings of life satisfaction, feeling the things we do in life are worthwhile and happiness for the UK overall. There was no change in average ratings of anxiety.

Figures 1a and 1b display the changes in personal well-being between the years ending March 2012 and June 2017. In the year ending June 2017, average ratings of life satisfaction, worthwhile and happiness reached their highest levels since we began measuring personal well-being in 2011. For anxiety, average ratings reached a low in the year ending September 2015 but subsequently rose. They have since levelled off and were unchanged between the years ending June 2016 and 2017 and remain lower compared with the years ending June 2012 and 2013.

Figure 1a: Average life satisfaction, worthwhile and happiness ratings, year ending March 2012 to year ending June 2017

UK

Source: Annual Population Survey, Office for National Statistics

Notes:

1. Chart axis does not start at zero.

Figure 1b: Average anxiety ratings, year ending March 2012 to year ending June 2017

UK

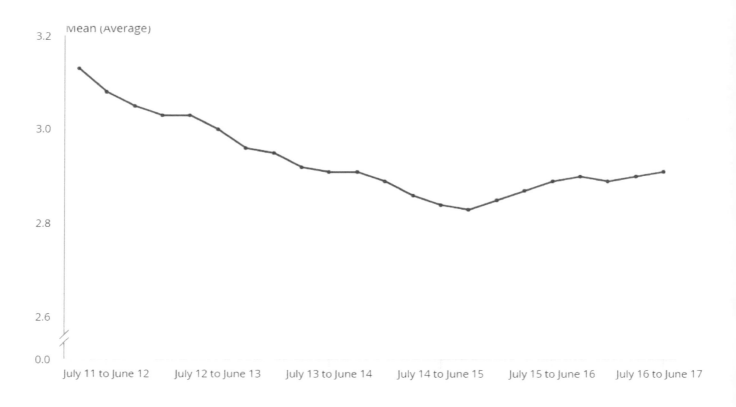

Source: Annual Population Survey, Office for National Statistics

Notes:

1. Chart axis does not start at zero.

4 . Increase in the proportion of people reporting very high levels of life satisfaction, worthwhile and happiness ratings

A higher proportion of people reported very high levels of life satisfaction, worthwhile and happiness in the year ending June 2017 compared with the previous year. The proportion rating their anxiety as very low did not change between the year ending June 2016 and June 2017.

Figure 2 displays changes in the proportion of people reporting the highest levels of personal well-being between the years ending June 2012 and 2017. In the year ending June 2017 a higher proportion of people reported very high levels of life satisfaction, worthwhile and happiness compared with the year ending June 2012. In addition to this, there is also an increase in the proportion of people who reported very low levels of anxiety between the years ending June 2012 and 2017.

Figure 2: Proportion of respondents reporting very high ratings of life satisfaction, worthwhile and happiness and very low ratings of anxiety

UK, year ending June 2012 and year ending June 2017

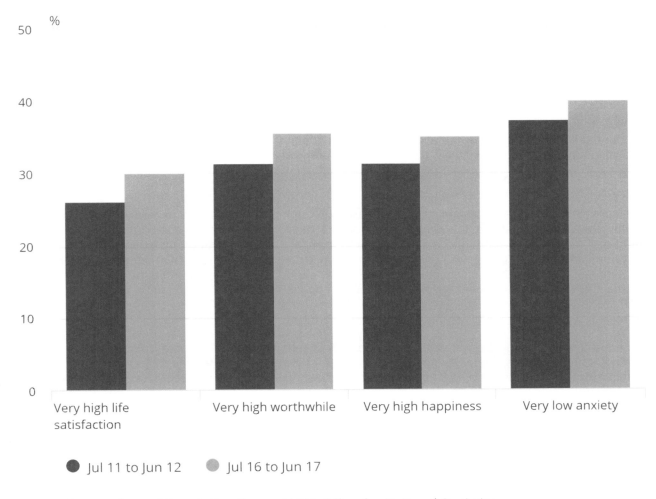

Figure 2: Proportion of respondents reporting very high ratings of life satisfaction, worthwhile and happiness and very low ratings of anxiety

UK, year ending June 2012 and year ending June 2017

Source: Annual Population Survey (APS), Office for National Statistics

Source: Annual Population Survey (APS), Office for National Statistics

Notes:

1. Very high life satisfaction, worthwhile and happiness are defined as those reporting 9 or 10 out of 10.

2. Very low anxiety is defined as those reporting 0 or 1 out of 10.

5 . England was the only country to show improvements across any measures of personal well-being

Between the years ending June 2016 and 2017, improvements in life satisfaction, worthwhile and happiness ratings in the UK were driven by England, where average (mean) ratings improved across all three measures. England also had an increase in the proportion of respondents reporting very high levels of personal well-being across each of these measures. No changes in reported personal well-being were found in Scotland, Wales or Northern Ireland.

However, people in Northern Ireland continued to report higher average levels of personal well-being across all four measures compared with the UK average in the year ending June 2017.

6 . What may explain these results?

Research shows that a number of factors influence our quality of life and well-being. Employment and job satisfaction, our health, the quality of our relationships and our financial situation are just some of the aspects of our lives shown to have an effect. Over time, changes and differences in the four measures could be related to these factors.

Some of the increases in well-being ratings may be explained through the improvement in certain economic indicators within the UK. For example, the employment rate is at its highest level since comparable records began in 1971 and the unemployment rate is at its joint lowest since 1975. Additionally, there were improvements in both gross domestic product (GDP) per head and net national disposable income (NNDI) per head. Despite these improvements, real household disposable income (RHDI) per head fell for the fourth quarter in a row and, for the first time in two years, consumers reported a worsening perception of their own financial situation in April to June 2017.

Over the year that this publication covers, various situations of uncertainty, not least in political terms, have unfolded in the UK. For example, alongside the appointment of a new prime minister, the 12-month period covered by this release also allows the first opportunity to consider how personal well-being has fared in the year following the UK's vote to leave the European Union (EU). Ipsos MORI's Political Monitor asked people in the UK "Now that Britain has voted to leave the EU, to what extent do you think it will be better or worse for your own standard of living, or will it make no difference?" March 2017 saw 40% report that it would make no difference, which is up from 24% in October 2016, possibly implying that as time goes on people are becoming more relaxed about the implications of Brexit. Another thing to note is that although Article 50 has been triggered, we have not yet left the EU and hence the implications on the daily lives of people in the UK remain to be seen.

In addition to the political uncertainties mentioned previously, the UK has witnessed a number of other incidents over the year, including several terror attacks. Considering this, it may be surprising that levels of personal well-being are increasing. However, it is important to note these figures are only reported at a country and national level, and are presented over the year. It is therefore possible that any sudden or individual change in personal well-being may not be seen in the data.

We are always looking for ways to improve our releases and make them more useful and helpful. Please contact the Quality of Life team via email at QualityOfLife@ons.gsi.gov.uk with any comments or suggestions, including your views on improvements we could make.

7 . Links to related statistics

Recent Office for National Statistics (ONS) publications related to well-being:

7 . Links to related statistics

Recent Office for National Statistics (ONS) publications related to well-being:

Personal well-being in the UK, local authority release: April 2016 to March 2017

Measuring national well-being in the UK, domains and measures: April 2017

Measuring National Well-being: At what age is Personal Well-being the highest?

Measuring National Well-being, What matters most to Personal Well-being?

Economic Well-being: Quarter 1, January to March 2017

Wealth in Great Britain: Relationship between wealth, income and personal well-being, July 2011 to June 2012
Income, Expenditure and Personal Well-being, 2011 to 2012

Social capital in the UK: May 2017

Well-being dashboard

8 . Quality and methodology

The Personal well-being in the UK Quality and Methodology Information report contains important information on:

- the strengths and limitations of the data and how it compares with related data

- uses and users

- how the output was created

- the quality of the output including the accuracy of the data

How we measure personal well-being

Since 2011, we have asked personal well-being questions to adults aged 16 and over in the UK, to better understand how they feel about their lives. This release presents headline results for the year ending June 2017, along with changes over the last six years. It provides data at a national level and country level.

The four personal well-being questions are:

- Overall, how satisfied are you with your life nowadays?

- Overall, to what extent do you feel the things you do in your life are worthwhile?

  Overall, how happy did you feel yesterday?

  Overall, how anxious did you feel yesterday?

People are asked to respond on a scale of 0 to 10, where 0 is "not at all" and 10 is "completely". We produce estimates of the mean ratings for all four personal well-being questions, as well as their distributions, using thresholds.

For more information on personal well-being, please see the personal well-being user guide.

Table 1: Labelling of thresholds

Life satisfaction, worthwhile and happiness scores		Anxiety scores	
Response on an 11 point scale	Label	Response on an 11 point scale	Label
0 – 4	Low	0 – 1	Very low
5 – 6	Medium	2 – 3	Low
7 – 8	High	4 – 5	Medium
9 – 10	Very high	6 – 10	High

Source: Office for National Statistics

The statistical significance of differences noted within the release are approximate because they are determined on the basis of non-overlapping confidence intervals.

Comparisons have been based on unrounded data.

We are able to compare with the same period last year (July 2015 to June 2016) to identify any changes that may have occurred. However, we are not able to reliably compare with the preceding period (April 2016 to March 2017) as they include overlapping time periods that contain the same data.

Personal well-being data are now included within the main Annual Population Survey (APS) dataset rather than released as a separate dataset. As part of this transition, personal well-being estimates now go through the regular APS re-weighting timetable. For the series published in this release, the estimates for the years ending June 2013 through to 2017 have been weighted to 2015 mid-year population estimates (MYPEs). For more information, see Impact of transition to Annual Population Survey dataset.

Contact details for this statistical bulletin

David Tabor, Lauren Stockley

QualityOfLife@ons.gsi.gov.uk

Telephone: +44 (0)1633 455871

Article

Social protection: European comparisons of expenditure, 2007 to 2014

How UK social protection compares to other European countries, and how it has changed over time.

Contact:
Gerard Carolan
gerard.carolan@ons.gov.uk

Release date:
1 March 2017

Next release:
To be announced

Table of contents

1 . Introduction

Social protection is comprised of the various benefits provided to households, usually by public bodies, to help with their needs[1]. Social protection benefits can either be in cash or in kind. Benefits in kind include such things as hospital stays, free school meals and home care.

The European System of Integrated Social Protection Statistics (ESSPROS) provides internationally comparable data on social protection in 32 countries – the 28 European Union states together with Switzerland, Iceland, Norway and Serbia. Throughout this publication, these will be referred to as "selected countries".

To ensure meaningful comparisons over time, 2014 prices have been used throughout this publication to describe UK expenditure[2]. Eurostat constant price data has been used where expenditure growth in other countries is described.

Notes for: Introduction

1. Eurostat give a more complete definition: Social protection encompasses interventions from public or private bodies intended to relieve households and individuals of the burden of a defined set of risks or needs, provided that there is neither a simultaneous reciprocal nor an individual arrangement involved.

2. Unless otherwise stated, the Consumer Price Index (CPI) has been used as a deflator for UK data.

2 . Main points

- The UK spent 17.5% per capita more than the European average on social protection in 2014.

- UK Social protection expenditure in the children and families categories fell every year between 2010 and 2014.

- Social protection expenditure in the old age category fell by 0.2% per recipient in the year to 2014.

3 . International comparisons

Figure 1 compares social protection expenditure among the selected countries in 2014. Purchasing Power Standards (PPS) are used to compare per capita expenditure. These are an artificial currency unit used for international comparisons. One PPS will, in theory, buy exactly the same amount in each country at a common point in time.

Figure 1: 2014 Social protection expenditure per capita, and growth since 2013

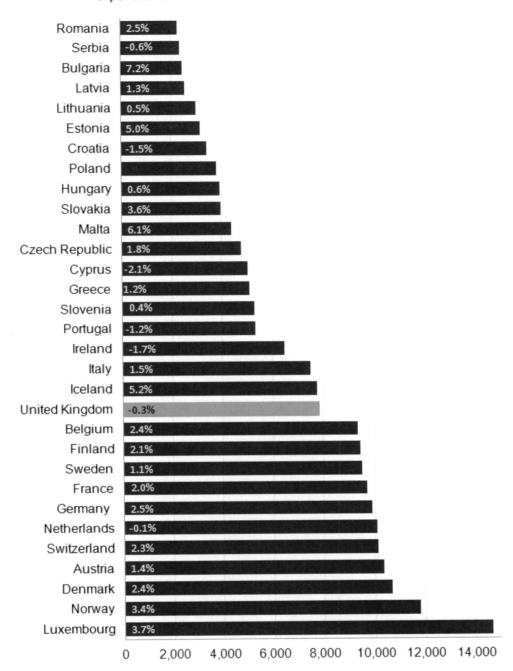

Percentage growth rate of total expenditure

Country	Growth
Romania	2.5%
Serbia	-0.6%
Bulgaria	7.2%
Latvia	1.3%
Lithuania	0.5%
Estonia	5.0%
Croatia	-1.5%
Poland	
Hungary	0.6%
Slovakia	3.6%
Malta	6.1%
Czech Republic	1.8%
Cyprus	-2.1%
Greece	1.2%
Slovenia	0.4%
Portugal	-1.2%
Ireland	-1.7%
Italy	1.5%
Iceland	5.2%
United Kingdom	-0.3%
Belgium	2.4%
Finland	2.1%
Sweden	1.1%
France	2.0%
Germany	2.5%
Netherlands	-0.1%
Switzerland	2.3%
Austria	1.4%
Denmark	2.4%
Norway	3.4%
Luxembourg	3.7%

Purchasing power standards per capita

Luxembourg had the highest social protection expenditure per capita in 2014. However, Luxembourg can be seen as a special case given the high percentage of its workforce that are not residents. Next highest was Norway which had expenditure of 11,797 PPS per capita. This was nearly 1.8 times the average expenditure – 6,647 PPS per capita. The next 2 highest spending countries spent 1.6 times the average. These were Denmark and Austria which spent 10,654 PPS per recipient and 10,344 PPS per recipient respectively. Romania had the lowest expenditure of the selected countries, 2,273 PPS per recipient, slightly more than one-third of the average.

The UK had expenditure of 7,809 PPS per capita, the 12th highest of the selected countries and 17.5% higher than the average.

The percentages of growth in total social protection expenditure for the selected countries between 2013 and 2014 are also included in figure 1.

Of the 30 countries for which growth rates are available [1], Bulgaria and Malta had the highest, 7.2% and 6.1% respectively.

Eight countries reduced spending in 2014 compared with 2013. The largest drop in social protection expenditure was in Cyprus where expenditure fell by 2.1%. The 2 countries with the smallest reduction in expenditure were the Netherlands and UK with falls of 0.1% and 0.3% respectively.

Notes for: International comparisons

1. Growth data were not available for Spain and Poland.

4 . Social protection in the UK

The European System of Integrated Social Protection Statistics (ESSPROS) system distinguishes between means tested and non-means tested benefits.

Table 1 shows that in 2014, the latest year for which data are available, nearly £495 billion was spent on social protection in the UK , a real terms decrease of 0.3% compared with 2013.

Table 1: Social protection expenditure in the UK in 2013 and 2014

	2013	2014	Change
Means-tested	67,667	62,096	-8.20%
Non Means-tested	428,547	432,815	1.00%
Total	496,214	494,911	-0.30%

Source: Office for National Statistics

Notes:

1. 2014 prices.

Expenditure on means-tested benefits fell by 8.2% between 2013 and 2014. This was partially offset by a 1.0% increase in non-means tested expenditure. However, means-tested benefits as a proportion of total expenditure fell by 1.1 percentage points between 2013 and 2014 to 12.5%.

The ESSPROS system divides social protection into 8 broad categories. Figure 2 illustrates the 2013 and 2014 percentage of total social protection expenditure in each category.

Figure 2: UK social expenditure by category, 2007 to 2014

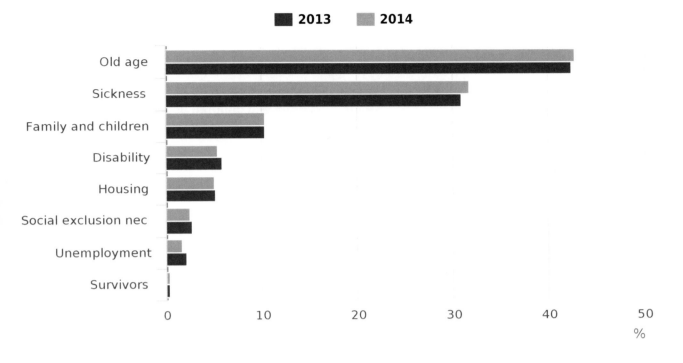

Source: Office for National Statistics

The old age and sickness categories, which between them account for around three-quarters of social protection expenditure, increased their share between 2013 and 2014 by 0.2 percentage points and 0.8 percentage points respectively.

Expenditure on disability and unemployment fell between 2013 and 2014 by 0.5 percentage points and 0.4 percentage points respectively[1]. The other categories were broadly unchanged.

Notes for Social protection in the UK

1. The disability figures for 2014 were compiled using a new methodology. This may have impacted on the growth rate described.

5 . Children and families

The family and children category of social protection includes benefits that provide:

- financial support to households for bringing up children

- financial assistance to people who support relatives other than children

- social services specifically designed to assist and protect the family, particularly children [1]

In 2014, £51.3 billion was spent in the UK on social protection in this category, equivalent to 10.4% of total social protection expenditure. Figure 3 illustrates how real terms expenditure changed year-on-year between 2008 and 2014. In 2008 and 2009 growth was fairly constant, 7.1% and 7.2% respectively. However, from 2009 onwards growth began to decline. Growth slowed to 5.5% in 2010, followed by annual decreases in real terms expenditure for each of the remaining 4 years. In 2011 there was a decrease of 1.5%, followed by 2.0% in 2012 and 4.3% in 2013. There was a relatively small decrease of 0.1% in 2014.

Figure 3: Year-on-year growth in UK total expenditure in the family and children sector

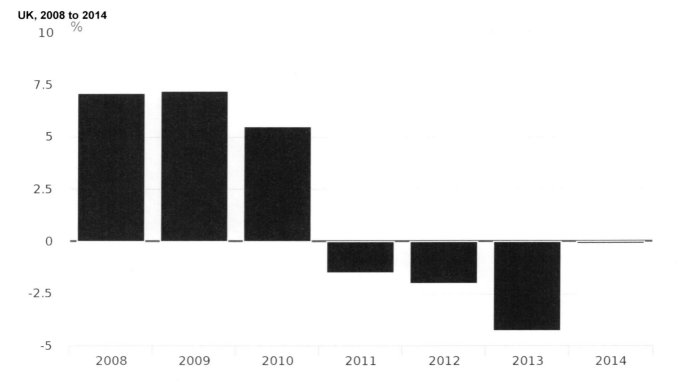

UK, 2008 to 2014

Source: Office for National Statistics

Notes:

1. 2014 prices.

Notes for: Children and families

1. This definition is taken from The ESSPROS Manual and User Guidelines.

6 . Old age

In this section the UK's expenditure on old age social protection will be compared to other countries. This international comparison should be interpreted with caution as the recipients of one type of social protection are likely to benefit from other types of social protection as well. For example, older people will potentially also benefit from social protection expenditure outside the old age category, such as sickness or housing, which have different patterns of expenditure by country.

The old age category of ESSPROS covers the provision of social protection against the risks linked to old age: loss of income, inadequate income, lack of independence in carrying out daily tasks, reduced participation in social life, and so on[1].

In terms of expenditure, the old age category of social protection is the largest. It accounted for 42.8% of total social protection expenditure in 2014. Pensions, both private and public, accounted for 88.3% of old age expenditure in 2014.

Table 2 gives the number of UK residents receiving benefits in the old age category of ESSPROS in 2014. It also gives the percentage changes in these numbers from 2013 and 2014; and the change from 2007 to 2014.

Table 2: Number of old age beneficiaries in the UK

	Total	Female	Male
Number in 2014	13,287,420	7,721,820	5,565,600
Change since 2013	0.5%	-0.8%	2.5%
Change since 2007	8.5%	0.7%	21.4%

Source: Office for National Statistics

The total number of recipients grew by 8.5% between 2007 and 2014, and by 0.5% between 2013 and 2014. There was a large difference between the growth rate of the number of female recipients and that of male recipients between 2007 and 2014 where the number of female recipients grew at 0.7%, compared with a growth rate of 21.4% in the number of males. In the year to 2014, the number of female recipients fell by 0.8%, while the number of male recipients grew at 2.5%. This difference was likely to have been driven by changes to the state pension rules introduced in 2010. In that year, incremental increases in state pension age for women designed to bring the state pension of females into line with that of males by 2018 were introduced.

From April 2012 onwards, the basic state pension in the UK, the largest single component of old age social protection expenditure, was subject to a new rule known as the "triple lock". In that and following years, it was increased by whichever was the highest of 3 percentages:

1. The growth in average earnings, as measured by the Average Weekly Earnings Index.

2. Price inflation (as measured by the Consumer Price Index).

3. 2.5%

Figure 4 illustrates 3 aspects of old age social protection expenditure. State pension expenditure and total old age social protection expenditure are considered on a per recipient basis. The UK's rank among the selected countries in terms of its expenditure on old age per capita is also considered.

Figure 4: UK expenditure on social protection and international rank

2007 to 2014

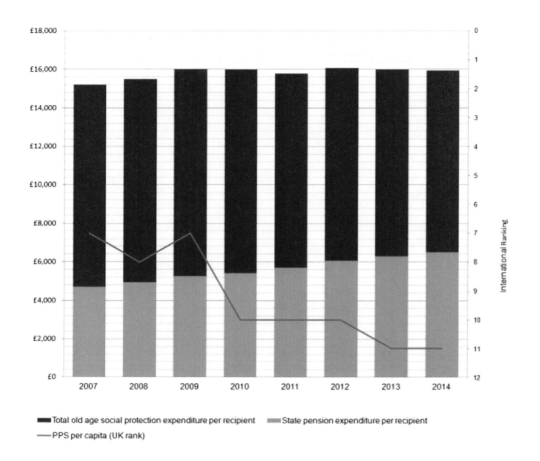

■ Total old age social protection expenditure per recipient ■ State pension expenditure per recipient
— PPS per capita (UK rank)

State pension expenditure per recipient has increased throughout 2007 to 2014. The strongest growth was recorded in 2009 and 2012 – an increase of 6.4% in both years. In the years between these peaks, 2010 and 2011, there was growth of 3.3% and 5.2% respectively. Growth was steady in 2013 and 2014, which saw increases of 3.6% and 3.5% respectively.

Growth in total expenditure per recipient on old age social protection was at its strongest in 2009 when it was 3.4%. After a relatively flat year in 2010, this expenditure fell by 1.3% in 2011. There was growth of 1.8% in 2012. This was followed by 2 years of declining expenditure. It decreased by 0.5% in 2013 and 0.2% in 2014.

These changes were partly driven by an increase in the number of beneficiaries. Total expenditure on old age social protection grew in real terms by 0.3% between 2013 and 2014, driven mainly by 1.1% growth in total expenditure on state and private pensions. This was partially offset by benefits in kind, mainly in the categories of accommodation and assistance in carrying out daily tasks. These decreased overall growth by 0.3 percentage points and 0.5 percentage points respectively.

The third time series illustrated in Figure 4 gives some international context to the old age expenditure described above. Purchasing Power Standards (PPS) have been used to rank the UK's expenditure per capita on old age social protection. Given that one PPS will, in theory, buy exactly the same amount in each country at a common point in time, this time series gives some insight into how well UK old age social protection is funded compared with other European countries.

The UK's rank as measured in PPS per capita fell 3 places to tenth in 2010. It remained in that position until 2013 when it fell to eleventh, where it remained the following year.

Notes for: Old age

1. This definition is taken from The ESSPROS Manual and User Guidelines.

Contact details for this statistical bulletin

Gerard Carolan

gerard.carolan@ons.gov.uk

Telephone: +44 (0)1633 456077

Office for
National Statistics

Article

Measuring national well-being in the UK: international comparisons, 2017

Compares the UK to the member countries of the Organisation for Economic Co-operation and Development (OECD) or the countries of the European Union (EU) to better understand how it is faring in key areas of well-being.

Contact:
Tess Carter / Chris Randall
qualityoflife@ons.gsi.gov.uk

Release date:
9 March 2017

Next release:
To be announced

Table of contents

1 . Main points

The UK is positioned around the middle of the distribution of countries for the majority of well-being measures. The countries that tend to appear in the top of the distribution include Denmark, Norway and Sweden, compared to Greece and Bulgaria who tend to appear at the bottom.

The harmonised unemployment rate for the UK was 5.3% in 2015. This compared to Greece which had the highest (25.0%) and Japan with the lowest (3.4%).

In 2015, 16% of UK households reported either difficulty or great difficulty in making ends meet, lower than the EU average of 26%. People in Greece (78%) were most likely to report difficulty while people in Sweden (5%) were least likely.

59% of people in the UK agreed or agreed strongly that they felt close to other people in the area where they lived, slightly higher than Germany (58%), the lowest-ranking country in 2012. The highest-ranked country was Cyprus (81%).

6% of the UK's total primary energy supply came from renewable sources in 2014. Iceland was the highest ranking country, where 89% of total primary energy supply was from renewable sources and Korea the lowest at 1%.

In 2014, 5% of people aged 15 and over in the UK reported feeling lonely most or almost all of the time. This compared with Poland which had the largest proportion (12%), and the Netherlands which had the lowest proportion (3%).

Asked to rate general satisfaction with life from 0 to 10, people in the UK gave 6.5 in 2015, the same as the Organisation for Economic Co-operation and Development (OECD) average. People in Norway and Switzerland were most satisfied (7.6) while people in Portugal were the least satisfied (5.1).

2 . Things you need to know about this release

This article explores how areas of well-being in the UK compares with the 35 member countries of the Organisation for Economic Co-operation and Development (OECD) using international well-being measures similar to those adopted as part of the UK's Measuring National Well-being (MNW) programme. We publish measures of national well-being, covering areas including our health, natural environment, personal finances and crime.

Looking at the measures within these domains from an international perspective gives us a sense of whether quality of life in the UK is better or worse than in other countries. This article includes data for the UK or Great Britain as a whole. It is worth noting that different groups or different areas of the UK may feel very differently about their lives and have different experiences. We will be publishing an update to the UK Measuring National Well-being programme in April 2017, which will allow comparisons across groups and geographies in the UK.

If international data are not available then a comparison with countries in the European Union (EU) is included if available. The article uses the latest data available in the last 5 years from sources including the OECD, Eurobarometer, European Social Survey, European Quality of Life Survey, Eurostat, Gallup World Poll, the International Institute for Democracy and Electoral Assistance, the United Nations and the World Health Organisation. Data for sections 3 to 12 are for adults aged 16 and over (unless otherwise stated) and cover different survey dates which are defined in the text. A lot of the data comes from household surveys so people not living in households are not included in the data (for example people who live in communal establishments).

For more information on the data and sources used for this article, please see <u>MNWB International Comparisons</u> <u>data</u>.

3 . Personal well-being

"Being able to measure people's quality of life is fundamental when assessing the progress of societies. There is now widespread acknowledgement that measuring subjective well-being is an essential part of measuring quality of life alongside other social and economic dimensions" (OECD, 2013).

Life satisfaction

Life satisfaction measures how people evaluate their life as a whole rather than their current feelings. According to data from the Organisation for Economic Co-operation and Development (OECD) conducted by Gallup World Poll, the average (mean) rating of life satisfaction for people in the UK was 6.5 out of 10 in 2015 (Figure 1). This was the same rating as the OECD average and Chile and was similar to France and Spain (6.4 out of 10) and the Czech Republic (6.6 out of 10). The highest-ranked countries were Norway and Switzerland (7.6 out of 10), while Portugal was the lowest-ranked country (5.1 out of 10).

Figure 1: Average rating of life satisfaction, 2015

OECD countries

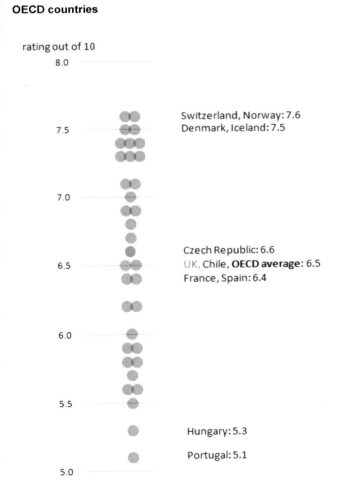

rating out of 10

8.0

Switzerland, Norway: 7.6
Denmark, Iceland: 7.5

7.5

7.0

Czech Republic: 6.6
UK, Chile, **OECD average**: 6.5
France, Spain: 6.4

6.5

6.0

5.5

Hungary: 5.3

Portugal: 5.1

5.0

Happiness

People aged 15 and over were asked on the 2014 European Social Survey, "Taking all things together, how happy would you say you are?" where 0 was extremely unhappy and 10 was extremely happy. In the UK a third of respondents (33%) reported a high rate of happiness (9 or 10 out of 10), the same proportion to Israel. Denmark had the largest proportion of people reporting a high rate of happiness (47%), while Lithuania had the lowest proportion (15%).

Worthwhile

According to the 2012 European Quality of Life Survey, over 8 in 10 people in the UK (82%) strongly agreed or agreed they generally felt that what they did in life was worthwhile. This was higher than the EU–28 average of 78%, the same as Spain (82%) and similar to France and Belgium (81%). The highest-ranking countries were Denmark and the Netherlands, where over 9 in 10 (92%) strongly agreed or agreed that they generally felt that what they did in life was worthwhile, while the lowest-ranking country was Greece (48%).

World Health Organisation (WHO) -5 mental well-being index

People thinking and feeling good about themselves and feeling able to cope with their problems can be described as having positive mental health. The WHO–5 mental wellbeing index comprises 5 positively worded items answered on a 6-point scale. Items included cheerfulness, calmness, activity, feeling rested and levels of interest. A higher score on this measure indicates better mental wellbeing. On the 2012 European Quality of Life Survey, people in the UK scored an average (mean) of 59 out of 100 on the WHO-5 mental wellbeing index. This was the same score as Slovakia and Poland and was lower than the EU–28 average of 63 out of 100. Denmark had the highest mean score (70 out of 100) and Latvia the lowest (56 out of 100).

4 . Our relationships

"Humans are social creatures. The frequency of their contacts with others and the quality of their personal relationships are crucial determinants of well-being" (OECD, 2011).

Satisfaction with personal relationships

Previous research has shown that the amount and quality of social connections with people around us are vitally important to an individual's well-being and should be considered when making any assessment of national well-being. On a survey run by Eurostat in 2013, respondents were asked to rate their satisfaction with their personal relationships on a scale from 0 (not satisfied at all) to 10 (fully satisfied). The average (mean) rating in the UK was 8.3 out of 10, this was the same as Finland, Slovenia and Sweden and higher than the EU-28 average of 7.8 out of 10. Ireland had the highest rating of satisfaction with their personal relationships (8.6 out of 10) while Bulgaria had the lowest (5.7 out of 10).

Loneliness

Inadequate social connectedness or poor relationships may lead to people experiencing loneliness in life. However the feeling of loneliness is subjective and a person may experience this even when in the company of family and friends. Loneliness increases the likelihood of mortality (Holt-Lunstad, 2015) and puts individuals at greater risk of cognitive decline (James et al, 2011). In the UK, 5% of people aged 15 and over reported feeling lonely most or almost all of the time in the week prior to interview according to the 2014 European Social Survey. This was the same proportion as Sweden and Ireland. Poland had the largest proportion of people reporting loneliness most or almost all of the time (12%), while the Netherlands had the lowest proportion (3%).

Social network support

People were asked on the Gallup World Poll in 2015, if they had relatives or friends they could count on to help when needed if they were in trouble. Over 9 in 10 people in the UK (93%) reported that they could count on someone, which was higher than the OECD average of 88%. This was the same proportion as Austria, Luxembourg, Norway and Switzerland. The highest and lowest proportions were in New Zealand (99%) and Mexico (75%) respectively.

5 . Health

"The relationship between health and well-being is fundamental and reciprocal, and the well-being of populations has important implications for the health sector" (World Health Organisation, 2015).

Healthy life expectancy at birth

Healthy life years are the average number of years that a person can expect to live in "full health" by taking into account years lived in less than full health due to disease and (or) injury. According to data for the Organisation for Economic Co-operation and Development (OECD) countries from the World Health Organisation (WHO), males in the UK had an estimated 70.3 healthy life years at birth in 2015, the same number of years as Ireland. Females in the UK had an estimated 72.5 healthy life years at birth in 2015, similar to New Zealand (72.4). Japan was the highest-ranking country for both males and females (72.5 and 77.2 healthy life years respectively). Latvia was the lowest-ranking country for males (63.2 healthy life years), while Turkey was the lowest-ranking country for females (67.8 healthy life years).

Perceived health status

Our previous research has shown that how people view their health was the most important factor related to their overall personal well-being. Data from the OECD shows that 70% of adults aged 15 and over in the UK reported to be in good or better than good health in 2014, the same proportion as Austria. Over 9 in 10 (91%) people in New Zealand reported good or better than good health, compared to 33% in Korea. Please note that data from New Zealand are not directly comparable with those for other countries, due to methodological differences in the survey questionnaire.

6 . What we do

"Participation in both physical and non-physical leisure activities has been shown to reduce depression and anxiety, produce positive moods and enhance self-esteem and self-concept, facilitate social interaction, increase general psychological wellbeing and life satisfaction, and improve cognitive functioning" (John T. Haworth, 2010).

Cultural participation

Some research studies have found links between arts and culture and well-being, for instance that culture helps to strengthen social ties in the community which ultimately nurtures social well-being. A special Eurobarometer survey run from April to May 2013 looked at cultural access and participation. Just under 8 in 10 (79%) adults aged 15 and over in the UK had a combined score of either very high, high or medium cultural engagement. This was higher than the EU-27 average of 66% and similar to France and Luxembourg (both 81%) and Finland and Lithuania (both 77%). The country with the highest combined score of either very high, high or medium cultural engagement was Sweden (92%) while the lowest was Greece (37%).

Taking part in sports or physical exercise

A special Eurobarometer survey run from November to December 2013 looked at participation in some kind of sport or exercise regularly or with some regularity. In the UK, 46% of people aged 15 and over participated in some kind of sport or exercise regularly (at least 5 times a week) or with some regularity (1 to 4 times a week). This was a higher proportion than the EU–28 average of 41% and the same proportion as Spain. Sweden had the highest proportion of people participating in sport or exercise regularly or with some regularity (70%) while Bulgaria had the lowest participation (11%).

Unemployment

There is strong evidence showing that work is generally good for physical and mental health and well-being. Worklessness is associated with poorer physical and mental health and well-being (Waddell and Burton, 2006). In 2015, the harmonised unemployment rate for the UK was 5.3% according to data from the Organisation for Economic Co-operation and Development (OECD), lower than the OECD average of 6.8% (Figure 2). This was the same rate as the United States and a similar rate to New Zealand (5.4%) and Israel (5.2%). The countries with the highest harmonised unemployment rate were Greece (25.0%) and Spain (22.1%), while the countries with the lowest rate were Japan (3.4%) and Korea (3.6%).

Figure 2: Harmonised unemployment rates, 2015

OECD countries

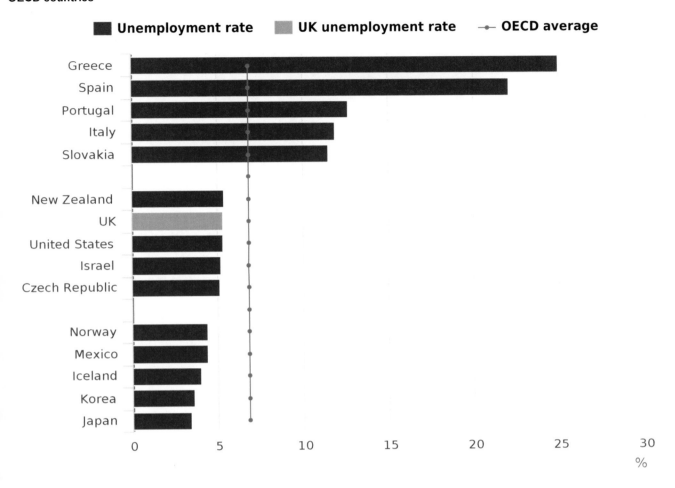

Source: Organisation for Economic Co-operation and Development

Notes:

1. Harmonised unemployment rates define the unemployed as people of working age who are without work, are available for work, and have taken specific steps to find work. The uniform application of this definition results in estimates of unemployment rates that are more internationally comparable than estimates based on national definitions of unemployment. This indicator is measured in numbers of unemployed people as a percentage of the labour force and it is seasonally adjusted. The labour force is defined as the total number of unemployed people plus those in civilian employment.

2. Chart shows the countries with the highest and lowest values along with the countries that have the same or similar values to the UK.

Job satisfaction

Work is an important part of most people's lives, it can provide structure and routine and a sense of self-worth which is essential for our well-being. There is evidence that happy and satisfied workers are more productive at work. It is also fair to say that the type of work, and job quality can have an impact on an employees' overall satisfaction with their job. On a survey run by Eurostat in 2013, respondents were asked to rate their satisfaction with their job on a scale from 0 (not at all satisfied) to 10 (fully satisfied). Fewer than 3 in 10 (28%) people in the UK reported a high satisfaction rating of rating 9 or 10 out of 10 with their job according to data from Eurostat, the same proportion as Malta and higher than the EU–28 average of 25%. Denmark had the highest proportion of people who had a high satisfaction with their job (44%), while the lowest proportion was in Greece (14%).

Volunteering

Volunteering may have benefits for both health and well-being and can make a difference to the lives of other people, the community or the environment. According to data from OECD conducted by Gallup World Poll in 2014, just under a third (32%) of people in Great Britain reported that they had volunteered some of their time during the 12 months prior to interview. This was higher than the OECD average of 26% and the same proportion as Austria, Germany and Norway. New Zealand had the highest proportion of people who reported that they had volunteered some of their time (45%), compared to just 7% in Greece.

7 . Where we live

"Where people live matters for their well-being and improving people's lives requires making where they live a better place" (OECD, 2014).

Feeling safe walking alone at night in the city or area where living

Personal security and safety is important to a person's sense of well-being and attitude to the area in which they live. According to the 2014 World Gallup Poll, over three-quarters of people in Great Britain (79%) felt safe walking alone at night in the city or area where they lived (Figure 3). This was higher than the Organisation for Economic Co-operation and Development (OECD) average of 69% and similar to Canada, Denmark and Germany (80%) and Iceland (78%). People in Norway felt the safest (86%), while people in Hungary felt the least safe (47%).

Figure 3: Proportion of people who feel safe walking alone at night in the city or area where living, 2014

OECD countries

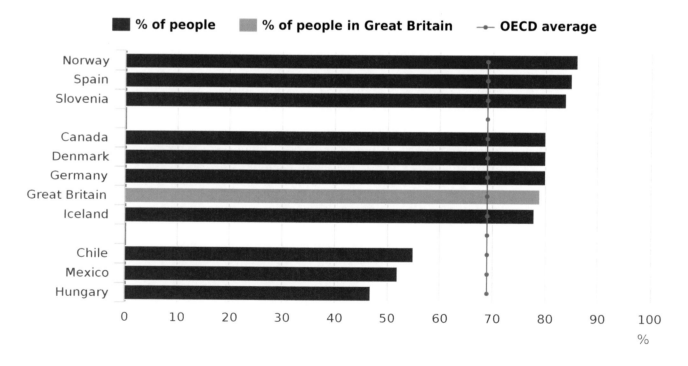

Source: Gallup World Poll

Notes:

1. Chart shows the countries with the highest and lowest values along with the countries that have the same or similar values to Great Britain.

Satisfaction with recreational and green areas

To have access to green and recreational areas plays an important role from the point of view of human well-being and health. On a survey run by Eurostat in 2013, respondents were asked to rate their satisfaction of recreational and green areas on a scale from 0 (not satisfied at all) to 10 (fully satisfied). In the UK, over a third (37%) rated their satisfaction as high (9 or 10 out of 10); this rating was similar to the Czech Republic (36%) and higher than the EU–28 average of 29%. Austria had the highest proportion of people rating their satisfaction with recreational and green areas as high (56%), while just 10% reported a high rating in Bulgaria.

Feeling close to people in the local area

Looking at whether people feel close to other people in the area where they live can give a sense of whether they feel a sense of belonging to their neighbourhood. According to the European Quality of Life Survey in 2012, 59% of people aged 16 and over in the UK reported that they agreed or agreed strongly with the statement that they felt close to other people in the area where they lived. This was lower than the EU–28 average of 67% and was similar to Germany (58%) which was the lowest-ranking country. The highest-ranked country was Cyprus (81%).

Satisfaction with accommodation

Satisfaction with accommodation is an important aspect of quality of life. Poor conditions such as overcrowding, damp, indoor pollutants and cold have all been shown to be associated with physical illnesses. They can also impact on mental health as people try to cope with the stress of living in cold, damp conditions.

On a survey run by Eurostat in 2013, respondents were asked to rate their satisfaction of their accommodation on a scale from 0 (not satisfied at all) to 10 (fully satisfied). In the UK, 44% rated their satisfaction as high (9 or 10 out of 10), higher than the EU–28 average of 33%. Finland had the highest proportion of people rating their satisfaction with their accommodation as high (54%), compared to just 17% in Latvia.

8 . Personal finance

"Household income and wealth are essential components of individual well-being. The ability to command resources allows people to satisfy basic needs and pursue many other goals that they deem important to their lives" (OECD, 2011).

At-risk-of-poverty rate

The well-being of people who are at-risk-of-poverty may be low as they may lack sufficient resources, be at risk of being in debt, suffer poor health, experience educational disadvantage and live in inadequate housing and environment. An individual is considered to be in poverty if they live in a household with an equivalised disposable income below 60% of the national median. Equivalisation adjusts the income to take into account the size and composition of the household. This type of relative indicator does not measure absolute wealth or poverty, but low income in comparison to other residents in that country, which does not necessarily imply a low standard of living. In 2015, 17% of the population of the UK were at-risk-of-poverty according to data from Eurostat, the same as the EU–28 average. The highest proportion of people at risk of poverty was in Romania (25%), while the lowest proportion of people was in the Czech Republic (10%).

Median net wealth per household

Financial wealth makes up an important part of a household's economic resources, and can protect from economic hardship and vulnerability. According to data from the Organisation for Economic Co-operation and Development (OECD), median net wealth per household[1] in Great Britain in 2012 was $187,380. This was higher than the OECD average (18 countries) of $132,615 and similar to Belgium ($188,149 in 2010). The country with the highest median net wealth per household was Luxembourg ($360,251 in 2010), while the Netherlands had the lowest median net wealth per household ($34,194 in 2010).

Median equivalised net income

Disposable income is the amount of money that households have available for spending and saving after direct taxes (such as income tax and council tax) have been accounted for, but before housing costs. It includes earnings from employment, private pensions and investments as well as cash benefits provided by the state. Data from Eurostat shows that in 2015 the median equivalised household disposable income (expressed in Purchasing Power Standard[2]) for the UK was €17,712, similar to Ireland (€17,704). Luxembourg had the highest median equivalised income (€29,285) while the lowest median equivalised income was in Romania (€4,357).

Satisfaction with financial situation

On a survey run by Eurostat in 2013, respondents were asked to rate their satisfaction of their financial situation on a scale from 0 (not satisfied at all) to 10 (fully satisfied). In the UK, 19% rated their financial satisfaction as high (9 or 10 out of 10); this rating was the same as Germany and higher than the EU–28 average of 13%. Denmark had the highest proportion of people rating their satisfaction with their financial situation as high (38%), while just 3% reported a high rating in Bulgaria.

Inability to make ends meet

To have the financial means to comfortably attain a satisfied lifestyle can be an important factor to many people's sense of well-being. According to data from Eurostat, 16% of all households in the UK reported great difficulty or difficulty in making ends meet in 2015 (Figure 4). This was lower than the estimated EU–28 average of 26%, and was the same as Estonia (16%). The countries with the highest proportion of households reporting great difficulty or difficulty in making ends meet were Greece (78%) and Bulgaria (64%), while the lowest proportion of households were in Sweden (5%) and Finland (7%).

Figure 4: Proportion of households making ends meet with difficulty or great difficulty, 2015

EU–28

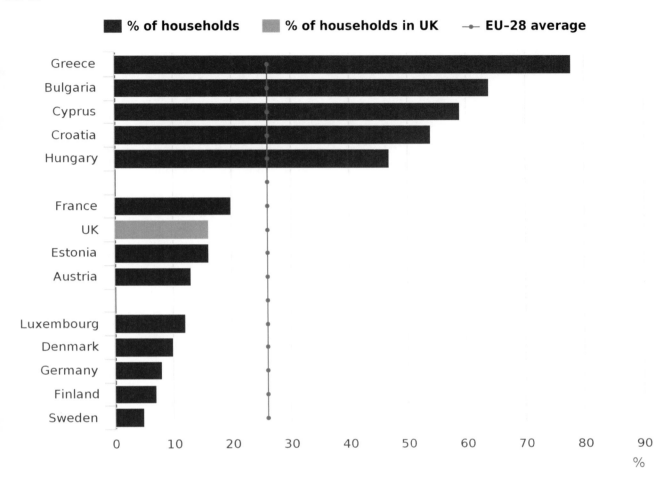

Source: Eurostat

Notes:

1. Chart shows the countries with the highest and lowest values along with the countries that have the same or similar values to the UK.

Notes for "Personal finance"

1. Wealth values are expressed in 2005 USD by, first, expressing values in prices of the same year (2005) through consumer price indexes and, second, by converting national values into a common currency through the use of purchasing power parities for household consumption. The median net wealth refers to the median wealth owned by households excluding pension schemes related to employment.

2. The purchasing power standard, abbreviated as PPS, is an artificial currency unit. Theoretically, one PPS can buy the same amount of goods and services in each country. However, price differences across borders mean that different amounts of national currency units are needed for the same goods and services depending on the country.

9 . The economy

"The economy makes an important contribution to national well-being. Financial stability and low inflation are important for economic growth. Without financial stability, banks are more reluctant to finance profitable projects which in turn affect jobs and wages" (ONS, 2016).

Net national income per capita

In 2014, ranking countries by net national income (NNI) [1] per capita, 16 Organisation for Economic Co-operation and Development (OECD) member countries were above or the same as the OECD average (100%), and 18 were below. The UK was just above the OECD average at 103%, and similar to Ireland (106%) and Finland (100%). The 4 highest-ranked countries were Norway (169%), Luxembourg (157%), Switzerland (145%) and the United States (140%). The lowest-ranked countries were Mexico (46%) and Latvia (54%).

Government consolidated gross debt

According to data from the OECD, the UK general government total gross [2] debt was 96% of gross domestic product (GDP) at current prices in July to September 2016. The highest rate of general government total gross debt as a percentage of GDP was in Japan (237%), while the lowest rate was in Estonia (13%).

Inflation rate

According to data from the OECD, the UK had a rate of inflation (Consumer Price Indices) in December 2016 of 1.6% which was the same as Spain and lower than the OECD average of 1.8%. Turkey had the highest inflation rate (8.5%), while Israel was the only OECD country that experienced falling prices in December 2016 (negative 0.2%).

Notes for "The economy"

1. Net national income (NNI) is equal to gross national income (GNI) net of depreciation. Gross National Income is defined as GDP plus net receipts from abroad of wages and salaries and of property income plus net taxes and subsidies receivable from abroad.

2. The definition and more information about general government debt is available

10 . Education and skills

"Education plays a key role in providing individuals with the knowledge, skills and competences needed to participate effectively in society and in the economy. In addition, education may improve people's lives in such areas as health, civic participation, political interest and happiness" (OECD, 2015)

Not in employment, education or training (NEET)

Helping young people to develop the drive, capacity and skills to enter employment is critical for the sustainability of societies. A young person identified as NEET is either unemployed or economically inactive and is either looking for work or is inactive for reasons other than being a student, an apprentice or a carer at home. In 2015, 16% of those aged 20 to 24[1] in the UK were NEET, lower than the Organisation for Economic Co-operation and Development (OECD) average (17%) and similar to Belgium and the United States (16%) (Figure 5). Italy and Turkey had the highest proportion of NEETS (34% and 33% respectively), while Iceland had the lowest proportion (7%).

Figure 5: Proportion of NEETs among those aged 20 to 24, 2015

OECD countries

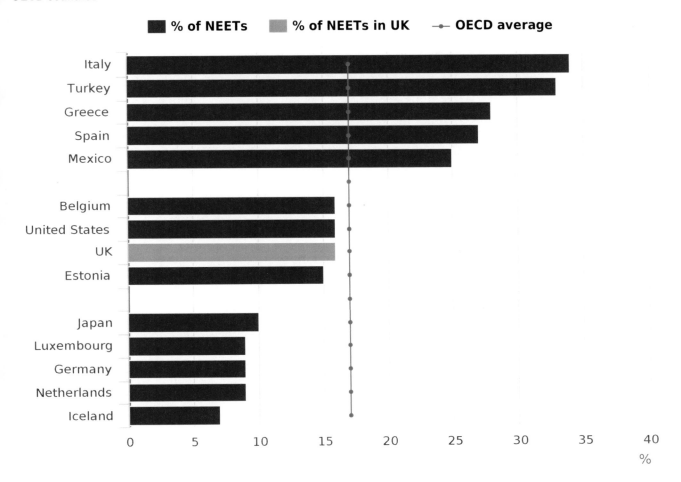

Source: Organisation for Economic Co-operation and Development

Notes:

1. NEET refers to young people that are not employed, in education or training.

2. Chart shows the countries with the highest and lowest values along with the countries that have the same or similar values to the UK.

Educational attainments below upper secondary education

Educational attainment can be a predictor of economic well-being. For example, people who have completed higher levels of education are more likely to achieve economic success than those who have not. According to data from the OECD, just over a fifth (21%) of people aged 25 to 64 in the UK had not completed upper secondary education in 2015. This included those who had pre-primary and primary education and lower secondary education only. This was slightly lower than the OECD average of 23% and the same proportion as Australia. Mexico had the highest proportion of people who had educational attainments below upper secondary education (65%), while the Czech Republic had the lowest proportion (7%).

Notes for "Education and skills".

1. OECD focuses mainly on 20- to 24-year-olds, as cross-country differences in the duration of compulsory education do not affect international comparisons of the transition from school to work at this age.

11 . Governance

"Civic engagement allows people to express their voice and to contribute to the political functioning of their society. In turn, in well-functioning democracies, civic engagement shapes the institutions that govern people's lives" (OECD, 2011).

Voter turnout

Voting is the most prominent form of political participation and, for many people, it is the only engagement with politics that they have. Political engagement and voicing political opinions matters to national well-being as it helps shape government activities, which in turn help build strong and resilient communities. According to data from the International Institute for Democracy and Electoral Assistance, two-thirds (66%) of registered voters in the UK voted in the parliamentary election in 2015. This was a similar proportion to Ireland in 2016 (65%) and Finland (67%) in 2015. Unsurprisingly, among the OECD countries, Luxembourg in 2013 and Australia in 2016 (where there is compulsory voting in both countries) had the highest proportion of registered voters who actually voted (91%). Of the countries with no compulsory voting, Denmark and Sweden in 2015 and 2014 respectively, had the highest proportion of voters (both 86%). Mexico in 2015 had the lowest proportion of voters (48%).

Confidence in national government

Trust in government is essential for social cohesion and well-being. It represents the confidence of citizens and businesses in the actions of the government. Just over 4 in 10 of people aged 15 and over in Great Britain (42%) reported having confidence in the national government in 2014 according to data from the Gallup World Poll (Figure 6). This was the same as the Organisation for Economic Co-operation and Development (OECD) average and similar to Estonia and Austria (41%). Switzerland had the highest proportion of people reporting confidence in their national government (75%), while Slovenia had the lowest proportion (18%).

Figure 6: Confidence in national government, 2014

OECD countries

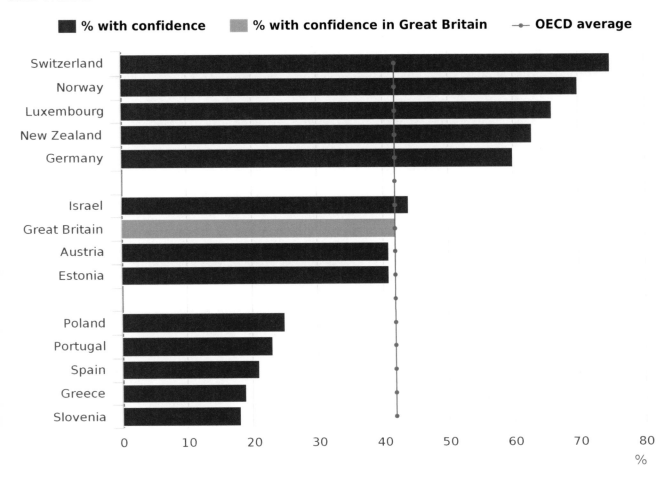

Source: Gallup World Poll

Notes:

1. Data refer to the percentage who answered "yes" to the question: "Do you have confidence in national government?"

2. Chart shows the countries with the highest and lowest values along with the countries that have the same or similar values to Great Britain.

12 . The natural environment

"Well-being is determined by physical and non-physical factors. The ability of a society to produce and consume goods and services determines its standard of living, but in the long-run even more critical is its ability to build and maintain the natural environment that meets basic needs like food, water, clean air and ensure the same for future generations" (ONS, 2012).

Greenhouse gas emissions

To mitigate climate change, countries around the world are developing policies to enhance environmental sustainability in areas such as transportation, housing and energy use, to reduce greenhouse gas emissions. In addition to their effects on greenhouse gas emissions, these policies are likely to have consequences for the well-being of their populations. Environmental statistics from the Organisation for Economic Co-operation and Development (OECD) show that the UK's greenhouse gas emissions[1] stood at 527.2 million tonnes of Carbon Dioxide equivalent (Mt of CO2e) in 2014. This figure was the fifth-highest among OECD countries and was similar to Australia (522.4 Mt of CO2e). The United States (6,870.5 Mt of CO2e) and Japan (1,363.9 Mt of CO2e) had the highest total emissions, while Iceland (4.6 Mt of Mt of CO2e) and Luxembourg (10.8 Mt of Mt of CO2e) had the lowest.

Protected Areas

Conservation policies usually involve protecting areas of land from human activity to preserve habitats and prevent species extinction. This in turn may have both a negative and positive effect on well-being for those who live near these areas, for example, loss of land can lead to loss of jobs while increased tourism can lead to the creation of jobs. According to data from the United Nations Statistical Division (Millennium Development Goals Database), 14% of marine and terrestrial areas were classed as protected[2] in the UK in 2014. This was the same as Finland. Slovenia had the highest proportion of protected marine and terrestrial areas (54%) and Turkey had the least (0%).

Energy from renewable sources

Using renewable sources[3] for supplying energy may enhance human welfare in terms of health and environmental improvements, and contribute to a climate safe future. In 2014, renewables accounted for 6% of the UK's total primary energy supply according to data from OECD. This was lower than the OECD average of 9% and similar to the United States, Australia and Belgium (7%) (Figure 7). The highest shares of renewable energy as a percentage of primary energy supply in 2014 were found in Iceland (89%) and Norway (43%). The lowest percentage shares were in Korea (1%) and Luxembourg (4%).

Figure 7: Contribution of renewables to primary energy supply, 2014

OECD countries

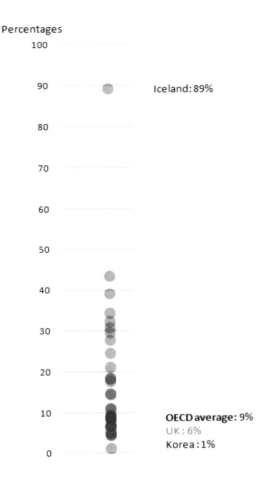

Percentages

Iceland: 89%

OECD average: 9%
UK : 6%
Korea : 1%

Recycling rate of municipal waste

According to data from OECD, 44% of the UK's municipal waste was recycled or composted [4] in 2014, the same proportion as Denmark. This was above the OECD average of 34%. The country with the highest proportion of recycled or composted municipal waste was Germany (64%). The countries with the lowest proportions were Turkey (0%) and Mexico (5% in 2012).

Notes for "The natural environment"

1. Data refer to total emissions of CO2 (emissions from energy use and industrial processes, for example, cement production), CH4 (methane emissions from solid waste, livestock, mining of hard coal and lignite, rice paddies, agriculture and leaks from natural gas pipelines), nitrous oxide (N2O), hydrofluorocarbons (HFCs), perfluorocarbons (PFCs), sulphur hexafluoride (SF6) and nitrogen trifluoride (NF3). Data exclude indirect CO2.

2. The units of measure in this indicator are terrestrial protected areas as well as marine protected areas in territorial waters (up to 12 nautical miles from the coast). The International Union for Conservation of Nature (IUCN) defines a protected area as "a clearly defined geographical space, recognized, dedicated and managed, through legal or other effective means, to achieve the long-term conservation of nature with associated ecosystem services and cultural values" (Dudley, 2008). For more information see Millennium Development Goals Indicators.

3. Renewable energy is defined as the contribution of renewables to total primary energy supply (TPES). Renewables include the primary energy equivalent of hydro (excluding pumped storage), geothermal, solar, wind, tide and wave sources. Energy derived from solid biofuels, biogasoline, biodiesels, other liquid biofuels, biogases and the renewable fraction of municipal waste are also included. Read more on renewable energy.

4. When interpreting these data, it should be noted that definitions and measurement methods vary among countries, and that inter-country comparisons require careful interpretation. For more information on each country's treatment and disposal method used see 'Municipal Waste Countries' Metadata'.

13 . Conclusion

This article has presented evidence of cross-country differences across 34 measures of well-being which are similar to those adopted as part of the UK's Measuring National Well-being programme. Among the Organisation for Economic Co-operation and Development (OECD) and European Union (EU) countries, quality of life varies widely according to these measures. The UK tends to rank at or near the OECD or EU average for each indicator and rarely appears at either the top or bottom of the rankings. This suggests that while the UK has strength on which to build, there is also room for improve in delivering a high quality of life for its citizens.

14 . Sources used in International comparisons, 2017

Eurobarometer

European Social Survey

European Quality of Life Survey

Eurostat

Gallup World Poll

International Institute for Democracy and Electoral Assistance

Organisation for Economic Co-operation and Development

United Nations Statistics Division

World Health Organisation

15 . OECD countries and member states of the EU

The Organisation for Economic Co-operation and Development (OECD)

The OECD is an international economic organisation of 35 countries, founded in 1961 to stimulate economic progress and world trade. It is a forum of countries describing themselves as committed to democracy and the market economy, providing a platform to compare policy experiences, seeking answers to common problems, identify good practices and coordinate domestic and international policies of its members.

OECD member countries are: Australia, Austria, Belgium, Canada, Chile, Czech Republic, Denmark, Estonia, Finland, France, Germany, Greece, Hungary, Iceland, Ireland, Israel, Italy, Japan, Korea (South Korea), Latvia, Luxemburg, Mexico, Netherlands, New Zealand, Norway, Poland, Portugal, Slovakia, Slovenia, Spain, Sweden, Switzerland, Turkey, the UK and the United States.

The European Union

The EU was created on 1 November 1993, when the Maastricht Treaty came into force. It encompasses the old European Community (EC) together with 2 intergovernmental "pillars" for dealing with foreign affairs and with immigration and justice. The European Union consists of 28 member states (EU–28), where the EU–27 is referred to in this article, Croatia is not included.

The 28 member states are as follows: Austria, Belgium, Bulgaria, Croatia, Cyprus, Czech Republic, Denmark, Estonia, Finland, France, Germany, Greece, Hungary, Ireland, Italy, Latvia, Lithuania, Luxembourg, Malta, Netherlands, Poland, Portugal, Romania, Slovakia, Slovenia, Spain, Sweden, and the UK.

Contact details for this statistical bulletin

Tess Carter / Chris Randall

QualityOfLife@ons.gsi.gov.uk

Telephone: +44 (0)1633 651812

Office for National Statistics

Statistical bulletin

Economic Well-being: Quarter 4, Oct to Dec 2016

Presents indicators that adjust or supplement more traditional measures such as GDP to give a more rounded and comprehensive basis for assessing changes in economic well-being.

Contact:
Dominic Webber/Vasileios Antonopoulos
economic.wellbeing@ons.gsi.gov. uk
+44 (0)1633 456246

Release date:
31 March 2017

Next release:
6 July 2017

Table of contents

1 . Main points

- In Quarter 4 (Oct to Dec) 2016, gross domestic product (GDP) in the UK per head increased by 0.5% compared with the previous quarter and 1.2% compared with the same quarter a year ago (Quarter 4 2015).

- Net national disposable income per head increased by 5.9% between Quarter 4 2015 and Quarter 4 2016, mainly due to a £7.6 billion increase in the income received from the UK's foreign direct investment abroad.

- Real household disposable income per head declined by 0.5% between Quarter 4 2015 and Quarter 4 2016, largely driven by increasing prices of goods and services.

- In Quarter 4 2016, real household spending per head increased 0.5% compared with the previous quarter – despite a fall in real household disposable income of 0.1% over the same period – meaning that it reached its pre-economic downturn level for the first time.

- Looking at economic well-being internationally, growth in real household disposable income (including non-profit institutions serving households (NPISH)) was slower in the UK compared with the OECD countries between Quarter 1 (Jan to Mar) 2010 and Quarter 3 (July to Sept) 2016 – 0.1% and 0.4% average quarterly growth respectively.

- Between Quarter 3 2016 and Quarter 4 2016, consumers reported a worsening in their perception of both the general economic situation and their own financial situation over the last year.

2 . Summary of latest economic well-being indicators

This quarter's data paints a mixed picture for economic well-being in the UK. Overall, whole economy indicators were positive; with growth in gross domestic product (GDP) per head and net national disposable income per head. This hasn't translated fully to households though; with incomes declining this quarter due mainly to a rise in prices. Despite the fall in income per person, spending increased and returned to the pre-2008 downturn level for the first time. Finally, economic sentiment worsened this quarter with consumers' confidence in the general economic situation falling and consumers also feeling less favourable about their own financial situation.

3 . Things you need to know about this release

This release reports measures of economic well-being in the UK . Rather than focusing on traditional measures such as gross domestic product (GDP) alone, these indicators aim to provide a more rounded and comprehensive basis for assessing changes in material well-being.

We prefer to measure economic well-being on a range of measures rather than a composite index. The framework and indicators used in this release were outlined in Economic Well-being, Framework and Indicators, published in November 2014.

Our 10 main economic well-being indicators are:

- gross domestic product (GDP) per head – the value of goods and services produced, adjusted for changes in population

- net national disposable income per head – the income available to all residents in the UK, which differs from GDP per head mainly due to adjustments for capital depreciation – such as the day-to-day wear and tear on vehicles and machinery – and the flows of income with the rest of the world - such as inward-income earned by UK investors on assets overseas, and outward-income foreign investors earn on assets in the UK

- real household disposable income per head – the amount of money households have to spend on consumption, or to save and invest, after taxes, National Insurance, pension contributions and interest have been paid

- real household final consumption expenditure per head – household spending on goods and services

- real median equivalised household income – represents the middle of the income distribution and is a good indication of the standard of living of the "typical" household in terms of income

- whole economy net wealth – represents the market value of financial and non-financial assets in the UK and provides an indication of the sustainability of current levels of production and corresponding income flows

- household and non-profit institutions serving households (NPISH) net wealth – market value of financial and non-financial assets in the household and NPISH sector

- consumers' perception of their personal financial situation over the past 12 months

- unemployment rate – the proportion of those actively looking for a job who are unemployed

- inflation – change in prices over the last month as measured by the Consumer Prices Index including a measure of owner occupiers' housing costs (CPIH))

This edition of the economic well-being release introduces a number of improvements. First, it focuses more on new data published this quarter, while providing a summary of already existing data in the "Economic well-being indicators already published" section. Second, we will include a "Spotlight" section, which will investigate issues relating to economic well-being in more detail. This quarter we present international comparisons of economic well-being. We welcome any feedback on the new style and any suggestions for further analysis at economic.wellbeing@ons.gov.uk.

4 . What were the main changes in economic well-being in Quarter 4 2016?

Figure 1: 4 measures of economic well-being Q1 (2008) to Q4 (2016)

United Kingdom

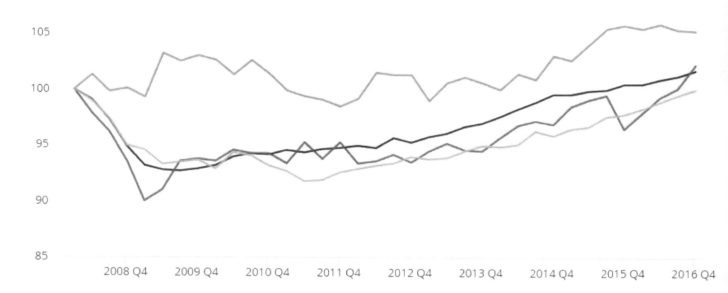

Source: Office for National Statistics

Notes:

1. Q1 refers to Quarter 1 (January to March), Q2 refers to Quarter 2 (April to June), Q3 (July to September) and Q4 refers to Quarter 4 (October to December).

Real GDP per head

Real gross domestic product (GDP) per head increased by 0.5% in Quarter 4 (Oct to Dec) 2016 compared with the previous quarter. This was a slightly slower growth rate than the 0.7% quarterly increase seen in GDP, but 0.2 percentage points higher than quarterly growth recorded in Quarter 3 (July to Sept) 2016. GDP per head grew by 1.1% between 2015 and 2016 – down 0.3 percentage points from growth of 1.4% between 2014 and 2015.

Real net national disposable income (NNDI) per head

Real net national disposable income (NNDI) increased by 5.9% between Quarter 4 2016 and Quarter 4 2015, compared with a 1.2% increase in GDP per head over the same period. Looking at 2016 as a whole, NNDI per head increased by 1.5% between 2015 and 2016, down 0.3 percentage points from growth between 2014 and 2015.

There are 2 main differences between GDP per head and NNDI per head.

First, not all income generated by production in the UK will be payable to UK residents. For example, a country whose firms or assets are predominantly owned by foreign investors may well have high levels of production, but a lower national income once profits and rents flowing abroad are taken into account. As a result, the income available to residents would be less than that implied by measures such as GDP.

Second, NNDI per head is adjusted for capital consumption. GDP is "gross" in the sense that it does not adjust for capital depreciation, that is, the day-to-day wear and tear on vehicles, machinery, buildings and other fixed capital used in the productive process. It treats such consumption of capital as no different from any other form of consumption, but most people would not regard depreciation as adding to their material well-being.

Figure 2: Cumulative contributions to growth in Net National Disposable Income per head since Q1 2008, Chain volume measure, Quarter 1 (Jan to Mar) 2008 to Quarter 4 (Oct to Dec) 2016

United Kingdom

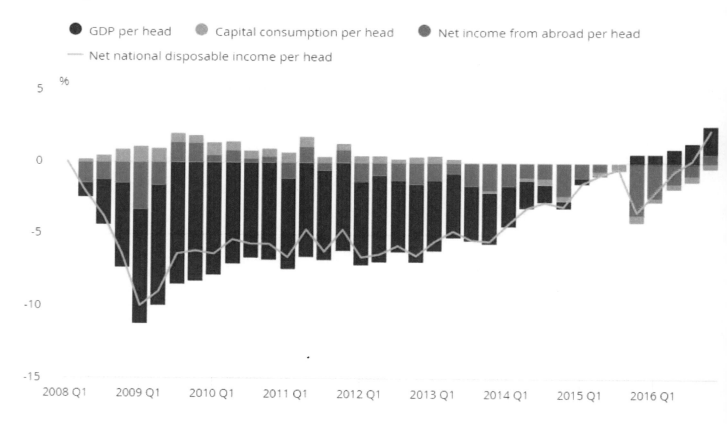

Source: Office for National Statistics

Notes:

1. Q1 refers to Quarter 1 (January to March), Q2 refers to Quarter 2 (April to June), Q3 refers to Quarter 3 (July to September) and Q4 refers to Quarter 4 (October to December).

Figure 2 examines how changes in GDP per head, capital consumption per head and net income from abroad per head have influenced NNDI per head since Quarter 1 2008. It should be noted that net income from abroad is comprised of a number of components which aren't published on a quarterly basis. In the analysis above, net income from abroad is derived using published information on net national disposable income, GDP and capital consumption.

Net income from abroad = Net national disposable income - GDP + capital consumption

Figure 2 shows that the contraction in GDP per head during the economic downturn provided the largest negative cumulative contribution towards a 10% decline in NNDI per head between Quarter 1 2008 and Quarter 1 2009. After Quarter 1 2009, GDP per head recovered – highlighted in the chart by the reduced negative cumulative contribution from GDP per head – while net income from abroad remained steady. As a result, NNDI per head grew by an average of 0.2% between Quarter 1 2009 and Quarter 4 2011. However, following this, the UK's net income balance with the rest of the world deteriorated. Figure 3 will look more closely at this; however, the effect was to introduce a gap between GDP per head and NNDI per head. Between Quarter 4 2011 and Quarter 4 2015, GDP per head increased by an average of 0.4% per quarter compared with average quarterly growth in NNDI per head of 0.1%. This meant that while GDP per head reached its pre-economic downturn peak in Quarter 3 2015, NNDI per head didn't reach this yardstick until Quarter 3 2016. More recently, there has been an improvement with the UK's net income from abroad, so that NNDI per head was 2.2% above its pre-economic downturn level in Quarter 4 2016 compared with GDP per head, which was 1.7% above its pre-economic downturn level in the same quarter.

Figure 3: Balance of primary incomes and components, £millions, from Quarter 1 (Jan to Mar) 2010 to Quarter 4 (Oct to Dec) 2016

United Kingdom

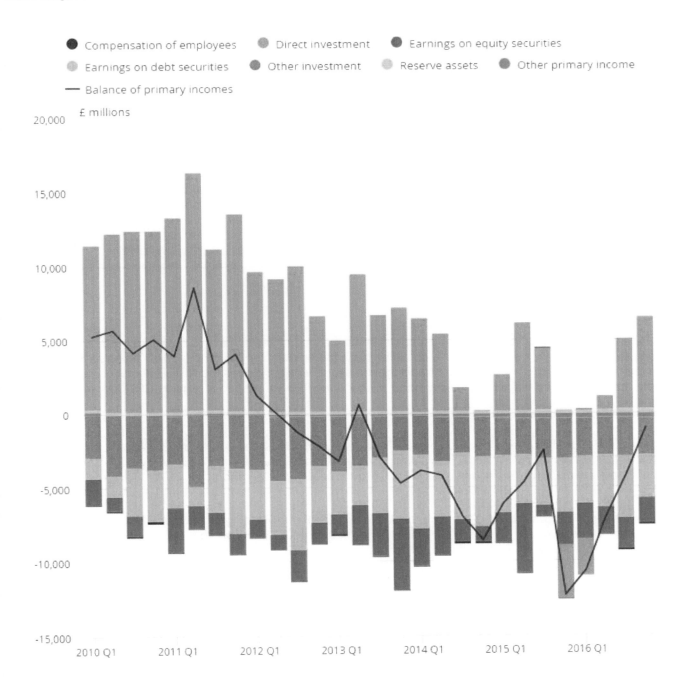

Source: Office for National Statistics

Notes:

1. Q1 refers to Quarter 1 (January to March), Q2 refers to Quarter 2 (April to June), Q3 refers to Quarter 3 (July to September) and Q4 refers to Quarter 4 (October to December).

Looking at the deterioration in net income from abroad, Figure 3 presents the balance of primary incomes and its main components. It should be noted that the balance of primary incomes is only one component of net foreign income from abroad, although it is generally the largest. Further, balance of primary incomes is in current prices, whereas net income from abroad is calculated from series that have been adjusted for the change in prices.

Figure 3 shows that the balance of primary incomes declined from £8,580 million in Quarter 2 2011 to reach a deficit of £12,353 million in Quarter 4 2015. After this it increased by £11,318 million to a deficit of £1,035 million in Quarter 4 2016. A major factor in the decline in the balance of primary income was a fall in the direct investment earnings balance – earnings from cross-border investments made by residents and businesses from one country into another, with the aim of establishing a lasting relationship.

Since 1997, the balance of earnings on foreign direct investment (FDI) (the difference between earnings from direct investment abroad and from foreign direct investment in the UK) made a positive contribution to the UK current account, partly offsetting negative contributions from the other major components. However, the surplus in FDI earnings has fallen since 2011, turning negative in late 2015 – the first deficit since Quarter 4 2008. This deterioration is attributed to falling earnings for UK residents from direct investment abroad and an increase in foreign earnings on direct investment in the UK. More information is available in our analysis of the drivers behind the fall in direct investment earnings and their impact on the UK's current account deficit release.

Household income

Unless stated otherwise, analysis of real household disposable income (RHDI) in this bulletin excludes non-profit institutions serving households (NPISH). We consider this a better indicator of economic well-being as it focuses more on the household experience than the traditional measure, which includes the NPISH sector. Real household and NPISH disposable income per head will continue to be published alongside RHDI per head (excluding NPISH) in the datasets.

In Quarter 4 2016, RHDI per head declined by 0.5% compared with the same quarter a year ago (Quarter 4 2015), but was 5.2% above its pre-economic downturn level. On an annual basis, RHDI per head increased 1.0% in 2016 compared with 2015. This is down from 3.1% growth between 2014 and 2015.

Looking at the historical context, as GDP began to fall in mid-2008, Figure 1 highlights that RHDI per head remained relatively resilient. By Quarter 2 2009, RHDI per head was 3.2% above its pre-economic downturn level. This initial improvement in real household income per head was a result of several factors.

Firstly, household incomes were buoyed by falling mortgage repayments as a result of historic lows in the interest rate. Additionally, automatic stabilisers – such as reduced Income Tax payments and increased benefits as a result of lower employment – supported incomes during worsening conditions in the labour market. However, moving into early 2011, the impact of these factors wore off and inflation rose. Prices grew more strongly than household income and therefore, over time, people found that their income purchased a lower quantity of goods and services.

More recently, growth in household income has begun to wane – average quarterly growth between Quarter 3 2015 and Quarter 4 2016 was 0.0% compared with 0.9% between Quarter 1 2014 and Quarter 3 2015. As explained in the previous edition of the economic well-being bulletin, recent slowing in household income per head has been mainly driven by an increase in the general price level.

Household expenditure

While income is an important measure of material well-being, it is important to also consider how much households actually consume. ONS analysis presented new findings on the relationship between personal well-being, household income and expenditure. Using regression analysis, it concluded that household expenditure appeared to have a stronger relationship with personal well-being than household income.

In Quarter 4 2016, real household spending per head (excluding non-profit institutions serving households) grew 0.5% compared with the previous quarter, continuing the general upward trend seen since Quarter 3 2011. As highlighted in Figure 1, real household spending per head (excluding NPISH) reached its pre-economic downturn level in Quarter 4 2016 for the first time after Quarter 1 2008. This is despite real household disposable income per head (excluding NPISH) being 5.2% above its pre-economic downturn level in Quarter 4 2016.

5 . Spotlight: International comparisons of economic well-being

Figure 4: GDP per head, UK and a range of selected countries, Quarter 1 (Jan to Mar) 2007 to Quarter 3 (July to Sept) 2016

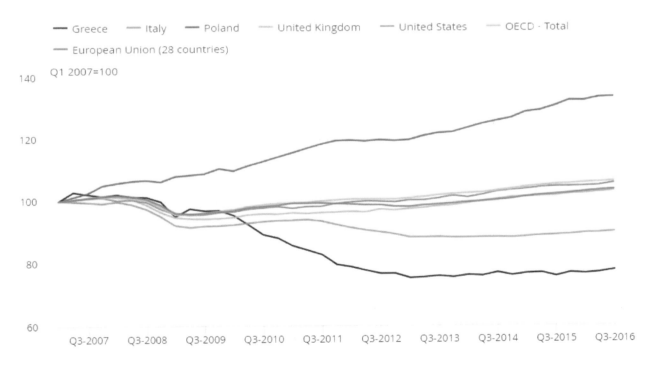

Source: Office for National Statistics, OECD

This section compares 2 headline indicators of economic well-being – gross domestic product (GDP) per head and real household disposable income (RHDI) (including non-profit institutions serving households (NPISH)) – in the UK and a selection of EU and Organisation for Economic Co-operation and Development (OECD) countries.

107

Figure 4 shows that the recovery in GDP per head in the UK has been weaker than the total of the OECD countries and more comparable with the European Union. Average quarterly growth in GDP per head was 0.2% across the OECD countries between Quarter 1 (Jan to Mar) 2007 and Quarter 3 (July to Sept) 2016, compared with 0.1% in the UK and EU over the same period.

However, the UK, EU and the total of OECD countries have followed different growth paths since 2007. Compared with the total of OECD countries and EU, GDP per head contracted more sharply in the UK during the economic downturn, but then recovered more quickly. Between Quarter 1 2007 and Quarter 4 (Oct to Dec) 2011, average quarterly growth in GDP per head in the UK was negative 0.2%, compared with 0.0% in the EU and the total of OECD countries respectively. Between Quarter 1 2012 until Quarter 3 2016, growth in GDP per head in the UK was 0.4% per quarter, compared with 0.3% and 0.2% in the total of OECD countries and EU respectively.

Poland and Greece represent 2 extremes in growth in GDP per head since 2007. Poland was largely unaffected by the economic downturn and recorded 0.8% average annual growth in GDP per head between Quarter 1 2007 and Quarter 3 2016 – the largest average annual growth of all OECD countries. GDP per head in Greece, on the other hand, contracted by 0.7% on average per quarter between Quarter 1 2007 and Quarter 3 2016. Further, GDP per head in Greece contracted in 25 of the 38 quarters between Quarter 1 2007 and Quarter 3 2016 – the highest number of all OECD countries.

Figure 5: Real household (including NPISH) disposable income per head, UK and selected countries, Quarter 1 (Jan to Mar) 2007 to Quarter 3 (July to Sept) 2016

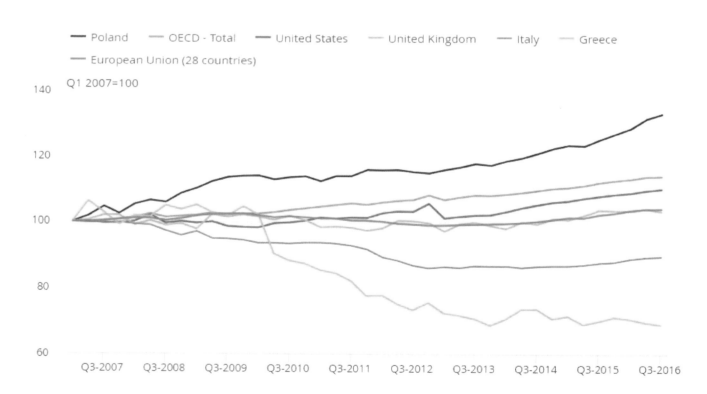

Source: Office for National Statistics, OECD, Eurostat

RHDI (including NPISH) growth in the UK was relatively weak compared with other OECD countries following the economic downturn. Figure 5 highlights that, between Quarter 1 2010 and Quarter 3 2016, RHDI (including NPISH) per head in the UK grew by 0.1% per quarter on average compared with 0.4% in the total of OECD countries.

Stronger growth in the OECD total of countries is largely accounted for by Chile, Poland and Norway – 1.1%, 0.6%, and 0.5% average quarterly growth between Quarter 1 2010 and Quarter 3 2016 respectively. On the other hand, Greece, which recorded the lowest growth rate of GDP per head over recent years, also recorded the lowest growth rate in RHDI (including NPISH) per head. RHDI (including NPISH) per head contracted by an average of 1.5% per quarter between Quarter 1 2010 and Quarter 3 2016.

Figure 6: Contributions to real household (including NPISH) disposable income growth, UK, Greece and Poland, Quarter 1 (Jan to Mar) 2003 to Quarter 3 (July to Sept) 2016

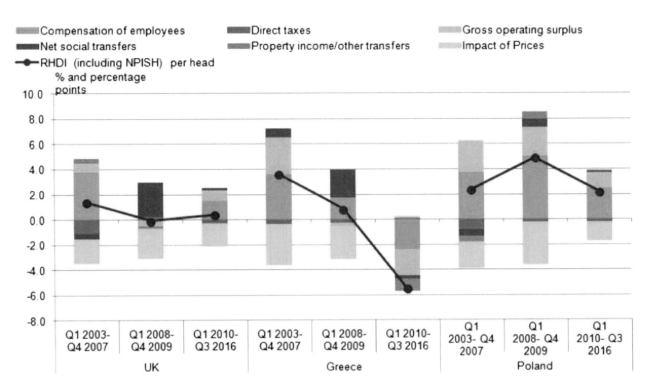

Figure 6 examines the role of different contributions to RHDI (including NPISH) per head growth for the UK, Greece and Poland between Quarter 1 2003 and Quarter 3 2016. It shows that for all 3 countries, growth in compensation of employees per head provided the strongest contribution to RHDI (including NPISH) growth per head before the economic crisis. Compensation of employees includes the wages and salaries payable in cash or in kind to an employee in a return for work done and the social insurance contributions payable by employers.

During the years of economic downturn – 2008 and 2009 – RHDI (including NPISH) per head in UK and Greece was supported by an increase in net social transfers amidst falling contributions from compensation of employees. The story in Poland, on the other hand, was remarkably different. As shown in Figure 5, GDP per head did not contract in Poland during 2008 and 2009, which perhaps explains stronger contributions from compensation of employees.

After 2009, the impact of net transfers began to decline in Greece and the UK. However, the UK's recovering economy supported a return to positive contributions from compensation of employees and gross operating surplus (which includes mixed income). The only component to support growth in RHDI (including NPISH) per head in Greece was a fall in prices. As a result RHDI (including NPISH) per head contracted by an average of 5.5% per quarter compared with growth of 0.4% in the UK.

6 . Economic sentiment

It is important to consider sentiment, along with other measures of economic well-being, to better understand how changes in official measures of the economy are perceived by individuals. Information regarding perceptions of the economy are sourced from the Eurobarometer Consumer Survey, conducted by GFK on behalf of the European Commission. The Quality and Methodology section provides more information regarding the Eurobarometer Consumer Survey.

General economic situation and perception of financial situation

The Eurobarometer Consumer Survey asks consumers their views on the state of the general economic situation over the previous 12 months. A positive balance means that consumers perceived an improvement within the economy, a zero balance indicates no change and a negative balance indicates a perceived worsening.

Figure 7: Consumer perceptions of general economic situation and their own financial situation over last 12 months, January 2006 to December 2016

Source: European Commission

Notes:

1. The source is the Eurobarometer Consumer Survey, which is collected by GfK for the European Commission. Further information can be found in background note 5.

2. A negative balance means that, on average, respondents reported the general economic situation. A positive balance means they reported it improved and a zero balance indicators no change.

Between Quarter 3 (July to Sept) 2016 and Quarter 4 (Oct to Dec) 2016, the balance fell from negative 18.8 to negative 23.3, suggesting that households' perception of the general economic situation has worsened, potentially as a result of the decline in UK's currency and rising inflation.

The series had been on a general upwards trend in recent years until April 2015, before the trend turned negative in July 2015. Analysis by GFK suggests that the negative trend could potentially be explained by economic uncertainty abroad and later, in 2016, reduced confidence following the European referendum.

The survey also asks respondents about their own financial situation. This has generally been positive since May 2015 (it was negative in July and August 2016), ending a 7 year negative balance since February 2008. In the latest quarter, the balance fell from 1.6 in September 2016 to 0.7 in December 2016, indicating that consumers are less positive about their financial situation. Overall, these indicators taken together suggest that respondents feel that the general economic situation has worsened in recent quarters and that their own financial situation is less certain.

Perception of inflation

The Eurobarometer Consumer Survey also asks respondents about their perception of prices over the previous 12 months. A positive balance suggests that consumers perceive prices to have increased over the previous 12 months, while a negative balance suggests the opposite. In Quarter 4 2016, the balance increased to positive 7.8 from negative 5.3 in Quarter 3 2016.

Figure 8: Comparison between CPIH and individual's perception of price trends over the last 12 months, January 2006 to December 2016

United Kingdom

Source: Office for National Statistics, European Commission

Notes:

1. The Eurobarometer Consumer Survey is collected by GfK for the European Commission.

Consumers' perception of inflation remained negative for 19 months between April 2015 and November 2016. This corresponds with a low CPIH rate during this period – the 12-month rate was under 1% from December 2014 to July 2016 and has steadily increased since October 2015.

7 . Economic well-being indicators already published

Between 2014 and 2015, the total net worth of the UK increased by 5.9% to £8.3 trillion. The largest contribution to this was from the household and non-profit institutions serving households (NPISH) sector, which contributed 4.9 percentage points to the total growth.

Between 2014 and 2015, household wealth increased by 4.1%. This was as a result of a 6.5% increase in the amount of wealth in non-financial assets (for example, buildings and machinery).

In the year to December 2016, the 12-month CPIH (Consumer Prices Index with owner occupiers' housing costs) rate increased from 1.3% to 1.8% to reach its highest level since June 2014. The increase in prices was mainly driven by a rise in prices for transport and restaurant and hotels.

The unemployment rate for those aged 16 to 64 remained unchanged at 4.9% between the 3 months to September 2016 and the 3 months to December 2016. The employment rate (the proportion of people aged from 16 to 64 who were in work) was 74.6% in the 3 months to December 2016 – the highest rate since comparable records began in 1971.

The median UK household disposable income was £26,300 in the financial year ending 2016 (2015/16); this was £600 higher than the previous year and £1,000 higher than the pre-downturn value of £25,400 in the financial year ending 2008 (2007/08) (after accounting for inflation and household composition).

The wealthiest 10% of households owned 45% of aggregate total wealth in July 2012 to June 2014 and were 2.4 times wealthier than the second wealthiest 10%. Over the same period the wealthiest 10% of households were 5.2 times wealthier than the bottom 50% of households (the bottom 5 deciles combined), who owned 9% of aggregate total wealth.

8 . Links to related statistics

Internal

United Kingdom Economic Accounts, Table 1.1.5 (ONS)

The National Balance Sheet (ONS)

Wealth and Assets Survey (ONS)

Household disposable income and inequality (ONS)

Labour Market Statistics (ONS)

Consumer Price Indices (ONS)

External

Eurobarometer Consumer Survey (produced by GFK on behalf of the European Commission)

International comparisons of real household (including NPISH) disposable income per head index (OECD)

International comparisons of GDP per head index (OECD)

Contributions to growth in real household (including NPISH) disposable income per head (European Central Bank)

9 . Quality and methodology

1. **Release policy**

   The data used in this version of the release are the latest available at 31 March 2017. This release uses the latest population estimates with the exception of the latest year where population projections are used and are consistent with mid-year estimates published 23 June 2016. These may be revised later once ONS publishes headline population estimates for 2017.

2. **Basic quality and methodology information**

   Basic quality and methodology information for all indicators in this statistical bulletin can be found on our website:

   - National Accounts Quality and methodology Information report

   - Consumer Price Indices Quality and methodology Information report

   - Wealth and Assets Survey Quality and methodology Information report

   - Effects of Taxes and Benefits Quality and methodology information report

   - Labour Market Quality and methodology Information reports

   These contain important information on:

   - the strengths and limitations of the data and how it compares with related data

   - users and uses of the data

   - how the output was created

   - the quality of the output including the accuracy of the data

3. **Revisions and reliability**

All data in this release will be subject to revision in accordance with the revisions policies of their original release. Estimates for the most recent quarters are provisional and are subject to revision in the light of updated source information. We currently provide an analysis of past revisions in statistical bulletins, which present time series. Details of the revisions are published in the original statistical bulletins.

Most revisions reflect either the adoption of new statistical techniques or the incorporation of new information, which allows the statistical error of previous estimates to be reduced.

Only rarely are there avoidable "errors", such as human or system failures and such mistakes are made quite clear when they do occur.

For more information about the revisions policies for indicators in this release:

- National Accounts revisions policy – covers indicators from the Quarterly National Accounts, UK Economic Accounts and the National Balance Sheet

- Wealth and Assets Survey revisions policy – covers indicators on the distribution of wealth

- Effect of Taxes and Benefits on household incomes revisions policy – covers indicators on the distribution of income

- Labour Market Statistics revisions policy – covers indicators from labour market statistics

- Consumer Price Inflation - revisions policy – covers indicators from consumer price indices

Our Revisions policies for economic statistics webpage is dedicated to revisions to economic statistics and brings together our work on revisions analysis, linking to articles, revisions policies and important documentation from the former Statistics Commission's report on revisions.

Data that come from the Eurobarometer Consumer Survey and Understanding Society releases are not subject to revision as all data are available at the time of the original release. These data will only be revised in light of methodological improvements or to correct errors. Any revisions will be made clear in this release.

4. Interpreting the Eurobarometer Consumer Survey

The Eurobarometer Consumer Survey, sourced from GFK on behalf of the European Commission, asks respondents a series of questions to determine their perceptions on a variety of factors, which collectively give an overall consumer confidence indicator. For each question, an aggregate balance is given which ranges between negative 100 and positive 100.

Balances are the difference between positive and negative answering options, measured as percentage points of total answers. Values range from negative 100, when all respondents choose the negative option (or the most negative one in the case of 5-option questions) to positive 100, when all respondents choose the positive (or the most positive) option.

The questions used in this release are:

Question 1: How has the financial situation of your household changed over the last 12 months? It has...

- got a lot better

- got a little better

- stayed the same

- got a little worse

- got a lot worse

- don't know

Question 3: How do you think the general economic situation in the country has changed over the past 12 months? It has...

- got a lot better

- got a little better

- stayed the same

- got a little worse

- got a lot worse

- don't know

Question 5: How do you think that consumer prices have developed over the last 12 months? They have...

- risen a lot

- risen moderately

- risen slightly

- stayed about the same

- fallen

- don't know

Further information on this consumer survey is available from the Business and Consumer Survey section of the European Commission website.

5. **Measuring national well-being**

This article is published as part of our Measuring National Well-being programme. The programme aims to produce accepted and trusted measures of the well-being of the nation – how the UK as a whole is doing. Further information on Measuring National Well-being is available on our website with a full list of well-being publications.

Contact details for this statistical bulletin

Dominic Webber / Vasileios Antonopoulos

economic.wellbeing@ons.gsi.gov.uk

Telephone: +44 (0)1633 456246

Statistical bulletin

Economic Well-being: Quarter 1 (Jan to Mar) 2017

Presents indicators that adjust or supplement more traditional measures such as GDP to give a more rounded and comprehensive basis for assessing changes in economic well-being.

Contact:
Dominic Webber and Vasileios Antonopoulos
economic.wellbeing@ons.gsi.gov. uk
+44 (0)1633 456246

Release date:
6 July 2017

Next release:
3 October 2017

Table of contents

1 . Main points

- Gross domestic product (GDP) per head in the UK was unchanged (0.0% growth) compared with the previous quarter and increased by 1.3% compared with the same quarter a year ago (Quarter 1 (Jan to Mar) 2016).

- Net national disposable income (NNDI) per head increased by 4.3% between Quarter 1 2016 and Quarter 1 2017, mainly due to a £6.9 billion increase in the income received from the UK's foreign direct investment from abroad.

- Despite improvements in both GDP per head and NNDI per head, real household disposable income (RHDI) per head declined by 2.0% in Quarter 1 2017 compared with the same quarter a year ago – the largest decrease since the end of 2011, driven by increasing prices of goods and services.

- Average quarterly growth in social transfers in kind – for example, education and health care services provided for free, or at little cost by the government – was 0.2% between Quarter 1 2010 and Quarter 1 2017 compared with 1.9% between Quarter 1 2002 and Quarter 4 (Oct to Dec) 2010.

- Between Quarter 4 2016 and Quarter 1 2017, consumers reported an improvement in their perception of their own financial situation and the general economic situation over the last year, despite falling growth in GDP per head and a decline in RHDI per head.

2 . Economic well-being indicators at a glance

Figure 1: Economic well-being indicators, UK, Quarter 1 (Jan to Mar) 2017

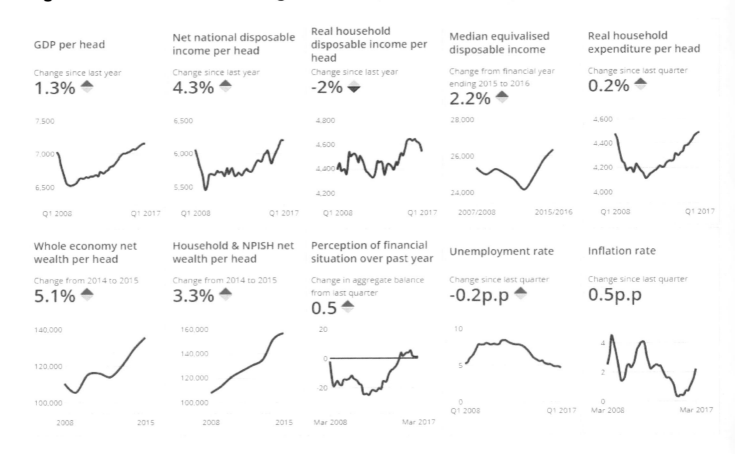

3 . Things you need to know about this release

This release reports measures of economic well-being in the UK. Rather than focusing on traditional measures such as gross domestic product (GDP) alone, these indicators aim to provide a more rounded and comprehensive basis for assessing changes in material well-being.

We prefer to measure economic well-being on a range of measures rather than a composite index. The framework and indicators used in this release were outlined in Economic Well-being, Framework and Indicators, published in November 2014.

4 . What were the main changes in economic well-being in Quarter 1 2017?

Figure 2: Four measures of economic well-being, Quarter 1 (Jan to Mar) 2008 to Quarter 1 2017

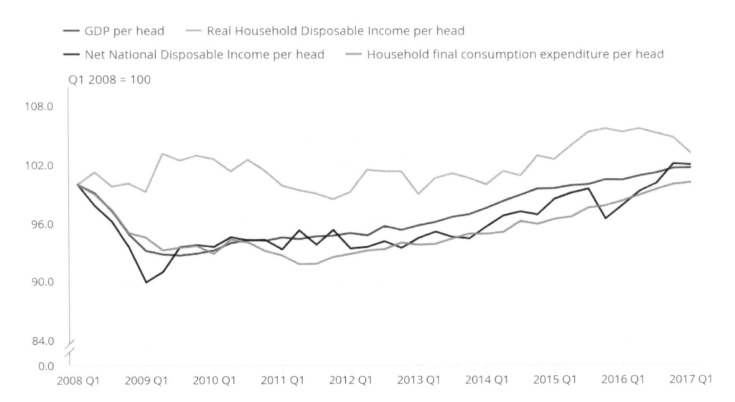

Source: Office for National Statistics

Notes:

1. Q1 refers to Quarter 1 (January to March), Q2 refers to Quarter 2 (April to June), Q3 (July to September) and Q4 refers to Quarter 4 (October to December).

2. Households do not include non-profit institutions serving households (NPISH).

3. The above indicators are presented in real prices.

Real gross domestic product per head

Growth in real gross domestic product (GDP) per head was 0.0% in Quarter 1 (Jan to March) 2017 compared with the previous quarter – down 0.5 percentage points on growth in the previous quarter. This was a slower growth rate than the 0.2% quarterly increase in GDP.

The growth rate in GDP per head in Quarter 1 2017 was the joint-lowest recorded over the past 4 years and was 0.4 percentage points lower than average growth over this period.

Real net national disposable income per head

Real net national disposable income (NNDI) per head increased by 4.3% between Quarter 1 2017 and Quarter 1 2016, compared with a 1.3% increase in GDP per head over the same period. Growth in NNDI per head recorded in Quarter 1 2017 continues the marked improvement in the series beginning at the end of 2016 and is 2.5 percentage points above average growth over the past 4 years.

As shown in the "Economic well-being indicators at a glance" section, NNDI per head represents the income available to all residents in the UK. There are two main differences between GDP per head and NNDI per head.

First, not all income generated by production in the UK will be payable to UK residents. For example, a country whose firms or assets are predominantly owned by foreign investors may well have high levels of production, but a lower national income once profits and rents flowing abroad are taken into account. As a result, the income available to residents would be less than that implied by measures such as GDP.

Second, NNDI per head is adjusted for capital consumption. GDP is "gross" in the sense that it does not adjust for capital depreciation, that is, the day-to-day wear and tear on vehicles, machinery, buildings and other fixed capital used in the productive process. It treats such consumption of capital as no different from any other form of consumption, but most people would not regard depreciation as adding to their material well-being.

Following 2 quarters of negative growth in Quarter 4 (Oct to Dec) 2015 and Quarter 1 2016, NNDI per head increased continuously. During this period, average growth was 2.7% per quarter (compared with the same quarter a year ago), compared with 1.2% average growth in GDP per head. This means that the growth in income available to residents to spend or save is greater once cross-border flows are taken into account.

The improvement in NNDI per head over recent quarters is mainly driven by an increase in the income to UK residents from investments abroad. Compared with the same quarter a year ago, the income to UK residents from investments abroad has increased by an average £1.4 billion per quarter between Quarter 2 (July to Sept) 2016 and Quarter 1 2017. This is in contrast with the period between Quarter 1 2012 and Quarter 1 (Apr to June) 2016, when the income that UK residents received from investments abroad fell by an average £0.7 billion per quarter.

More detailed analysis on the contributions to growth in NNDI and the relationship with the balance of primary incomes was presented in Economic well-being: Quarter 4, Oct to Dec 2016.

Household income

Unless stated otherwise, analysis of real household disposable income (RHDI) in this bulletin excludes non-profit institutions serving households (NPISH). We consider this a better indicator of economic well-being as it focuses more on the household experience than the traditional measure, which includes the NPISH sector. Real household and NPISH disposable income per head will continue to be published alongside RHDI per head (excluding NPISH) in the datasets.

In Quarter 1 2017, RHDI per head declined by 2.0% compared with the same quarter a year ago (Quarter 1 2016) – 3.0 percentage points lower than the 4-year average growth rate, but still 3.3% above its pre-economic downturn level.

Figure 3: Contributions to quarter-on-same-quarter-a-year-ago growth in real household disposable income per head, chain volume measure, Quarter 1 (Jan to Mar) 2013 to Quarter 1 2017

UK

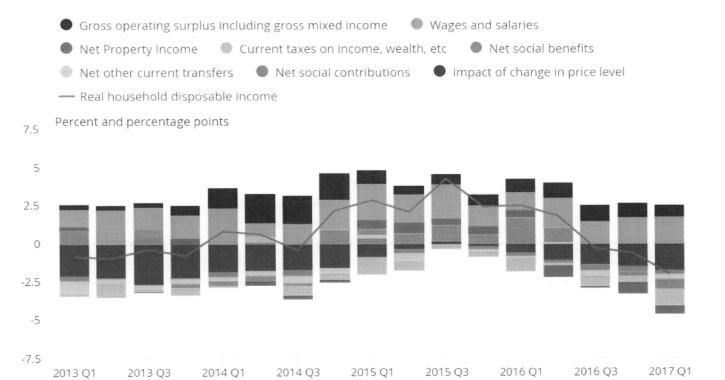

Source: Office for National Statistics

Notes:

1. Real household disposable income includes non profit institutions serving households (NPISH).

2. Q1 refers to Quarter 1 (January to March), Q2 refers to Quarter 2 (April to June), Q3 refers to Quarter 3 (July to September) and Q4 refers to Quarter 4 (October to December).

3. Contributions may not sum due to rounding.

Despite growth in both NNDI per head and GDP per head in Quarter 1 2017, RHDI decreased at the fastest rate since the end of 2011. Figure 2 highlights the contributions to growth from different components of RHDI (including NPISH). It shows that, higher prices facing households had a negative contribution to RHDI (including NPISH) growth in Quarter 1 2017 compared with the same quarter a year ago – contributing negative 1.8 percentage points. However, growth in wages and salaries (in nominal terms) supported RHDI (including NPISH), contributing 1.7 percentage points.

Adjusted household income

One of the limitations of RHDI per head as a measure of economic well-being is that it does not take into account transfers-in-kind – such as education and health care services – that households receive.

To examine the role of these types of benefits more closely, this section of the bulletin compares changes in real adjusted gross household disposable income (RAHDI) with RHDI (including NPISH). RAHDI is an adjusted version of RHDI, which incorporates social transfers in kind (STIK).

STIK consist of individual goods and services provided as transfers-in-kind to individual households by government units and non-profit institutions serving households (NPISHs), whether purchased on the market or produced as non- market output by government units or NPISHs.

Figure 4: Growth rates of real household and NPISH disposable income (RHDI)per head and adjusted RHDI per head, and impact of social transfers in kind

Quarter 1 (Jan to Mar) 2004 to Quarter 1 2017, UK

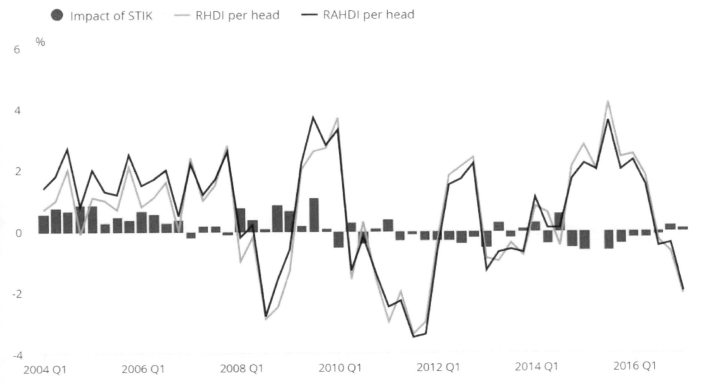

Source: Office for National Statistics

Notes:

1. Real household disposable income includes non profit institutions serving households (NPISH).

2. Q1 refers to Quarter 1 (January to March), Q2 refers to Quarter 2 (April to June), Q3 refers to Quarter 3 (July to September) and Q4 refers to Quarter 4 (October to December).

3. Data are presented in real prices.

4. Quarter-on-same-quarter-a-year-ago growth rate

Figure 4 highlights that during the period between Quarter 1 2004 and Quarter 4 2008, average RAHDI per head growth was higher than RHDI per head growth – 1.1% per quarter compared with 0.7% per quarter respectively. This suggests that over this period, households were receiving additional benefits not captured in RHDI, with positive implications for economic well-being.

However, from Quarter 1 2009 to Quarter 1 2017, the growth of STIK waned, meaning that both measures of income followed similar trajectories – each growing at an average of 0.4% per quarter (compared with the same quarter a year ago).

Figure 5: Contributions to year-on-year growth in social transfers in kind per head by individual components, 2004 to 2015

UK

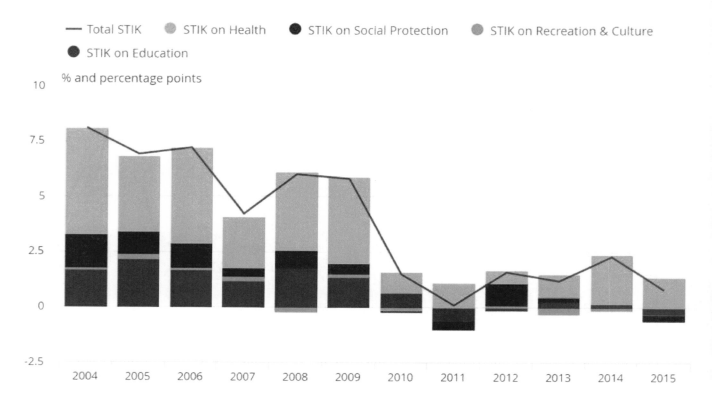

Source: Office for National Statistics

Notes:

1. The STIK are presented in current prices.

Figure 5 examines the reversal in the growth of STIK per head analysing, in current prices, contributions from health and education services, social protection (such as social housing), and recreation and culture (for example, libraries).

It highlights that in the period leading up to 2010, all components provided positive contributions to growth in STIK per head, with government expenditure on healthcare and education services the main drivers. Average annual growth in STIK per head was 6.0% between 2004 and 2009, with average contributions of 3.5 and 1.7 percentage points from healthcare services and education services respectively.

However, following 2009, average annual growth in STIK per head was 4.8 percentage points lower compared with the period prior to 2009. This was mainly driven by a fall in the growth rate in the value of education services provided – contributing 0.0 percentage points on average per year since 2009.

Household expenditure

In Quarter 4 2016, real household spending per head (excluding non-profit institutions serving households (NPISH)) grew 0.2% compared with the previous quarter, continuing the general upward trend seen since Quarter 3 2011. As highlighted in Figure 1, real household spending per head (excluding NPISH) was 0.2% higher than its pre-economic downturn level in Quarter 1 2017. This is despite real household disposable income per head (excluding NPISH) being 3.3% above its pre-economic downturn level in Quarter 1 2017.

The increase in household spending and the decrease in household income had a negative impact on the saving ratio. The household and NPISH saving ratio decreased from 6.1 to 1.7 from Quarter 1 2016 to Quarter 1 2017.

5 . Economic sentiment

It is important to consider sentiment, along with other measures of economic well-being, to improve our understanding of how changes in official measures of the economy are perceived by individuals. The Eurobarometer Consumer Survey, conducted by GFK on behalf of the European Commission, provides information regarding perceptions of the economic environment. The "Quality and methodology" section provides more information regarding the Eurobarometer Consumer Survey.

General economic situation and perception of financial situation

The Eurobarometer Consumer Survey asks consumers their views on the state of the general economic situation over the previous 12 months. A positive balance means that consumers perceived an improvement within the economy, a zero balance indicates no change and a negative balance indicates a perceived worsening.

Figure 6: Consumer perceptions of general economic situation and their own financial situation over last 12 months, January 2006 to March 2017

UK

Source: European Commission

Notes:

1. The source is the Eurobarometer Consumer Survey, which is collected by GFK for the European Commission. Further information can be found in Quality and Methodology section.

2. A negative balance means that, on average, respondents reported the general economic situation worsened. A positive balance means they reported it improved and a zero balance indicates no change.

Between Quarter 4 (Oct to Dec) 2016 and Quarter 1 (Jan to March) 2017, the perception of the general economic situation improved slightly from a balance of negative 23.3 to negative 21.8. Despite the small improvement, the negative balance is still suggesting that households perception of the general economic situation is unfavourable, potentially because of the decline in UK's currency and rising inflation.

The series had been on a general upwards trend in recent years until April 2015, before the trend turned negative in July 2015. Analysis by GFK suggests that the negative trend could potentially be explained by economic uncertainty abroad and later, in 2016, reduced confidence following the EU referendum.

The survey also asks respondents about their own financial situation. This has generally been positive since May 2015 (it was negative in July and August 2016), ending a 7-year negative balance since February 2008. In the latest quarter, the balance increased from 0.7 in December 2016 to 1.2 in March 2017, indicating that consumers are still positive about their financial situation, despite an increase in the price level.

Perception of inflation

The Eurobarometer Consumer Survey also asks respondents about their perception of prices over the previous 12 months. A positive balance suggests that consumers perceive prices to have increased over the previous 12 months, while a negative balance suggests the opposite. In Quarter 1 2017, the balance increased to positive 20.8 from positive 7.8 in Quarter 4 2016.

Figure 7: Comparison between CPIH and individual's perception of price trends over the last 12 months, January 2006 to March 2017

January 2006 to March 2017, UK

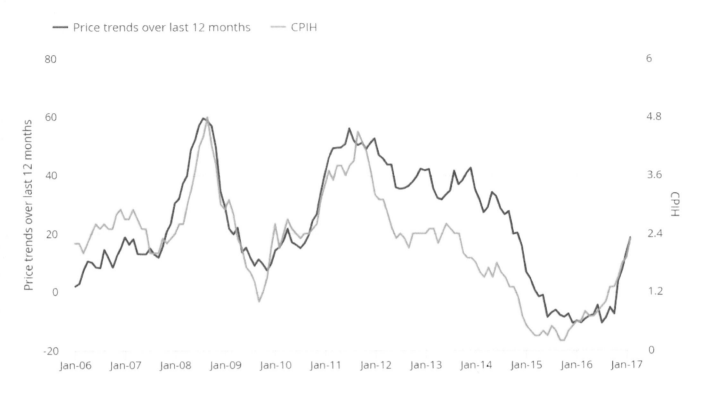

Source: Office for National Statistics, European Commission

Notes:

1. CPIH has been re-assessed to evaluate the extent to which it meets the professional standards set out in the Code of Practice for Official Statistics. The assessment report includes a number of requirements that need to be implemented for CPIH to regain its status as a National Statistic and we are working to address these.

2. The source is the Eurobarometer Consumer Survey, which is collected by GfK for the European Commission. Further information can be found in Quality and Methodology.

3. A negative balance means that, on average, respondents reported that the price level decreased. A positive balance means they reported it increased and a zero balance indicators no change.

Consumers' perception of inflation remained negative for 19 months between April 2015 and November 2016. This corresponds with a low Consumer Prices Index including owner occupiers' housing costs (CPIH) rate during this period – the 12-month rate was under 1% from December 2014 to July 2016 and has steadily increased since October 2015.

6 . Spotlight: developments in measuring economic well-being

The headline indicators presented in this bulletin were selected for their suitability in providing broad coverage of the economic well-being framework. Inevitably, factors such as data availability, frequency and timeliness mean that we cannot yet report regularly on all the issues covered in the well-being framework.

The situation continues to improve though. We are currently working on a number of developments, which aim to improve the existing suite of indicators and to introduce new ways of informing on economic well-being in the UK. This section of the bulletin will provide a snapshot of some of the main developments ongoing at the Office for National Statistics (ONS).

Natural capital

The UK, along with several international bodies and in-line with recommendations in the Stiglitz Report, considers sustainability through the "capitals approach". The capitals approach states that economic, natural, human and social capitals are all resources that matter for the present and future well-being of individuals.

We plan to publish estimates of human capital for 2016 later this year and regularly present indicators of social capital as part of the wider programme of measuring national well-being.

More recently, the concept of natural capital and the need to keep track of it through accounts is building momentum in the UK. Natural capital is simply the natural wealth of the UK, for example, woodland, mountains or natural coastal areas. It is from this natural capital that humans receive a wide range of services. In partnership with the UK Department for Environment, Food and Rural Affairs (Defra), we are working to produce natural capital accounts, with the aim to incorporate them into the UK Environmental Accounts by 2020.

Why is measuring natural capital Important?

A wide range of benefits are provided by natural capital, which make human life possible, such as the provision of food and water, regulating air quality and providing opportunities for recreation. Many of the benefits that society receives are free, so the value of natural assets is often hidden, partial or missing from the nation's balance sheet.

By providing valuations for the UK's natural capital, decision-makers can include the environment into their plans and include them in their policy interests. The accounts enable us to monitor the services that residents receive from natural assets and track changes to them over time. Our SlideShare summarises some of the changes identified so far.

In 2011 the government committed to working with ONS to incorporate natural capital into the UK Environmental Accounts by 2020, so that the benefits of nature would be better recognised. In the lead-up to this, our current commitments are:

- Scoping the development of natural capital accounts for mountains, moorland and heath – 6 July 2017

- UK natural capital accounts by habitat (woodland, farmland and freshwater) – 21 July 2017

- Natural capital accounts for the UK – November 2017

- Initial urban natural capital accounts – late 2017

For more information on the natural capital accounts see the "Natural capital" section of the ONS website, or contact us via email at environment.accounts@ons.gsi.gov.uk.

Distributional analysis within the national accounts framework

The importance of developing statistics on the distribution of income, consumption and wealth is widely recognised both in the UK and internationally. As part of an Organisation for Economic Co-operation and Development (OECD) Expert Group on Disparities within the national accounts framework, we have been working on producing distributional national accounts totals. The process involves mapping micro data on household income and consumption, largely derived from the Living Cost and Food Survey (LCFS), to national accounts concepts.

Figure 8: Savings as proportion of adjusted disposable income, by equivalised disposable income quintile, 2008, 2012 and 2013

UK

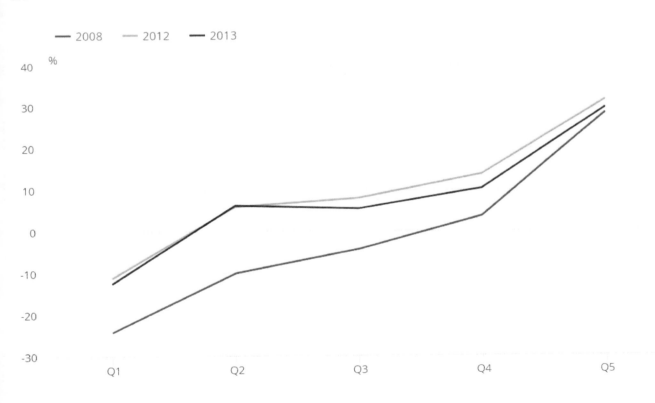

Source: Office for National Statisitcs

Notes:

Q1 equals Quintile 1, Q2 equals Quintile 2, Q3 equals Quintile 3, Q4 equals Quintile 4, Q5 equals Quintile 5.

As an indication of the findings that are possible from this kind of analysis, Figure 7 presents savings (the difference between disposable income and actual consumption) as a percentage of adjusted disposable income for the 3 years covered in an initial exercise published by both ONS and the OECD.

As distributional information for national accounts data does not currently exist, these experimental estimates are unique to the UK. A particularly striking finding is that, in 2008, the average savings rate for the second and middle quintiles were negative (minus 10% and minus 4% respectively). However, by 2012 and 2013 they became positive (varying between 5% and 8% respectively). This is explained by nominal levels of adjusted disposable income for the lower quintiles increasing at a faster rate than actual consumption.

We are aiming to further this initial distributional work by investigating the gaps between macro and micro totals and allocating them to relevant households, depending on the underlying reasons for the discrepancies. We are also looking to extend the scope of this work to include financial wealth, which will be largely based on data from the Wealth and Assets Survey (WAS). The refined methodology will build on recent national accounts developments, allowing national accounts aggregates to be adjusted in ways that were not previously possible. This will enable closer conceptual alignment between the macro and micro estimates.

Results from this exercise will be published by the end of 2017. For more information, please contact us via email at hie@ons.gsi.gov.uk.

Joint analysis of income, consumption and wealth

Stiglitz et al. (2009) highlighted the importance of considering income and consumption jointly with wealth. However, the complexity of collecting accurate income, consumption or wealth data, particularly through surveys, means that micro data sources generally contain data on at most two of these dimensions.

One option for facilitating joint analysis, which we have been taking forward, is the creation of synthetic datasets containing all the variables of interest through statistical matching techniques. Work to date has looked at the statistical matching of data from EU-SILC (income) with Household Budget Survey (consumption) data (Webber and Tonkin, 2013; Serafino and Tonkin, 2017) and with wealth data from our Wealth and Assets Survey (Tonkin, Serafino and Davies, 2016).

As a longer-term development, and as part of our Data Collection Transformation Programme (DCTP), we are moving towards an integrated Household Finance Survey, underpinned by administrative data. This process has started in 2017 through harmonising the sampling, collection and processing of the Living Costs and Food Survey (LCF) and the Survey on Living Conditions (SLC), exploiting existing commonalities and overlap between the sources. Harmonising the surveys will allow the resulting datasets to be combined to produce precise, coherent income, consumption and social exclusion statistics.

7 . Economic well-being indicators already published

Between 2014 and 2015, the total net worth per head of the UK increased by 5.1%. The largest contribution was from the household and non-profit institutions serving households (NPISH) sector.

Between 2014 and 2015, household wealth per head increased by 3.3%, mainly driven by a 6.5% increase in the wealth in non-financial assets (for example, buildings and machinery).

Between the year to December 2016 and the year to March 2017, the 12-month Consumer Prices Index with owner occupiers' housing costs (CPIH) rate increased from 1.8% to 2.3% to reach its highest level since September 2013. The increase in prices was mainly driven by a rise in prices for food, alcohol and tobacco, clothing and footwear.

The unemployment rate for those aged 16 and over decreased by 0.2 percentage points to 4.6% between the 3 months to December 2016 and the 3 months to March 2017. The employment rate (the proportion of people aged from 16 to 64 who were in work) was 74.8% in the 3 months to March 2017 – the highest rate since comparable records began in 1971.

The median UK household disposable income was £26,332 in the financial year ending 2016 (2015 to 2016); this was £564 higher than the previous year and £977 higher than the pre-downturn value of £25,355 in the financial year ending 2008 (2007 to 2008) – after accounting for inflation and household composition.

The wealthiest 10% of households owned 45% of aggregate total wealth in July 2012 to June 2014 and were 2.4 times wealthier than the second wealthiest 10%. Over the same period, the wealthiest 10% of households were 5.2 times wealthier than the bottom 50% of households (the bottom 5 deciles combined), who owned 9% of aggregate total wealth.

8 . Links to related statistics

More information on the topic of economic well-being is available, including the following publications:

- UK Economic Accounts, Table 1.1.5

- The National Balance Sheet

- Wealth and Assets Survey

- Household disposable income and inequality

- Labour market statistics

- Consumer Price Indices

- Eurobarometer Consumer Survey (produced by GFK on behalf of the European Commission)

- International comparisons of real household (including non-profit institutions serving households (NPISH)) disposable income per head index (Organisation for Economic Co-operation and Development)

- International comparisons of gross domestic product (GDP) per head index (Organisation for Economic Co-operation and Development)

- Contributions to growth in real household (including NPISH) disposable income per head (European Central Bank)

9 . Quality and methodology

Release policy

The data used in this version of the release are the latest available at 30 June 2017. The UK resident population mid-year estimates used in this publication are those published on 23 June 2016. The latest population estimates published on 22 June 2017 will be included in quarterly national accounts on 29 September 2017.

Basic quality and methodology information

Basic quality and methodology information for all indicators in this statistical bulletin is available:

- National Accounts Quality and Methodology Information report

- Consumer Price Indices Quality and Methodology Information report

- Wealth and Assets Survey Quality and Methodology Information report

- Effects of Taxes and Benefits Quality and Methodology information report

- Labour Market Quality and Methodology Information report

These Quality and Methodology Information reports contain important information on:

- the strengths and limitations of the data and how it compares with related data

- users and uses of the data

- how the output was created

- the quality of the output including the accuracy of the data

Revisions and reliability

All data in this release will be subject to revision in accordance with the revisions policies of their original release. Estimates for the most recent quarters are provisional and are subject to revision in the light of updated source information. We currently provide an analysis of past revisions in statistical bulletins, which present time series. Details of the revisions are published in the original statistical bulletins.

Most revisions reflect either the adoption of new statistical techniques or the incorporation of new information, which allows the statistical error of previous estimates to be reduced.

Only rarely are there avoidable "errors", such as human or system failures and such mistakes are made quite clear when they do occur.

More information about the revisions policies for indicators in this release is available:

- National Accounts revisions policy – covers indicators from the Quarterly National Accounts, UK Economic Accounts and the National Balance Sheet

- Wealth and Assets Survey revisions policy – covers indicators on the distribution of wealth

- Effect of taxes and benefits on household incomes revisions policy – covers indicators on the distribution of income

- Labour market statistics revisions policy – covers indicators from labour market statistics

- Consumer Price Inflation revisions policy – covers indicators from consumer price indices

Our revisions policies for economic statistics web page is dedicated to revisions to economic statistics and brings together our work on revisions analysis, linking to articles, revisions policies and important documentation from the former Statistics Commission's report on revisions.

Data that come from the Eurobarometer Consumer Survey and Understanding Society releases are not subject to revision, as all data are available at the time of the original release. These data will only be revised in light of methodological improvements or to correct errors. Any revisions will be made clear in this release.

Interpreting the Eurobarometer Consumer Survey

The Eurobarometer Consumer Survey, sourced from GFK on behalf of the European Commission, asks respondents a series of questions to determine their perceptions on a variety of factors, which collectively give an overall consumer confidence indicator. For each question, an aggregate balance is given that ranges between negative 100 and positive 100.

Balances are the difference between positive and negative answering options, measured as percentage points of total answers. Values range from negative 100, when all respondents choose the negative option (or the most negative one in the case of five-option questions) to positive 100, when all respondents choose the positive (or the most positive) option.

The questions used in this release are as follows:

Question 1: How has the financial situation of your household changed over the last 12 months? It has...

- got a lot better

- got a little better

- stayed the same

- got a little worse

- got a lot worse

- don't know

Question 3: How do you think the general economic situation in the country has changed over the past 12 months? It has...

- got a lot better

- got a little better

- stayed the same

- got a little worse

- got a lot worse

- don't know

Question 5: How do you think that consumer prices have developed over the last 12 months? They have...

- risen a lot

- risen moderately

- risen slightly

- stayed about the same

- fallen

- don't know

Further information on this consumer survey is available from the Business and Consumer Survey section of the European Commission website.

Measuring national well-being

This article is published as part of our Measuring National Well-being programme. The programme aims to produce accepted and trusted measures of the well-being of the nation – how the UK as a whole is doing. Further information on Measuring National Well-being is available, with a full list of well-being publications.

Contact details for this statistical bulletin

Dominic Webber / Vasileios Antonopoulos

economic.wellbeing@ons.gsi.gov.uk

Telephone: +44 (0)1633 456246

Statistical bulletin

Economic Well-being: April to June 2017

Presents indicators that adjust or supplement more traditional measures such as GDP to give a more rounded and comprehensive basis for assessing changes in economic well-being.

Contact:
Dominic Webber and Vasileios Antonopoulos
economic.wellbeing@ons.gsi.gov. uk
+44 (0)1633 456246

Release date:
3 October 2017

Next release:
9 January 2018

Table of contents

1 . Main points

- Gross domestic product (GDP) per head grew by 0.1% in Quarter 2 (Apr to June) 2017 compared with the previous quarter and increased by 0.9% compared with the same quarter a year ago (Quarter 2 2016).

- Net national disposable income (NNDI) per head increased by 2.0% between Quarter 2 2016 and Quarter 2 2017, due mainly to a £6.4 billion increase in the income received from the UK's foreign direct investment from abroad.

- Despite improvements in both GDP per head and NNDI per head, real household disposable income (RHDI) per head declined by 1.1% in Quarter 2 2017 compared with the same quarter a year ago; this was the fourth consecutive quarter that RHDI per head has decreased – the longest period of consistent negative growth since the end of 2011.

- For the first time in two years, consumers reported a worsening of their perception of their own financial situation in Quarter 2 2017.

2 . Economic well-being indicators at-a-glance

Figure 1: Economic well-being indicators, UK, Quarter 2 (Apr to June) 2017

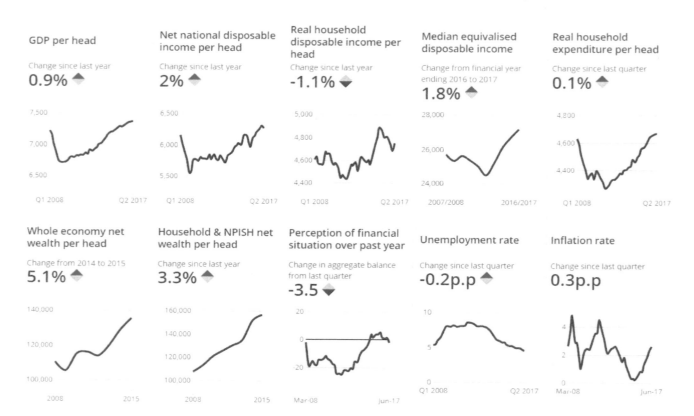

3 . Things you need to know about this release

This release reports measures of economic well-being in the UK. Rather than focusing on traditional measures such as gross domestic product (GDP) alone, these indicators aim to provide a more rounded and comprehensive basis for assessing changes in material well-being.

We prefer to measure economic well-being on a range of measures rather than a composite index. The framework and indicators used in this release were outlined in Economic Well-being, Framework and Indicators, published in November 2014.

4 . What were the main changes in economic well-being in Quarter 2 2017?

Figure 2: Four measures of economic well-being, Quarter 1 (Jan to Mar) 2008 to Quarter 2 (Apr to June) 2017

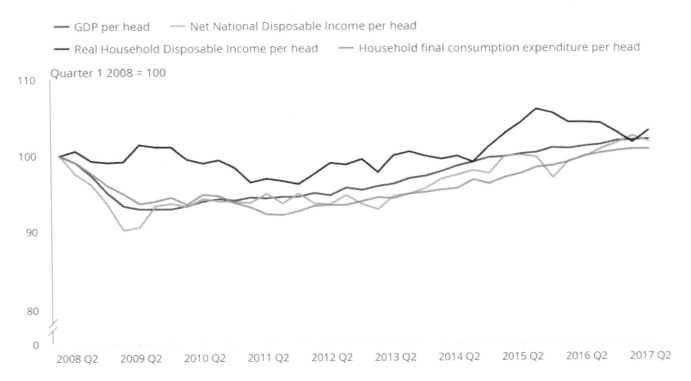

Source: Office for National Statistics

Notes:

1. Q1 refers to Quarter 1 (January to March), Q2 refers to Quarter 2 (April to June), Q3 (July to September) and Q4 refers to Quarter 4 (October to December).

Real GDP per head

Growth in real gross domestic product (GDP) per head was 0.1% in Quarter 2 (Apr to June) 2017 compared with the previous quarter – unchanged from the growth rate in Quarter 1 (Jan to Mar) 2017. This was a slower growth rate than the 0.3% quarterly increase in GDP, due to population growth over the same period.

GDP per head growth in Quarter 2 2017 was 0.2 percentage points lower than the average quarterly growth rate over the past four years.

Real net national disposable income (NNDI) per head

Real net national disposable income (NNDI) per head increased by 2.0% between Quarter 2 2016 and Quarter 2 2017, compared with a 0.9% increase in GDP per head over the same period. Growth in NNDI per head recorded in Quarter 2 2017 continues the marked improvement in the series beginning in Quarter 3 (July to Sept) 2016.

As shown in the "Economic well-being indicators at a glance" section, NNDI per head is a better representation than GDP of the income available to all residents in the UK to spend or save. There are two main differences between GDP per head and NNDI per head.

First, not all income generated by production in the UK will be payable to UK residents. For example, a country whose firms or assets are predominantly owned by foreign investors may well have high levels of production, but a lower national income once profits and rents flowing abroad are taken into account. As a result, the income available to residents would be less than that implied by measures such as GDP.

Second, NNDI per head is adjusted for capital consumption. GDP is "gross" in the sense that it does not adjust for capital depreciation, that is, the day-to-day wear and tear on vehicles, machinery, buildings and other fixed capital used in the productive process. It treats such consumption of capital as no different from any other form of consumption, but most people would not regard depreciation as adding to their material well-being.

As highlighted in Figure 2, NNDI per head and GDP per head have followed slightly different growth paths in recent years. The differences between these two series' growth rates are largely explained by changes in the amount of income earned from UK residents' investments overseas. For instance, between Quarter 4 2015 and Quarter 2 2017, NNDI per head grew by 5.0%, compared with 1.1% growth in GDP per head. Over this period, the amount of income earned by UK residents on their foreign direct investments increased, on average, by £1.2 billion per quarter. This contrasts with period during Quarter 2 2011 and Quarter 4 2015, during which GDP per head and NNDI per head grew by 7.0% and 2.1% respectively. Slower growth in NNDI per head compared with GDP per head is largely accounted for by an average decline of £1.1 billion per quarter in the income that UK residents received from investments abroad.

More detailed analysis on the contributions to growth in NNDI and the relationship with the balance of primary incomes was presented in Economic well-being: Quarter 4, Oct to Dec 2016.

Household income

In Quarter 2 2017, real households disposable income (RHDI) per head declined by 1.1% compared with the same quarter a year ago (Quarter 2 2016). Quarter 2 2017 marks the fourth consecutive quarter that RHDI per head has decreased – the longest period of consistent negative growth since the end of 2011. Despite this fall, RHDI per head still remains 3.2% above its pre-economic downturn level.

Figure 3: Contributions to quarter-on-same-quarter-a-year-ago growth in real household disposable income, Quarter 1 (Jan to Mar) 2013 to Quarter 2 (Apr to June) 2017

UK

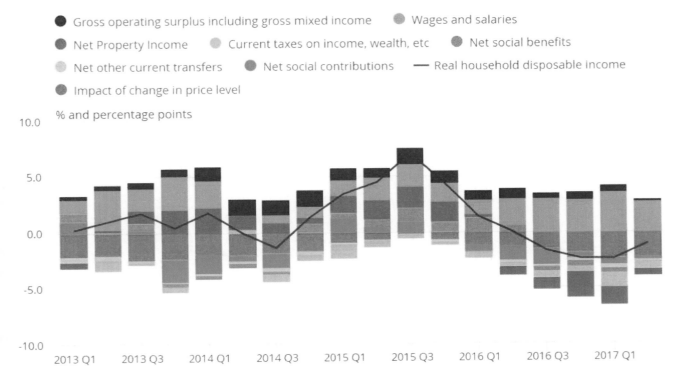

Source: Office for National Statistics

Notes:

1. Q1 refers to Quarter 1 (January to March), Q2 refers to Quarter 2 (April to June), Q3 (July to September) and Q4 refers to Quarter 4 (October to December).

2. Real household disposable income includes non profit institutions serving households (NPISH).

3. Contributions may not sum due to rounding.

Despite growth in both NNDI per head and GDP per head in Quarter 2 2017 compared with the same quarter a year ago, RHDI per head continued to decline. Figure 2 highlights the contributions to growth from different components of RHDI per head. It shows that, higher prices facing households had a negative contribution to RHDI growth in Quarter 2 2017 compared with the same quarter a year ago – contributing negative 2.3 percentage points to the 1.1% decline. However, growth in wages and salaries (in nominal terms) supported RHDI per head, contributing 2.7 percentage points.

Changes to measures of real household disposable income

This quarter we publish, for the first time, separate income accounts for the households and NPISH sectors. As part of the process of separating these accounts, we took the opportunity to improve the measurement of both sectors, by updating methodologies and drawing on new data sources. Improving the household, private non-financial corporations and non-profit institutions serving households sectors' non-financial accounts, provides more information on the changes introduced.

Figure 4: Quarter-on-same-quarter-a-year-ago growth in real households disposable income per head, and impact of methodological improvements, chain volume measure

UK, Quarter 1 (Jan to Mar) 2008 to Quarter 2 (Apr to June) 2017

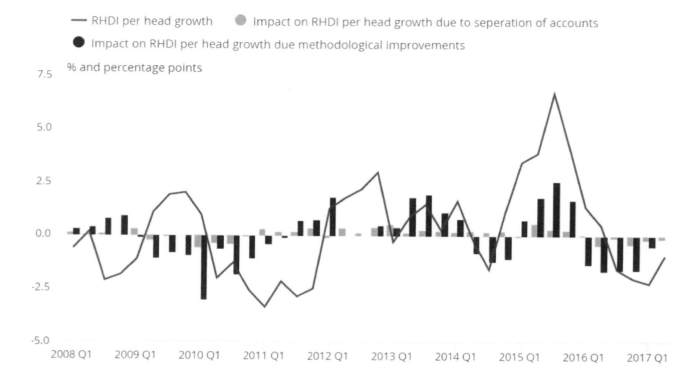

Source: Office for National Statistics

Notes:

1. Q1 refers to Quarter 1 (January to March), Q2 refers to Quarter 2 (April to June), Q3 refers to Quarter 3 (July to September) and Q4 refers to Quarter 4 (October to December).

Figure 4 presents three series. The first reports the quarterly growth rate, on an annual basis, of RHDI per head. The second and third series demonstrate the impact of separating the household and NPISH sectors, and the methodological improvements introduced respectively. The impact on RHDI per head growth due to the separation of accounts has been relatively minor over the period since Quarter 1 2008. Over this period, average quarterly growth in both RHDI per head and RHDI and NPISH per head was 0.1%.

The impact of methodological improvements on the measurement of RHDI is more noticeable. While average annual growth in both the revised and previous measure of RHDI per head is 0.1% per head since Quarter 1 2008, there are distinct periods where these revisions had greater impact. For instance, between Quarter 2 2009 and Quarter 4 2010, RHDI per head growth was revised by an average of negative 1.3% per quarter. Similarly, between Quarter 2 2013 and Quarter 3 2015, growth was revised upwards by an average of 0.8% per quarter.

These revisions have altered the path of RHDI per head, telling a slightly different story of economic well-being following the economic downturn. As GDP began to fall in mid-2008, Figure 2 highlights that RHDI per head remained relatively resilient. By Quarter 2 2009, the revised measure of RHDI per head was 1.4% above its pre-economic downturn level, compared with 3.1% as indicated by the previously published measure.

This initial improvement in real household income per head was a result of several factors. Firstly, household incomes were buoyed by falling mortgage repayments as a result of historic lows in the interest rate. Additionally, automatic stabilisers – such as reduced Income Tax payments and increased benefits as a result of lower employment – supported incomes during worsening conditions in the labour market. However, moving into early 2010, the impact of these factors wore off and inflation rose. Prices grew more strongly than household income and therefore, over time, people found that their income purchased a lower quantity of goods and services.

Following this, RHDI per head remained under its pre-economic downturn level for 14 consecutive quarters (compared with five quarters according to the previous estimate) from Quarter 1 2010 until Quarter 2 2013. Between Quarter 3 2014 and Quarter 3 2015, RHDI per head had a general upward trend because of the lower impact of prices, increasing by 7.0%. However, the series decreased by 2.7% from Quarter 3 2015 to Quarter 1 2017, due mainly to the onset of price pressures.

Household expenditure

Growth in real household spending per head (excluding non-profit institutions serving households (NPISH)) was 0.1% in Quarter 2 2017 compared with the previous quarter. This means that household spending per head has grown for 10 quarters in a row – the longest period of consecutive growth since 2003.

As highlighted in Figure 1, real household spending per head (excluding NPISH) in Quarter 2 2017 was 0.8% higher than its pre-economic downturn level. This is despite real household disposable income per head (excluding NPISH) in Quarter 2 2017 being 3.2% above its pre-economic downturn level. As a result, the household-only saving ratio decreased from 7.3 to 5.4 between Quarter 2 2016 to Quarter 2 2017.

5 . Spotlight: Regional trends in economic well-being

The economic well-being indicators described so far are reported at the national level. This section will examine regional differences, using previously published data, for the indicators where data is available: gross disposable household income (GDHI) per head and median income.

Regional GVA per head and GDHI per head

The nearest equivalent metric to GDP per head that is available at regional level is gross value added (GVA) per head. At the national level GDP per head is regarded as a useful indicator for economic well-being and the health of the economy. However, at regional level, we advise that GVA per head should not be used as either an estimate or proxy for economic well-being. This is because the value of GVA per head at regional level is impacted by the level of net-commuting flows and for places with high levels of net in- or out- commuting, GVA per head ceases to be a useful economic well-being (or economic performance) proxy.

Instead, when assessing regional economic well-being the preferred regional accounts measure is gross disposable household income (GDHI) per head. This measures the total amount of money that households have for spending or saving, after they have paid direct and indirect taxes and received any direct benefits, divided by the population of each region.

Figure 5: Gross disposable household income (GDHI) per head in 2015 and average annual growth, by UK region, 2005 to 2015, current prices

UK

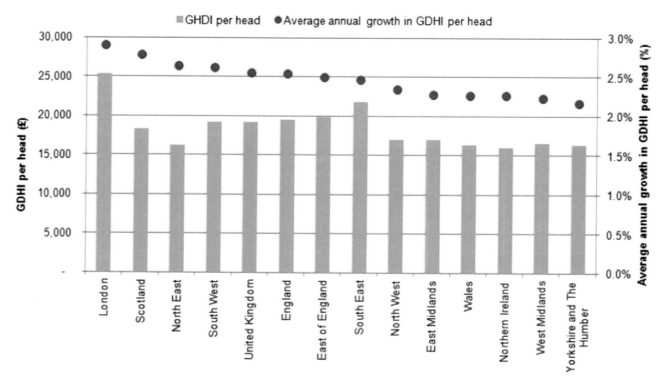

Source: Office for National Statistics

Notes:

1. Figures may not sum to totals as a result of rounding.

2. 2015 estimates are provisional.

London had the highest GDHI per head in 2015 where, on average, each person had £25,293 available to spend or save. Northern Ireland had the lowest at £15,913. This compares with a UK average of £19,106.

Between 2005 and 2015, London and Scotland had the highest average annual growth in GDHI per head among all UK regions – 2.9% and 2.8% per year respectively. West Midlands, and Yorkshire and The Humber, on the other hand, had the lowest average annual growth – both at 2.2%.

Figure 6: Contributions to gross disposable household income growth, North East, East of England, Yorkshire and The Humber, East Midlands, 2003 to 2015, current prices

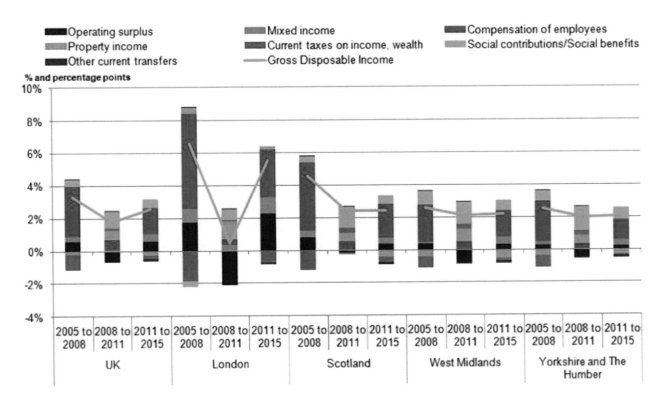

Source: Office for National Statistics

Notes:

1. Figures may not sum to totals as a result of rounding.

2. 2015 estimates are provisional.

Figure 6 provides more insight into the variations in growth rates of GDHI per head across regions. It examines the role of different contributions to GDHI per head growth for the regions that had the highest GDHI growth between 2005 to 2015 – London and Scotland – and the lowest growth – West Midlands, and Yorkshire and The Humber.

In all the regions considered, growth in compensation of employees per head provided the greatest contribution to GDHI growth per head before the economic crisis. Compensation of employees includes the wages and salaries payable in cash or in kind to an employee in a return for work done and the social insurance contributions payable by employers.

During the years of economic downturn – 2008 to 2011 – average GDHI per head fell in all four regions. However, the fall in income was mitigated by an increase in social contributions and social benefits, as automatic stabilisers via the taxes and benefits system supported households, amidst falling contributions from compensation of employees. After 2012, the impact of social contributions and social benefits declined. Larger contributions from compensation of employees during these years characterised the recoveries of London and Scotland, compared with the West Midlands, and Yorkshire and The Humber.

Regional median income

The analysis presented so far has focused on an aggregate measure of income. While this measure was presented on a per person basis, it is important to note that GDHI per head is not a direct estimate of the income of a typical individual or household. As such, for measures of median income, or for data on distributions of income, it is necessary to examine alternative sources. Regional measures of median income are sourced from the households below average income data from Department for Work and Pensions (DWP), and are based on the Family Resources Survey. Due to limitations in sample size, median income by regions is calculated as a three-year average.

This section therefore compares regional growth rates of median income, allowing some assessment of the equality of overall economic gains. This analysis reports median income both before and after accounting for housing costs, therefore accounting for the regional variations in rents and other housing costs. Housing costs include: rent (gross of housing benefit); water rates, community water charges and council water charges; mortgage interest payments; structural insurance premiums; ground rent and service charges.

Figure 7: Weekly regional median income before and after housing costs, financial year ending 2014 to financial year ending 2016, three-year average, by UK region

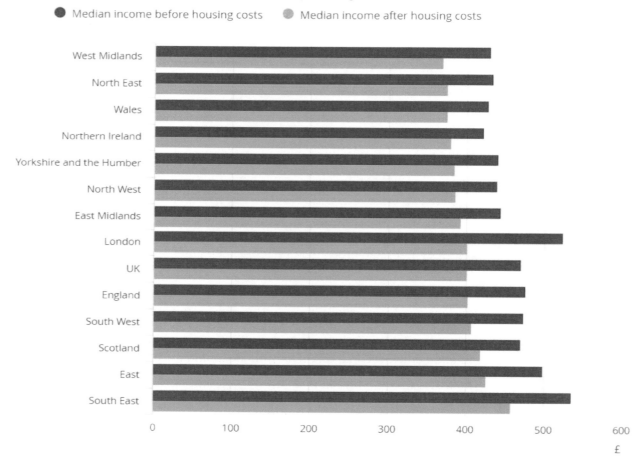

Source: Department for Work and Pensions, Households below Average Income.

Weekly median income after housing costs was greatest in the South East and East of England over the three years to the financial year ending 2016 – £459 and £427 respectively. Therefore, the South East ranked first in terms of household disposable income per head in 2015 and second for equivalised median income for the financial year ending 2016. However, users should exercise caution when directly comparing these results – these measures of income don't entirely overlap in terms of coverage and use different source data.

144

The North East and West Midlands had the lowest weekly median income after housing costs – £375 and £370 respectively.

Interestingly, median income before the deduction of housing costs in London was £524. This is a difference of 23% compared with median income after housing costs – the largest difference of all the UK regions. This clearly demonstrates the impact of high rents and other associated costs relating to dwellings, on economic well-being. On the other hand, Northern Ireland, Scotland and the East Midlands had the lowest difference between median incomes before and after housing costs over the three years to the financial year ending 2016.

6 . Economic sentiment

It is important to consider sentiment, along with other measures of economic well-being, to improve our understanding of how changes in official measures of the economy are perceived by individuals. The Eurobarometer Consumer Survey, conducted by GFK on behalf of the European Commission, provides information regarding perceptions of the economic environment. The "Quality and methodology" section provides more information regarding the Eurobarometer Consumer Survey.

General economic situation and perception of financial situation

The Eurobarometer Consumer Survey asks consumers their views on the state of the general economic situation over the previous 12 months. A positive balance means that consumers perceived an improvement within the economy, a zero balance indicates no change and a negative balance indicates a perceived worsening.

Figure 8: Consumer perceptions of general economic situation and their own financial situation over last 12 months, January 2006 to June 2017

UK

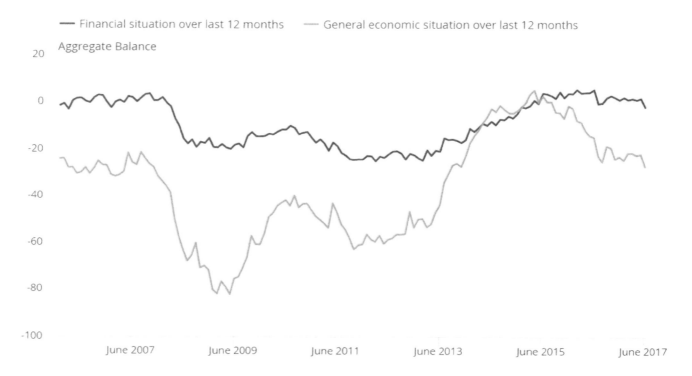

Source: European Commission

Notes:

1. The source is the Eurobarometer Consumer Survey, which is collected by GfK for the European Commission. Further information can be found in Quality and Methodology.

2. A negative balance means that, on average, respondents reported the general economic situation. A positive balance means they reported it improved and a zero balance indicators no change.

Between Quarter 1 (Jan to Mar) 2017 and Quarter 2 (Apr to June) 2017, the perception of the general economic situation declined from a balance of negative 21.8 to negative 27.5. This was the largest quarterly decline since Quarter 3 (July to Sept) 2013. Analysis by GFK suggests that the worsening in the balance may have been caused by the pressure of both higher prices and slow wage growth, which are acting to dampen household spending. GFK also cite economic uncertainty abroad and later, in 2016, reduced confidence following the EU referendum. In the year following the EU referendum, consumers' perception on the general economic situation has decreased by an average of 3.1 points per quarter.

The survey also asks respondents about their own financial situation. In Quarter 2 2017, the average aggregate balance was negative 2.3 – down from positive 1.2 in the previous quarter. This is the lowest level since Quarter 1 2015.

Perception of inflation

The Eurobarometer Consumer Survey also asks respondents about their perception of prices over the previous 12 months. A positive balance suggests that consumers perceive prices to have increased over the previous 12 months, while a negative balance suggests the opposite. In Quarter 2 2017, the balance increased to 24.3 from positive 20.8 in Quarter 1 2017, which was the highest value since October 2014.

Figure 9: Comparison between CPIH and individual's perception of price trends over the last 12 months, January 2006 to June 2017

UK

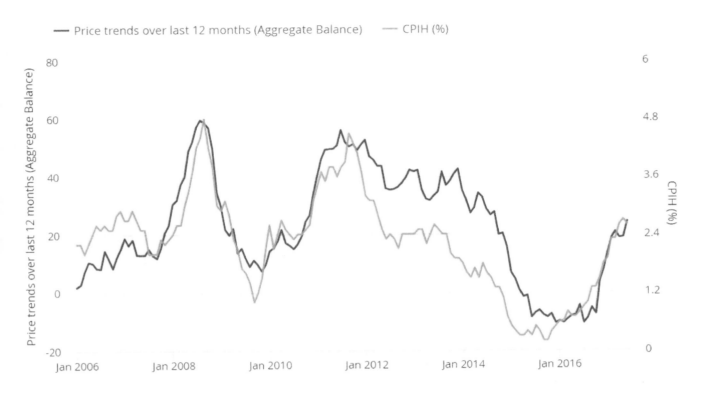

Source: European Commission

Notes:

1. CPIH has been re-assessed to evaluate the extent to which it meets the professional standards set out in the Code of Practice for Official Statistics. The assessment report includes a number of requirements that need to be implemented for CPIH to regain its status as a National Statistic and we are working to address these.

2. The source is the Eurobarometer Consumer Survey, which is collected by GfK for the European Commission. Further information can be found in Quality and Methodology.

3. A negative balance means that, on average, respondents reported that the price level decreased. A positive balance means they reported it increased and a zero balance indicators no change.

Since November 2016, inflation expectations have been positive, corresponding with an increased Consumer Prices Index including owner occupiers' housing costs (CPIH) rate during this period. The 12-month rate was over 1.5% from November 2016 and has steadily increased to reach 2.6% in June 2017.

7 . Economic well-being indicators already published

Between 2014 and 2015, the total net worth per head of the UK increased by 5.1%. The largest contribution was from the households and non-profit institutions serving households (NPISH) sector. Estimates for 2016 are expected towards the end of 2017.

Between 2014 and 2015, household wealth per head increased by 3.3%, driven mainly by a 6.5% increase in the wealth in non-financial assets (for example, buildings and machinery). Estimates for 2016 are expected towards the end of 2017.

In June 2017, the CPIH inflation 12-month rate fell to 2.6% compared with 2.7% in May 2017. This was for the first fall in the inflation rate since April 2016 but still remains relatively high compared with recent years. The main reason was falling prices for motor fuels and certain recreational and cultural goods and services.

The unemployment rate in the three months to June 2017 fell to 4.5% from 4.6%. The employment rate (the proportion of people aged from 16 to 64 who were in work) was 75.1% in the three months to June 2017 – the highest rate since comparable records began in 1971.

The median UK household disposable income was £27,170 in the financial year ending 2017; this was £487 higher than the previous year and £1,466 higher than the pre-downturn value of £25,704 in the financial year ending 2008 – after accounting for inflation and household composition.

The wealthiest 10% of households owned 45% of aggregate total wealth in July 2012 to June 2014 and were 2.4 times wealthier than the second wealthiest 10%. Over the same period, the wealthiest 10% of households were 5.2 times wealthier than the bottom 50% of households (the bottom five deciles combined), who owned 9% of aggregate total wealth.

8 . Links to related statistics

More information on the topic of economic well-being is available, including the following publications:

Internal

- UK Economic Accounts, Table 1.1.5 (ONS)

- The National Balance Sheet (ONS)

- Wealth and Assets Survey (ONS)

- Household disposable income and inequality (ONS)

- Labour market statistics (ONS)

- Consumer Price Indices (ONS)

External

- Eurobarometer Consumer Survey (produced by GFK on behalf of the European Commission)

- International comparisons of real households (including NPISH) disposable income per head index (OECD)

- International comparisons of GDP per head index (OECD)

- Contributions to growth in real households (including NPISH) disposable income per head (European Central Bank)

9 . Quality and methodology

1. Release policy

    - The data used in this version of the release are the latest available at 29 September 2017. The UK resident population mid-year estimates used in this publication are those published on 23 June 2016. The latest population estimates published on 22 June 2017 are included in quarterly national accounts on 29 September 2017.

2. Basic quality and methodology information

    Basic quality and methodology information for all indicators in this statistical bulletin can be found on our website:

    - National accounts Quality and methodology Information report

    - Consumer Prices Indices Quality and methodology Information report

    - Wealth and Assets Survey Quality and methodology Information report

    - Effects of taxes and benefits Quality and methodology information report

    - Labour market Quality and methodology Information reports

    These contain important information on:

    - the strengths and limitations of the data and how it compares with related data

    - users and uses of the data

    - how the output was created

    - the quality of the output including the accuracy of the data

3. Revisions and reliability

All data in this release will be subject to revision in accordance with the revisions policies of their original release. Estimates for the most recent quarters are provisional and are subject to revision in the light of updated source information. We currently provide an analysis of past revisions in statistical bulletins, which present time series. Details of the revisions are published in the original statistical bulletins.

Most revisions reflect either the adoption of new statistical techniques or the incorporation of new information, which allows the statistical error of previous estimates to be reduced.

Only rarely are there avoidable "errors", such as human or system failures and such mistakes are made quite clear when they do occur.

For more information about the revisions policies for indicators in this release:

- National accounts revisions policy – covers indicators from the quarterly national accounts, UK Economic Accounts and the national balance sheet

- Wealth and Assets Survey revisions policy – covers indicators on the distribution of wealth

- Effects of taxes and benefits on household incomes revisions policy – covers indicators on the distribution of income

- Labour market statistics revisions policy – covers indicators from labour market statistics

- Consumer Price Inflation - revisions policy – covers indicators from consumer price indices

Our Revisions policies for economic statistics webpage is dedicated to revisions to economic statistics and brings together our work on revisions analysis, linking to articles, revisions policies and important documentation from the former Statistics Commission's report on revisions.

Data that come from the Eurobarometer Consumer Survey and Understanding Society releases are not subject to revision as all data are available at the time of the original release. These data will only be revised in light of methodological improvements or to correct errors. Any revisions will be made clear in this release.

4. Interpreting the Eurobarometer Consumer Survey

The Eurobarometer Consumer Survey, sourced from GFK on behalf of the European Commission, asks respondents a series of questions to determine their perceptions on a variety of factors, which collectively give an overall consumer confidence indicator. For each question, an aggregate balance is given, which ranges between negative 100 and positive 100.

Balances are the difference between positive and negative answering options, measured as percentage points of total answers. Values range from negative 100, when all respondents choose the negative option (or the most negative one in the case of five-option questions) to positive 100, when all respondents choose the positive (or the most positive) option.

The questions used in this release are:

Question 1: How has the financial situation of your household changed over the last 12 months? It has...

- got a lot better

- got a little better

- stayed the same

- got a little worse

- got a lot worse

- don't know

Question 3: How do you think the general economic situation in the country has changed over the past 12 months? It has...

- got a lot better

- got a little better

- stayed the same

- got a little worse

- got a lot worse

- don't know

Question 5: How do you think that consumer prices have developed over the last 12 months? They have...

- risen a lot

- risen moderately

- risen slightly

- stayed about the same

- fallen

- don't know

Further information on this consumer survey is available from the Business and Consumer Survey section of the European Commission website.

5. Measuring national well-being

This article is published as part of our Measuring National Well-being programme. The programme aims to produce accepted and trusted measures of the well-being of the nation – how the UK as a whole is doing. Further information on Measuring National Well-being is available with a full list of well-being publications.

Contact details for this statistical bulletin

Dominic Webber / Vasileios Antonopoulos

QualityOfLife@ons.gsi.gov.uk

Telephone: +44 (0)1633 456246

Reinventing the 'Well-being' Wheel

Dawn Snape March 28, 2017

The Measuring National Well-being (MNW) programme began in 2010. Its aim is to provide a fuller picture of how society is doing by supplementing existing economic, social and environmental measures. The well-being wheel (pictured below in its most recent form) has been a familiar symbol and iconic feature of the programme and is published alongside each MNW update to illustrate how the UK is doing across the 41 headline indicators.

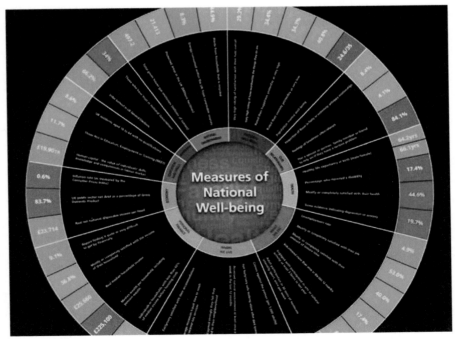

However, over the years, the wheel has become less suited to the challenges of presenting UK progress and is not in alignment with government wide accessibility standards. In an attempt to enable a better user experience, we have created a dashboard of well-being (indicative version pictured below) to replace the well-being wheel. Among other benefits, it will allow users to immediately see trend data for each indicator, allowing a more complete overview of all measures. It will also be compatible with smart devices, something which the wheel is not.

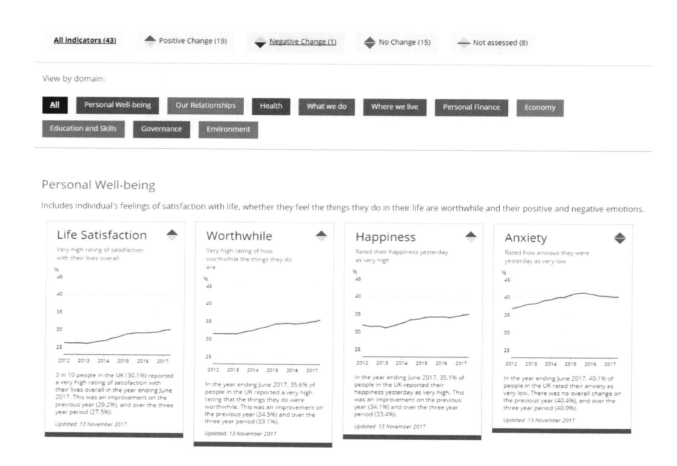

The new well-being dashboard will also provide a first step towards a 'live' well-being product. Where possible, indicators on the dashboard will update automatically as new data are published by the original data owner. We will be working hard in the background to ensure more and more data are updated automatically in this way. This is a major step away from the static essence of the wheel, which often was out of date shortly after being published.

The new dashboard will be published alongside our next update on 6 April 2017. Although it's in its infancy, we are hoping to develop it over time to suit user needs. As well as the national headline estimates, we also provide more detailed analysis by age, sex and region. Over the next few months we will be working on better ways to disseminate these different views of well-being.

Looking to the future, we aim to combine the best of what the wheel offered with newer technology and more accessible data visualisation methods. The dashboard will be in keeping with the programme's aim of presenting a more holistic view of how the UK is doing to supplement GDP.

Article

Measuring national well-being: Life in the UK, Apr 2017

An assessment of UK progress against a set of headline national well-being indicators, which include our health, natural environment, personal finances and crime. Change over time is also assessed to establish whether national well-being is improving or deteriorating.

Contact:
Tess Carter
qualityoflife@ons.gsi.gov.uk
+44 (0)1633 651812

Release date:
6 April 2017

Next release:
To be announced

Table of contents

1 . Main points

- The latest update provides a broadly positive picture of life in the UK, with the majority of indicators either improving or staying the same over the 1 year period.

- Considering the 43 national well-being indicators, 15 improved, 18 stayed the same and 2 deteriorated, compared with 1 year earlier.

- Satisfaction with our jobs, health, and leisure time all showed improvements on a 1-year and 3-year basis.

- Fewer people reported their anxiety as very low between the years ending September 2015 and 2016.

- On environmental sustainability, the proportion of waste from households that was recycled fell over a 1-year period, while remaining unchanged over the 3-year period.

2 . Things you need to know about this release

In November 2010, the Measuring National Well-being (MNW) programme was established. The aim was to monitor and report "how the UK as a whole is doing" by producing accepted and trusted measures of the well-being of the nation. Twice a year we report progress against a set of headline indicators covering areas of our lives including our health, natural environment, personal finances and crime. The measures include both objective data (for example, unemployment rate) and subjective data (for example, satisfaction with job) to provide a more complete view of the nation's progress than economic measures such as gross domestic product (GDP) can do alone.

This report is based on the most recent available data as of April 2017. It is important to recognise that the data underpinning the indicators are often from different sources with different timeliness and coverage. Please see the datasets for further information for each indicator. Alongside this release, we have also published:

- national well-being measures dataset containing: the latest data and back series, the indicators broken down by age, sex and region where applicable; and quality information

- an interactive dashboard showing trend data for each indicator alongside the assessment of change, compared with one year earlier

The dashboard replaces the Measuring National Well-being static wheel. Please see our recent blog for more information on this change.

We regularly review our indicators in response to changing coverage, frequency and other quality considerations affecting our data sources. Changes have been made to one of the indicators included within the Measuring National Well-being programme (Table 1).

Table 1: Summary of removed indicator and its replacement

Removed Indicator	Source	Reason
7.3 Inflation rate (as measured by CPI)	Consumer Prices, ONS	ONS is moving from CPI to CPIH as a preferred measure of inflation. CPIH is a measure of UK consumer price inflation that includes owner occupiers' housing costs (OOH). These are the costs of housing services associated with owning, maintaining and living in one's own home. OOH does not include costs such as utility bills, minor repairs and maintenance, which are already included in the index.

Replacement indicator	Source
7.3 Inflation rate (as measured by CPIH)	Consumer Prices, ONS

Source: Office for National Statistics

Please contact the Quality of Life team with any comments or suggestions, including your views on improvements we might make.

3 . Assessments of change

This report includes assessments showing the direction of change for each of the measures, whether they have improved, shown no overall change, or deteriorated (Figure 1). Comparisons have been made with the previous year's data, or the previously published figure where year-on-year data are not available, as well as an assessment of change over a 3-year period. For more information on how we assess change, please see the Quality and methodology section.

The latest update provides a broadly positive picture of life in the UK, with the majority of indicators either improving or staying the same over the 1-year period. Areas of life that are improving include satisfaction with our jobs, health and leisure time. Two areas deteriorated over the 1-year – the proportion reporting very low anxiety and waste from households that is recycled.

Figure 1: Assessment of change - national well-being measures

UK, April 2017

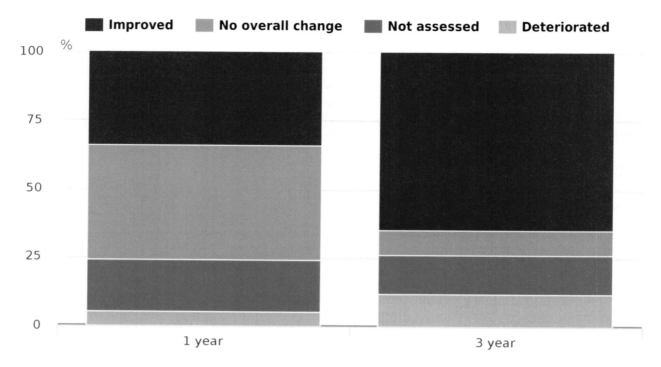

Source: Office for National Statistics

Notes:

1. Although there are 41 indicators of national well-being, measures of healthy life expectancy and feeling safe walking alone after dark are presented for both men and women, and so there are 43 measures to assess.

2. Figures may not add to 100% due to rounding.

Over the 1-year period:

- 35% (15 measures) had improved

- 42% (18 measures) showed no overall change

- 19% (8 measures) were not assessed for this publication

- 5% (2 measures) had deteriorated

Over the 3-year period:

- 65% (28 measures) had improved

- 9% (4 measures) showed no overall change

- 14% (6 measures) were not assessed for this publication

- 12% (5 measures) had deteriorated

A number of measures have not been assessed, either because data are not available for comparison, or where the direction of change is not a clear indication of either improvement or deterioration.

4 . Which areas of our lives have improved?

Areas of life which are getting better include what we do in life, with improvements in both satisfaction with our job and satisfaction with our leisure time. A higher proportion of people also felt that they belonged to their neighbourhood. The proportion of people volunteering has also shown improvements, however, a recent release by ONS found that while the number of people volunteering had increased in recent years, the average time spent volunteering per day has fallen.

There have also been improvements in people's financial situation, with real median household income increasing over both the 1 and 3 year periods. This improvement is also reflected in people's subjective view of their financial situation, with an increase in the proportion satisfied with their income and a smaller proportion stating they were struggling to get by financially. However, this data covers the reference period 2014 to 2015 while a recent release, based on data for the 12 months to December 2016 found that respondents reported a worsening in their perception of both the general economic situation and their own financial situation over the last year.

Other areas that are improving include education, decreases in the percentage of UK residents aged 16 to 64 with no qualifications, and the proportion of those classified as not in education, employment or training (NEETS) falling over a 3 year basis. There has also been an increase in those who reported trust in national government, while in regard to the natural environment, total greenhouse gas emissions have fallen and the proportion of energy consumed from renewable sources has increased.

5 . Which areas of our lives have deteriorated?

Not all areas of life are improving. The proportion of people reporting their anxiety as very low has fallen over the 1-year period. However, it is worth noting that there is still an improvement over the 3-year basis. The proportion of waste from households that was recycled also fell over a 1-year period, while remaining unchanged over the 3-year period.

Other areas that have deteriorated over a 3-year basis are the mental well-being of the population, the proportion of people in unhappy relationships, and the proportion of people with someone to rely on. Other areas that have shown deterioration are satisfaction with accommodation and the proportion of people participating in sport once a week.

6 . Which areas of our lives have stayed the same?

On a 1 year basis, the majority of headline indicators showed little to no change. There were no annual improvements in those reporting the highest ratings of personal well-being, covering levels of life satisfaction, worthwhile and happiness, between the years ending September 2015 and September 2016.

Healthy life expectancy remained unchanged for both males and females between 2011 to 2013 and 2013 to 2015, and while there was an improvement for male healthy life expectancy over the long-term, female healthy life expectancy remained unchanged.

Other areas include the percentage of people that have engaged with, or participated in, arts or cultural activity at least three times in the last year and the proportion of people feeling lonely often or always.

7 . Related links

Personal well-being in the UK: Oct 2015 to Sept 2016

Personal well-being in the UK: local authority update, 2015 to 2016

Economic Well-being: Quarter 4, Oct to Dec 2016

Changes in the value and division of unpaid volunteering in the UK: 2000 to 2015

Understanding Society

Community Life Survey

8 . Quality and methodology

The Measuring National Well-being (MNW) programme set out to establish measures that would help people to understand national well-being and also help monitor it. This report includes assessments showing the direction of change for each of the measures. Broadly speaking, indicators have only been assessed as having improved or deteriorated if the difference between the comparison periods is statistically significant using 95% confidence intervals. If a difference is said to be statistically significant, it is unlikely that it could have occurred by chance.

Confidence intervals give a measure of the statistical precision of an estimate and show the range of uncertainty around the estimate. As a general rule, if the confidence intervals around the estimate overlap with the intervals around another, there is no statistically significant difference between the estimates.

Some indicators have been assessed by experts, while voter turnout has been assessed using the actual increase or decrease as this is not an estimation. Other indicators have not been assessed. This is because either there are not enough data points to provide a comparison, or that the direction of change is not a clear indication of either an improvement or deterioration.

Contact details for this statistical bulletin

Tess Carter

QualityOfLife@ons.gsi.gov.uk

Telephone: +44 (0)1633 651812

Office for
National Statistics

Article

Young people's well-being: 2017

How young people aged 16 to 24 in the UK are faring in a range of areas that matter to their quality of life, reflecting both the circumstances of their lives and their own perspectives.

Contact:
Dawn Snape
QualityofLife@ons.gsi.gov.uk
+44 (0)1633 455674

Release date:
13 April 2017

Next release:
To be announced

Table of contents

1 . Main points

- Several aspects of young people's quality of life and well-being have improved in this latest update; many of these relate to education, employment and skills, while some measures of how young people feel about their lives provide a more mixed picture.

- Overall satisfaction with health has improved and the gap between young men's and young women's satisfaction with their health has narrowed.

- In 2016, the proportions of young people who were unemployed or not in education, employment or training (NEET) both reached their lowest levels since the most recent economic downturn.

- The proportion of young people reporting that they find it difficult to get by financially decreased to 7% in the period 2014 to 2015 from 15% in 2009 to 2010 but the proportion of young people living in households at risk of poverty increased from 19% in 2008 to 25% in 2015.

- The proportion of young people reporting symptoms of anxiety or depression increased from 18% in the period 2009 to 2010 to 21% in 2013 to 2014; young women were more likely than young men to report symptoms of anxiety or depression.

- On social connections, the proportion of young people who said they had someone to rely a lot on, decreased from 80% in the period 2010 to 2011 to 76% in 2013 to 2014 but the proportion of young people who agreed or strongly agreed that they belong to their neighbourhood, increased from 50% in 2009 to 2010 to 57% in 2014 to 2015.

2 . Things you need to know about this release

This article presents a picture of how young people aged 16 to 24 in the UK are faring in a range of areas that matter to their quality of life. We monitor young people's quality of life using a set of 28 headline indicators designed to shed light both on their current well-being and on their future prospects. The measures include objective data (for example, educational attainment) and subjective data (such as a sense of belonging in the neighbourhood where they live). The aim is to provide a holistic view of life in the UK for young people reflecting both the circumstances of their lives and their own perspectives.

The analysis uses the latest data available as of April 2017, however It is important to recognise that the data underpinning the indicators are from a range of different sources with different timeliness and coverage. Further information on the source of each indicator can be found in the dataset.

The measures for young people's personal well-being have been aligned with the data presented in the Personal well-being statistical bulletin. These changes offer more detailed data for young people. The measure is provided for 16- to 19-year-olds and 20- to24-year-olds, and the "high or very high" rating (low or very low for anxiety) is now only "very high" (9 or 10 out of 10) or "very low" (0 or 1 out of 10). In addition, the measure for long-term illness and disability has been changed from the Equality Act core disabled definition to the Government Statistical Service (GSS) Harmonised Standard definition.

The principles of the Government Statistical Service (GSS) Harmonised Standard are designed to be consistent with a conceptual framework of disability that encompasses medical, individual and societal factors as documented in the International Classification of Functioning (ICF), the World Health Organisation's definition of disability and the disablement process. This approach is consistent with the collection of traditional data on activity restriction, long-standing illness and impairment, as well as data on the importance of aspects of society which restrict the participation of people with impairments relative to those without impairments.

3 . Assessments of change

To give a sense of whether and how quality of life is improving for young people in the UK, we assess whether each indicator has improved, deteriorated or remained unchanged. Comparisons are made with the previous year's data, as well as change over a 3-year period. Where possible, the article also includes trends over a longer period to provide further context.

Figure 1: Assessment of young people's [1] well-being measures over 1 and 3 years

April 2017 release

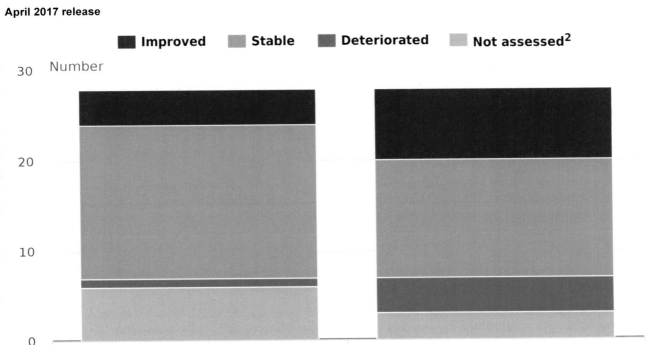

Source: Office for National Statistics

Notes:

1. Young people aged 16 to 24 years.

2. Where data are not available for the previous period, the measure has not been assessed.

Over a 1-year period, the majority (17) of indicators remained unchanged, while four improved and one deteriorated. Six indicators were not assessed for this publication because data were not available for the previous period.

Over a 3-year period eight indicators of young people's quality of life improved, while 13 remained unchanged, and four deteriorated. Three indicators were not assessed for this publication because data were not available for the previous period.

The overall picture is one of stability or improvement in young people's quality of life, though with some notable exceptions, particularly in relation to the proportion of young people in households at risk of poverty, young people's mental health and well-being and the social support available to them. A more in-depth review of these factors and their contribution to young people's quality of life is presented below.

4 . Personal well-being

Our personal well-being questions allow individuals to assess their own quality of life. People aged 16 and over are asked to evaluate their satisfaction with life overall, whether they feel the things they do in life are worthwhile, how happy they were yesterday and how anxious they were yesterday. The proportions of young people who gave very high ratings (9 or 10 out of 10) of life satisfaction, worthwhile and happiness and very low ratings (0 or 1 out of 10) of anxiety for financial year ending (FYE) 2016 are presented in Table 1.

Table 1: Proportions reporting very high life satisfaction, worthwhile and happiness and very low anxiety for those aged 16 to 19 and 20 to 24

	UK: financial year ending 2016	
	16 to 19	20 to 24
Life Satisfaction (very high)	36.4	26.8
Worthwhile (very high)	32.5	31.1
Happiness (very high)	39.6	32.7
Anxiety (very low)	42.2	41.4

Source: Annual Population Survey, Office for National Statistics

Notes:

1. For Life satisfaction, worthwhile and happiness, percentages for 'very high' relates to those who responded 9 or 10 on a scale of 0 to 10 where 0 was not at all and 10 was completely.

2. Percentages for 'very low' relates to those who responded 0 or 1 on a scale of 0 to 10 where 0 was not at all anxious and 10 was completely anxious.

In the FYE 2016, a larger proportion of people aged 16 to 19 in the UK reported very high levels of life satisfaction and happiness than those aged 20 to 24. There are no differences between the two age groups in the proportions giving very high ratings that the things they do in life are worthwhile and very low levels of anxiety. There has been no change in the proportions of both age groups reporting very high life satisfaction, worthwhile or happiness, or very low anxiety compared with the previous year (FYE 2015).

5 . Health

Previous analysis has found a strong relationship between self-reported health and personal well-being (What matters most to personal well-being? ONS, 2013). The most recent estimate shows that 56% of young people aged 16 to 24 were mostly or completely satisfied with their health in the period 2014 to 2015. This measure deteriorated between the periods 2009 to 2010 and 2013 to 2014, and was driven by a fall in the proportion of young men, who reported that they were mostly or completely satisfied with their health (59% to 52%). While satisfaction with health for both young men and young women improved between 2013 to 2014 and 2014 to 2015, young women's satisfaction increased more sharply from 50% to 56%. This has effectively closed the gap between young men's and young women's reported health satisfaction.

Figure 2: Proportion of young people[1] mostly or completely satisfied with health by sex, 2009 to 2010 through 2014 to 2015

UK

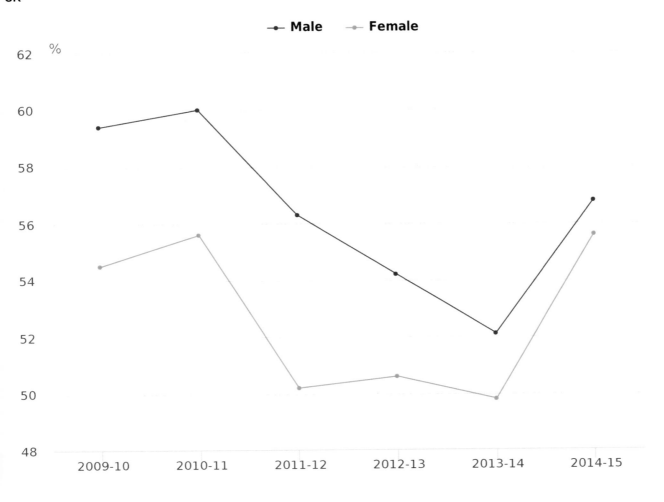

Source: Understanding Society: the UK Household Longitudinal Survey

Notes:

1. Young people aged 16 to 24 years.

In terms of objective measures of health, the Health Survey for England estimates around 39% of young people aged 16 to 24 in England were classified as overweight or obese in 2015. People in this age group are the least likely of all adult age groups to be overweight or obese, compared for example with those aged 25 to 34 (52%) and 55 to 64 (75%). The proportion of young people who are overweight or obese has remained largely stable since 2012.

The Labour Force Survey captures information about people's disability status using the principles of the Government Statistical Service (GSS) Harmonised Standard[1]. In 2015, around 12% of young people were classified as disabled or having a long-term illness, an increase from 9% in 2013.

Notes for: Health

1. The principles of the Government Statistical Service (GSS) Harmonised Standard are designed to be consistent with a conceptual framework of disability that encompasses medical, individual and societal factors as documented in the International Classification of Functioning (ICF), the World Health Organisation's definition of disability and the disablement process. This approach is consistent with the collection of traditional data on activity restriction, long-standing illness and impairment, as well as data on the importance of aspects of society which restrict the participation of people with impairments relative to those without impairments.

6 . Mental health and well-being

Recent longitudinal research on well-being over the life course suggests that mental ill-health may be an important contributory factor to subsequent life satisfaction, educational success, earnings, and physical health (Layard, 2013).

Overall, the proportion of young people with symptoms of anxiety or depression [1] increased from 18% to 21% between the periods 2009 to 2010 and 2013 to 2014. Although this fell to 19% in the period 2014 to 2015, the change was not statistically significant.

The increase to 2013 to 2014 was primarily due to an increase in the proportion of young women reporting symptoms of anxiety or depression; in 2013 to 2014 around 26% of young women reported symptoms compared with 22% in 2009 to 2010. Overall, young women were significantly more likely to report symptoms of anxiety and depression than young men; in 2014 to 2015, around 1 in 4 young women (25%) reported symptoms of anxiety or depression compared with fewer than 1 in 6 young men (15%).

Figure 3: Proportion of young people[1] showing signs of depression or anxiety by sex, 2009 to 2010 through 2014 to 2015

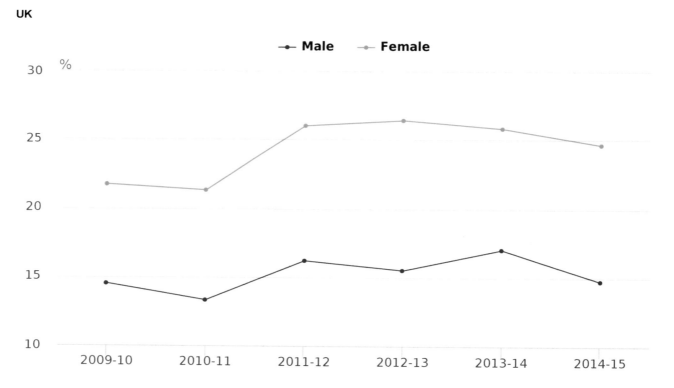

Source: Understanding Society: the UK Household Longitudinal Survey

Notes:

1. Young people aged 16 to 24 years.

In contrast to mental ill-health, mental well-being focuses on whether people are feeling and functioning well. It has been described as, "a dynamic state, in which the individual is able to develop their potential, work productively and creatively, build strong and positive relationships with others, and contribute to their community" (Foresight report, 2008).

The mental well-being indicator used here is based on the shortened version of the Warwick-Edinburgh Mental Well-being Scale (SWEMWBS) developed to measure the mental well-being of populations and groups over time. It provides a mean score (out of 35) of population mental well-being. Changes over time are assessed by examining differences in the mean score but it cannot be used to categorise good, average or poor mental well-being[2].

According to this measure, young people's mental well-being deteriorated between the periods 2009 to 2010 and 2012 to 2013 (from an average score of 25.0 to 24.2). Young women's mental well-being scores were significantly lower than young men's in both years and declined more than men's. In 2012 to 2013 the average score for young women was 23.8 compared with 24.6 for young men. It is important to note that this may not reflect the current situation as the most recent estimate is from 2012 to 2013.

Figure 4: Mean mental well-being score of young people [1] by sex, 2009 to 2010 through 2012 to 2013

UK

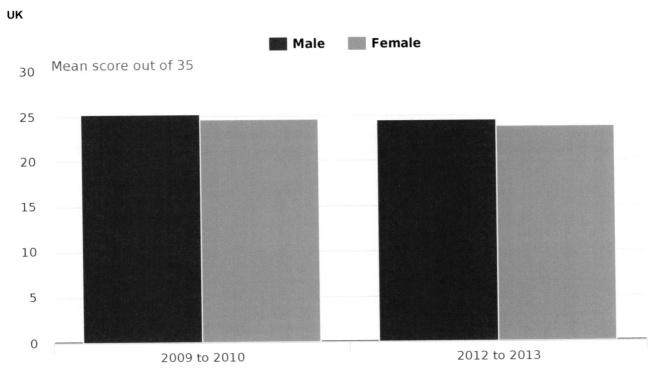

Source: Understanding Society; the UK Household Longitudinal Survey

Notes:

1. Young people aged 16 to 24 years.

Notes for: Mental health and wellbeing

1. The mental ill-health measure used here focusses on whether a person has a higher likelihood of a clinically diagnosable illness, from anxiety or depression to problems such as bi-polar disorder or schizophrenia.

2. As well as not being designed to identify people who have, or probably have a mental illness, WEMWBS does not a have a "cut-off" level to divide the population into those who have "good" and those who have "poor" mental well-being, in the way that scores on other mental health measures do, for example the GHQ 12.

7 . Employment, volunteering, education and skills

A crucial aspect of young people's current quality of life relates to whether they are engaged in fulfilling activities such as education, training, volunteering or work. These things also contribute to how well they are prepared to make the transition to the world of work and financial independence as they get older and as such, are important to their future well-being.

The Education and Skills Act 2008 made it compulsory to be in full-time education or training (such as an apprenticeship), or part-time education if they were employed or volunteering for at least 20 hours a week to age 17 in England from 2013 and to age 18 by 2015.

Recent labour market data show that the proportion of unemployed young people declined to 13% (around 1 in 8) in 2016 after peaking in 2012 at 21% (around 1 in 5). Similarly, the proportion of young people across the UK who were not in education, employment or training (NEET) increased between 2008 and 2012 (the lowest point of the economic downturn), before returning to pre-downturn levels in 2015. By 2016, both the unemployment rate for young people and the NEET rate were lower than before the economic downturn. This is likely to reflect the combined impacts of the Education and Skills Act coming into force as well as wider economic conditions.

Figure 5: Proportion of young people[1] unemployed and proportion of young people not in education, employment or training,[2] 2004 to 2016

UK

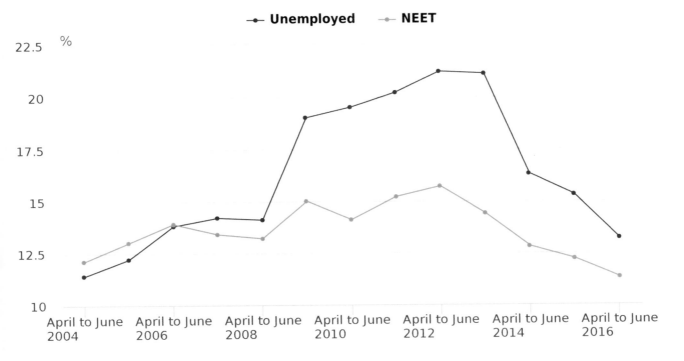

Source: Labour Force Survey; Office for National Statistics

Notes:

1. Young people aged 16 to 24 years.

2. A person identified as NEET will always be either unemployed or economically inactive, although not all unemployed and economically inactive persons will be NEET.

There has also been a steady increase in the proportion of 19-year-olds in England attaining a Level 2 qualification[1], up from 79% in 2009 to 87% in 2015. Furthermore, around 60% of 19-year-olds in 2015 had attained qualifications equivalent to level 3 of the NQF (for example, A-levels or the International Baccalaureate). This is an increase from 51% in 2009.

Figure 6: Educational attainment at age 19, [1] 2009 to 2015

England

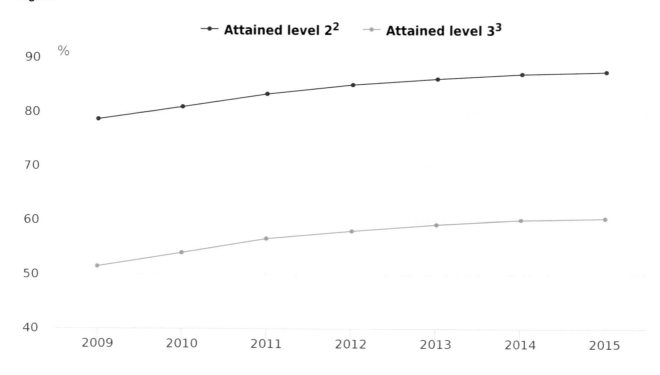

Source: Department for Education administrative data

Notes:

1. Those aged 19 in reference year.

2. Level 2 of the National Qualifications framework includes 5 A*-C GCSEs, and BTEC first Diplomas.

3. Level 3 of the National Qualifications framework includes A levels or the International Baccalaureate.

The proportion of young people aged 16 to 24 in the UK reporting that they volunteered several times a year or more remained stable between 2009 to 2010 and 2014 to 2015. However, recent analysis of volunteering using time-use data and other data sources presents a more detailed picture over the longer term. Data from the UK Harmonised European Time Use survey (HETUS) suggest that between 2000 and 2015, young people increased the time they devote to volunteering from an average of 8.6 minutes per day to 17.0 minutes per day. Data from the Community Life Survey also show that in England, young people saw the highest increase of any age group in volunteering participation (at least once a year) from 40% in 2000 to 51% in 2015.

Notes for: Employment, volunteering, education and skills

1. Qualifications equivalent of Level 2 of the National Qualifications Framework (NQF) include 5 GCSEs A*-C and BTEC first diplomas.

8 . Personal finance

The latest data provide a mixed picture of young people's personal finances. The subjective measures – how young people feel about their finances – have improved. At the same time, the objective measure of the proportion of young people living in households at risk of poverty has deteriorated.

The proportion of young people who say they are mostly or completely satisfied with their household income has increased from 31% in the period 2009 to 2010 to 45% in 2014 to 2015. However, a recent release on economic well-being looked at data for the 12 months to December 2016 and found that respondents (all adults aged 16 and over) reported a worsening in their perception of both the general economic situation and their own financial situation over the last year.

In the period 2014 to 2015, those aged 16 to 18 were significantly more likely to say they were mostly or completely satisfied with their household income (52%) than those aged 22 to 24 (37%). This probably reflects the fact that 16- to 18-year-olds are usually still living in the parental home, so continue to benefit from the household income of their parents. Those aged 22 to 24 are more likely to have their own financial responsibilities, such as rent and bills and a level of household income reflecting their individual earnings. However, a higher proportion of people aged 22 to 24 in 2014 to 2015 were satisfied with their household income than those of the same age in 2009 to 2010. This coincided with an increase in the proportion of young people in this age group still living with their parents. In 2009, around 39% of young people aged 22 to 24 lived with their parents; in 2016 the proportion increased to 46%.

The largest increase in the proportion reporting they were mostly or completely satisfaction with household income was among those aged 19 to 21 between the periods 2009 to 2010 and 2014 to 2015 (29% and 46% respectively). Among this age group the proportion living with their parents remained relatively stable.

Figure 7: Proportion of young people mostly or completely satisfied with their household income by age group, 2009 to 2010 to 2014 to 2015

UK

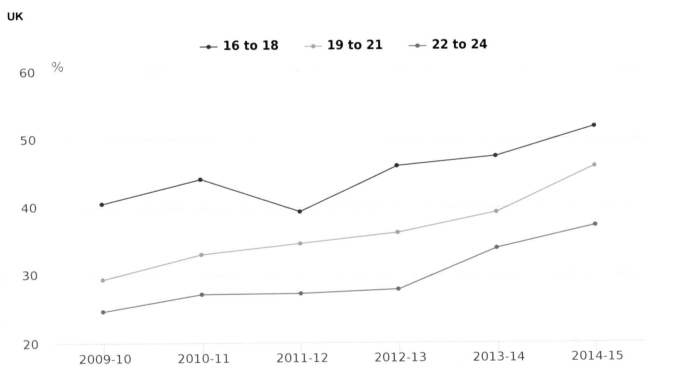

Source: Understanding Society; the UK Household Longitudinal Survey

Notes:

1. Young people aged 16 to 24 years.

Figure 8: Proportion of young people living with their parents by age group, 2008 to 2016

UK

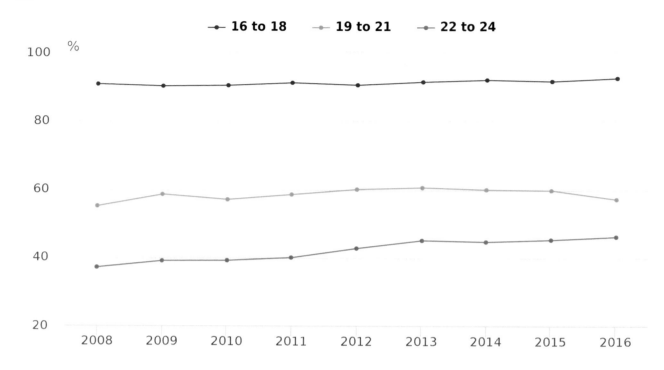

Source: Labour Force Survey, Office for National Statistics

Notes:

1. Young people aged 16 to 24 years.

2. Data has been rounded to the nearest thousand.

3. Once a person either lives with a partner or has a child, they are considered to have formed their own family and are no longer counted as being part of their parents' family even if they still live in the same household. Therefore such people are deemed to be not living with their parents here.

4. The term 'Parent' could include grandparents, step parents or foster parents.

5. Students living in halls of residence during term-time and living with their parents outside term-time are counted as not living with their parents here.

The proportion of young people reporting they are finding it difficult or very difficult to manage financially has decreased from 15% in the period 2009 to 2010 to 7% in 2014 to 2015 while the proportion reporting that they are financially "comfortable" increased from 22% to 31% over the same period.

Although those aged 16 to 18 were more likely than others in the 16 to 24 age range to report being financially comfortable in 2014 to 2015 (80% of those aged 16 to 18; 73% of those aged 19 to 21; and 70% of those aged 22 to 24), all age groups have shown significant decreases in the proportions reporting they are finding it difficult to manage financially.

Despite these positive developments in how young people are feeling about their finances, the proportion of young people living in households at risk of poverty has increased. Median household disposable income in the UK was estimated as £25,700 in the financial year ending (FYE) 2015. The level of 60% of median household income is used as a poverty "threshold"[1]. Estimates from the European Union Statistics on Income and Living Conditions survey show that in 2015, around 1 in 4 young people in the UK (25%) lived in households with less than 60% of the UK's median income. This proportion has increased since 2008 when around 1 in 5 (19%) of 16- to 24-year-olds lived in households with less than 60% of median income.

Figure 9: Proportion of young people[1] living in households with less than 60% median income,[2] 2009 to 2015

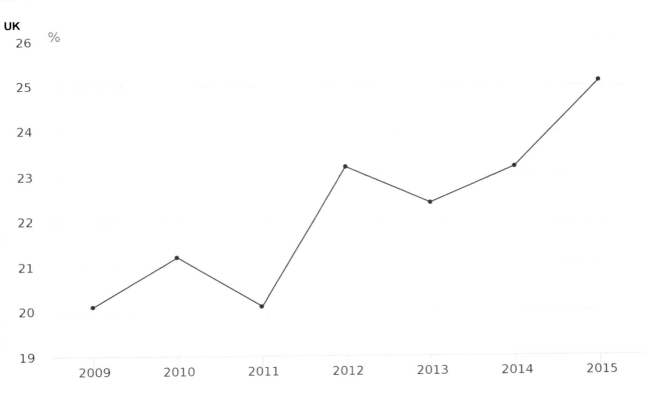

Source: Eurostat, Survey of Income and Living Conditions

Notes:

1. Young people aged 16 to 24 years.

2. After housing costs.

Although there appears to be a disparity between the increased proportion of 16- to 24-year-olds in households at risk of poverty and young people's subjective assessments of their financial situation, it may be that the aggregate indicators are masking differences in the experiences of young people. For example, recent analysis by ONS of young people's well-being and personal finance (May 2016) found that around 1 in 5 young people in social rental housing rated their current financial situation as difficult or very difficult compared with an average of 1 in 14 young people in other accommodation types in 2013 to 2014. This is something we aim to explore further as part of a wider focus on well-being inequalities.

Notes for: Personal finance

1. Median income is the middle point in the income range, with equal numbers of households on incomes above and below that point. The 60% level is chosen as an indicator of the income at which those below are likely to be suffering hardship.

9 . Social support, personal security and sense of belonging

Positive social connections and relationships are very important to quality of life and to physical and mental well-being. Public Health England's report, Reducing social isolation across the lifecourse (2015), highlights the positive benefits of social connectedness and the detrimental impact of prolonged social isolation on people of all ages. Using a life course approach, they describe how social isolation in childhood is associated with isolation in adolescence and adulthood, potentially casting a long shadow throughout life:

"Children who experience social isolation in childhood tend to have lower educational outcomes and lower adult social class (based on occupation), and higher likelihoods of smoking, obesity and psychological distress in adulthood."

One of the indicators that can help to assess this issue is whether young people feel they have a spouse, family member or friend they can rely on if they have a serious problem. The latest data available showed deterioration in 2013 to 2014 when 76% of young people aged 16 to 24 reported they had someone they could rely on a lot, down from 80% in the period 2010 to 2011. In 2013 to 2014, young women were significantly more likely than young men to say they had someone they could rely on a lot (81% and 72%, respectively).

Assessing young people's sense of belonging to their neighbourhood is another way of looking at their social connections. The proportion of young people who agreed or strongly agreed that they belong to their neighbourhood improved from 50% in the period 2009 to 2010 to 57% in 2014 to 2015.

Young people aged 16 to 18 are more likely to feel they belong to their neighbourhood than either those aged 19 to 21 or 22 to 24. This may be because those in the younger age group are more likely to be living in the parental home where they grew up.

Figure 10: Proportion of young people[1] who agree or strongly agree they belong to their neighbourhood by age group, 2009 to 2010 to 2014 to 2015

UK

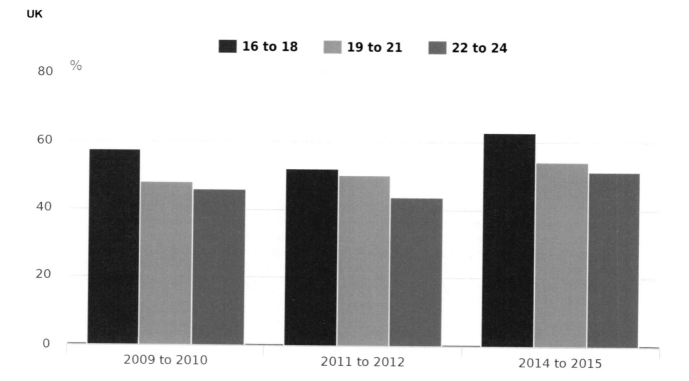

Source: Understanding Society; the UK Household Longitudinal Survey

Notes:

1. Young people aged 16 to 24 years.

Our analysis of the personal well-being of victims of crime published in 2015 shows that victims of crime have lower well-being than non-victims, and that the largest differences in well-being between victims and non-victims were found in the 16 to 24 age group. In addition, the most recent data from the Crime Survey for England and Wales financial year ending 2016 showed people aged 16 to 24 were more likely to be victims of crime – and particularly of violent crimes – than those aged 35 and over.

Despite this, the proportion of young people who have been victims of any type of crime declined from 26% in the financial year ending (FYE) 2013 to 21% in the FYE 2016. The proportion of young people who have been a victim of personal crime (for example, violence, robbery, theft from the person, and other theft of personal property) also decreased from 12% to 8% over this period.

10 . Quality and methodology

The aim of the young people's well-being indicator set is to help us better understand young people's quality of life and well-being, and to monitor it over time. This report includes assessments showing the direction of change for each of the measures, whether they have improved, shown no overall change, or deteriorated. Comparisons have been made with the previous year's data, as well as an assessment of change over a 3-year period, where data are available.

Broadly speaking, indicators have only been assessed as having improved or deteriorated if the difference between the comparison periods is statistically significant using 95% confidence intervals. If a difference is said to be statistically significant, it is unlikely that it could have occurred by chance.

Confidence intervals give a measure of the statistical precision of an estimate and show the range of uncertainty around the estimate. As a general rule, if the confidence intervals around the estimate overlap with the interval around another, there is no statistically significant difference between the estimates.

Some indicators such as educational attainment have been assessed using the actual increase or decrease as this is not an estimate. Other indicators such as parental relationships have not been assessed because there are not enough data points to provide a comparison.

For more information on how we assess change, please contact us via QualityofLife@ons.gov.uk. Further links to the data used in each measure can be found in the data table.

Contact details for this statistical bulletin

Dawn Snape

QualityOfLife@ons.gsi.gov.uk

Telephone: +44 (0)1633 455674

Statistical bulletin

Effects of taxes and benefits on UK household income: financial year ending 2016

The redistribution effects on households of direct and indirect taxation and benefits received in cash or kind analysed by household type, and the changing levels of income inequality over time.

Contact:
Paola Serafino / Nathan Thomas
hie@ons.gov.uk
+44 (0) 1633 651538

Release date:
25 April 2017

Next release:
To be announced

Table of contents

1 . Main points

In the financial year ending 2016, the average income of the richest fifth of households before taxes and benefits was £84,700 per year, 12 times greater than that of the poorest fifth (£7,200 per year). An increase in the average income from employment for the poorest fifth of households has reduced this ratio from 14 to 1 in the financial year ending 2015.

The ratio between the average income of the top and bottom fifth of households (£63,300 and £17,200 respectively) is reduced to less than 4 to 1 after accounting for benefits (both cash and in kind) and taxes (both direct and indirect).

On average, households paid £7,800 per year in direct taxes (such as Income Tax, National Insurance contributions and Council Tax), equivalent to 18.7% of their gross income. Richer households pay higher proportions of their income in direct taxes than poorer households.

The poorest households paid more of their disposable income in indirect taxes (such as Value Added Tax (VAT) and duties on alcohol and fuel) than the richest (27.0% and 14.4% respectively) and therefore indirect taxes cause an increase in income inequality.

There has been a 14% increase in the average amount paid in Insurance Premium Tax for all households, reflecting the November 2015 increase in the standard rate from 6% to 9.5%.

Overall, 50.5% of all households received more in benefits (including in kind benefits such as education) than they paid in taxes (direct and indirect). This is equivalent to 13.7 million households and continues the downward trend seen since the financial year ending 2011.

Households where the main earner is aged between 25 and 64 paid more in taxes (direct and indirect) than they received in benefits (including in kind benefits), whilst the reverse was true for those aged 65 and over.

Despite being less progressive (targeted towards reducing inequality) than many of the other benefits, the State Pension has consistently made the largest contribution to the overall progressivity of cash benefits over the past 22 years.

2 . Things you need to know about this release

This bulletin looks at two main measures of average household income, the mean and the median (Figure 1). The median is used when looking at the average income of a particular group of households, while the mean is used when looking at the sources of earnings, benefits and taxes that make up the overall income measures.

The mean simply divides the total income of households by the number of households. A limitation of using the mean for this purpose is that it can be influenced by just a few households with very high incomes and therefore does not necessarily reflect the standard of living of the "typical" household.

Many researchers argue that growth in median household incomes provides a better measure of how people's well-being has changed over time. The median household income is the income of what would be the middle household, if all households in the UK were sorted in a list from poorest to richest. As it represents the middle of the income distribution, the median household income provides a good indication of the standard of living of the "typical" household in terms of income.

Figure 1: Distribution of UK household disposable income, financial year ending 2016

UK

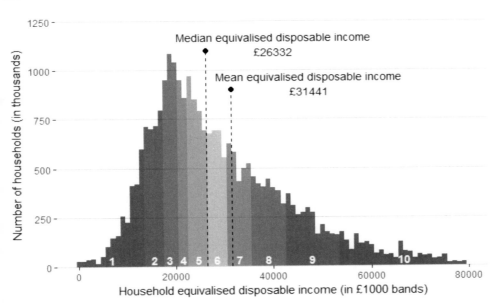

Household equivalised disposable income (in £1000 bands)

How is income redistributed across the population?

This release looks at how taxes and benefits affect the distribution of income in the UK and breaks this process into five stages. These are summarised in Figure 2 and in this section:

1. Household members begin with income from employment, private pensions, investments and other non-government sources. This is referred to as "original income".

2. Households then receive income from cash benefits. The sum of cash benefits and original income is referred to as "gross income".

3. Households then pay direct taxes. Gross income minus direct taxes is referred to as "disposable income".

4. Indirect taxes are then paid via expenditure. Disposable income minus indirect taxes is referred to as "post-tax income".

5. Households finally receive a benefit from services (benefits in kind). Benefits in kind plus post-tax income is referred to as "final income".

Figure 2: Stages in the redistribution of income

UK

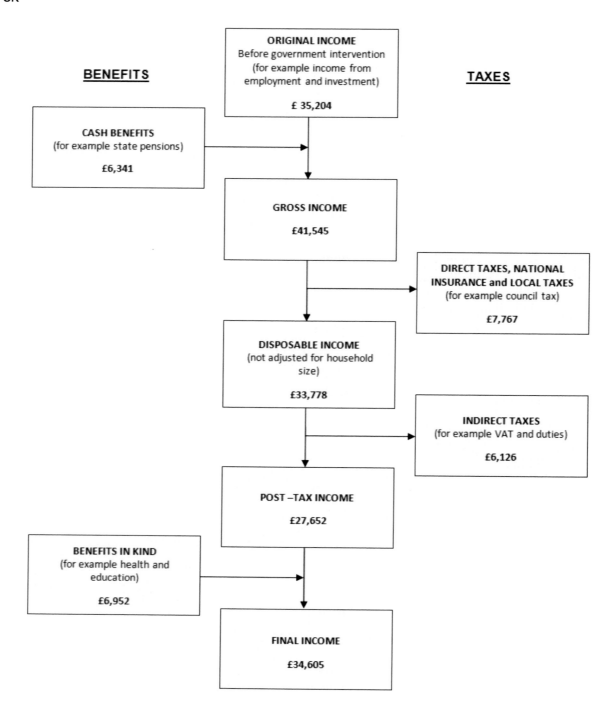

What does it mean for a benefit or tax to be progressive?

A tax is considered to be progressive when high-income groups face a higher average tax rate than low-income groups. If those with higher incomes pay a higher amount but still face a lower average tax rate, then the tax is considered regressive; similarly, cash benefits are progressive where they account for a larger share of low-income groups' income

Progressivity is measured through the Kakwani index (Kakwani, 1977). For taxes, a positive value indicates that the tax is progressive overall and acting to reduce inequality. The larger the value, the more progressive the tax is. A negative value would indicate that the tax is regressive and therefore contributing to increased inequality.

Conversely, for benefits, a negative value indicates that the benefits are progressive and acting to reduce the level of inequality. Again, the larger the negative value, the more progressive the benefit is.

How do we make comparisons over time?

This bulletin looks at how main estimates of household incomes and inequality have changed over time. To make robust comparisons historic data have been adjusted for the effects of inflation and are equivalised to take account of changes in household composition. More information on the details of these adjustments can be found in the Quality and Methodology section of this bulletin.

3 . Taxes and benefits lead to income being shared more equally

The overall impact of taxes and benefits are that they lead to income being shared more equally between households. In the financial year ending (fye) 2016 (April 2015 to March 2016), before taxes and benefits, the richest fifth (those in the top income quintile group) had an average original income of £84,700 per year, compared with £7,200 for the poorest fifth – a ratio of 12 to 1 (Figure 3). This ratio has decreased from 14 to 1 in fye 2015 indicating that inequality of original income has reduced slightly according to this measure. This was mainly due to an increase in the average income from employment for the poorest fifth, reflecting increases in both the wages and employment of people living in those households.

Figure 3: The effects of taxes and benefits on household income by quintile groups, all households, financial year ending 2016

UK

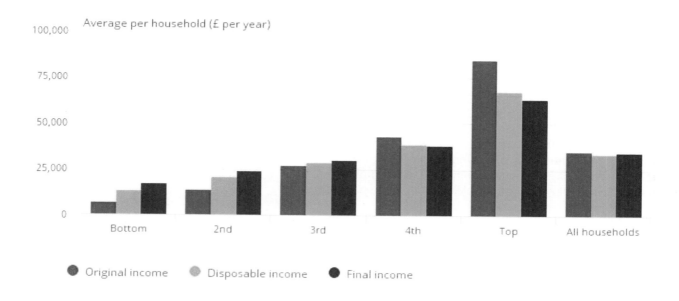

Figure 3: The effects of taxes and benefits on household income by quintile groups, all households, financial year ending 2016

UK

Source: Office for National Statistics

Source: Office for National Statistics

After cash benefits and direct taxes, the richest fifth of households had an average disposable income that was around five times that of the poorest fifth (£67,500 and £13,100 per year respectively).

After accounting for all taxes and benefits, including indirect taxes and benefits in kind, in fye 2016, the ratio of final income for the richest fifth of the population to the poorest fifth (£63,300 and £17,200 per year respectively) was further reduced to less than 4 to 1.

Effect of cash benefits

In contrast to original income, the amount received from cash benefits such as tax credits, Housing Benefit and Income Support tends to be higher for poorer households than for richer households. The highest amount of cash benefits were received by households in the second quintile group, £9,600 per year compared with £7,600 for households in the bottom group, a trend that has remained unchanged from fye 1996. This is largely because more retired households are located in the second quintile group, compared with the bottom group, and in this analysis the State Pension is classified as a cash benefit.

Figure 4: Summary of the effects of taxes and benefits by quintile groups [1], all households, financial year ending 2016

UK

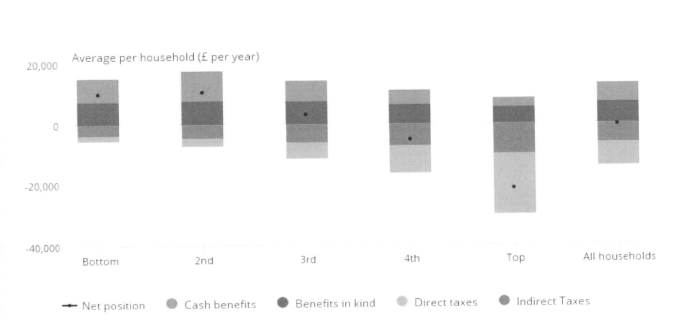

Figure 4: Summary of the effects of taxes and benefits by quintile groups 1 , all households, financial year ending 2016

UK

Source: Office for National Statistics

Source: Office for National Statistics

Notes:

1. Households are ranked by their equivalised disposable incomes, using the modified-OECD scale.

The distribution of cash benefits between richer and poorer households has the effect of reducing inequality of income. After cash benefits were taken into account, the richest fifth had an average income that was roughly 6 times the poorest fifth (gross incomes of £87,600 per year compared with £14,800, respectively), a proportion that was broadly unchanged on the previous year.

Looking at individual cash benefits, in fye 2016, the average combined amount of contribution-based and income-based Jobseeker's Allowance (JSA) received by the bottom quintile decreased compared with fye 2015 (Reference table 2 in the Effects of taxes and benefits dataset). This was largely due to fewer households receiving this benefit, consistent with a fall in unemployment between these years, as well as the ongoing implementation of the Universal Credit (UC) system which, by April 2016, had been rolled out to almost 250,000 claimants.

Effect of direct taxes

Direct taxes (Income Tax, employees' National Insurance contributions and Council Tax or Northern Ireland rates) also act to reduce income inequality. Richer households pay both higher amounts of direct tax and a higher proportion of their income in direct taxes.

In fye 2016, on average, households paid £7,800 per year in direct taxes, equivalent to 18.7% of their gross income (Figure 5). The richest fifth of households paid, on average £20,100 per year, which corresponds to 23.0% of their gross income. The majority of this (16.5% of gross income) was paid in Income Tax. The average tax bill for the poorest fifth of households, by contrast was £1,600 per year, which is equivalent to 11.0% of their gross household income. Council Tax or Northern Ireland rates made up the largest proportion of direct taxes for this group, accounting for half of all direct taxes paid by them, 5.6% of their gross income on average.

Figure 5: Direct taxes as a percentage of gross income by quintile groups, ALL households, financial year ending 2016

UK

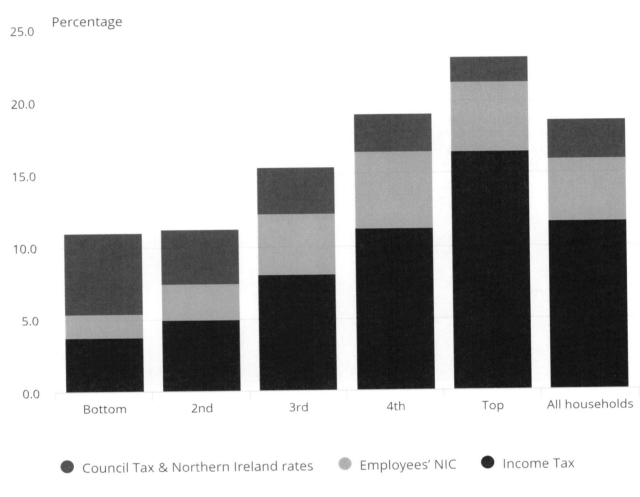

Figure 5: Direct taxes as a percentage of gross income by quintile groups, ALL households, financial year ending 2016

UK

Source: Office for National Statistics

Source: Office for National Statistics

The poorest fifth of households had the largest annual percentage increase in the average amount paid in Employees' National Insurance Contributions in fye 2016, increasing from £205 per year in fye 2015 (fye 2016 prices) to £240 per year in fye 2016, equivalent to an increase of 17%. However, the average amount paid as a proportion of their gross income was largely unchanged (1.6% in fye 2016 compared with 1.5% in fye 2015). This reflects an increase in both the wages and employment level of people living in these households. However, there has been no corresponding increase in the average amount of Income Tax paid by the poorest fifth of households as the tax-free personal allowance increased from £10,000 in fye 2015 to £10,600 in fye 2016.

Further analysis on the impact of cash benefits and direct taxes on disposable income can be found within the Household Disposable Income and Inequality, financial year ending 2016 publication.

Effect of indirect taxes

The amount of indirect tax (such as Value Added Tax (VAT) and duties on alcohol and fuel) each household pays is determined by their expenditure rather than their income. The richest fifth of households paid nearly three times as much in indirect taxes as the poorest fifth (£9,700 and £3,500 per year, respectively). This reflects greater expenditure on goods and services subject to these taxes by higher income households. However, although richer households pay more in indirect taxes than poorer ones, they pay less as a proportion of their income (Figure 6). This means that indirect taxes increase inequality of income. After indirect taxes, the richest fifth had post-tax household incomes that were six times those of the poorest fifth (£57,800 compared with £9,600 per year, respectively), this ratio has reduced slightly since fye 2015.

In fye 2016, the richest fifth of households paid 14.4% of their disposable income in indirect taxes, while the bottom fifth of households paid the equivalent of 27.0% of their disposable income. Across the board, VAT is the largest component of indirect taxes. Again, the proportion of disposable income that is spent on VAT is highest for the poorest fifth and lowest for the richest fifth.

Looking in detail at specific taxes there has been a 14% increase in the average amount paid in Insurance Premium Tax for all households, reflecting the November 2015 increase in the standard rate from 6% to 9.5%. There has also been an overall increase of 19% in the average amount paid on betting taxes. This increase is seen for all except the poorest households and is due in part to the Gambling Tax Reform.

Figure 6: Indirect taxes as a percentage of disposable income by quintile groups, ALL households, financial year ending 2016

UK

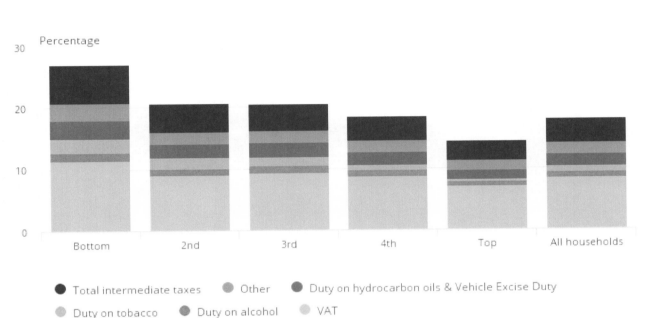

Figure 6: Indirect taxes as a percentage of disposable income by quintile groups, ALL households, financial year ending 2016

UK

Source: Office for National Statistics

Source: Office for National Statistics

Grouping households by their income is recognised as the standard approach to distributional analysis, as income provides a good indication of households' material living standards, but it is also useful to group households according to their expenditure, particularly for examining indirect taxes, which are paid on expenditure rather than income. Some households, particularly those at the lower end of the income distribution, may have annual expenditure that exceeds their annual income. For these households, their expenditure is not being funded entirely from income. During periods of low income, these households may maintain their standard of living by funding their expenditure from savings or borrowing, thereby adjusting their lifetime consumption.

Figure 7: Indirect taxes as a percentage of expenditure by quintile group, financial year ending 2016

UK

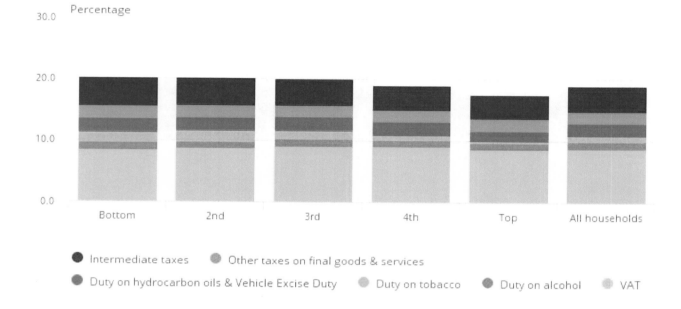

Figure 7: Indirect taxes as a percentage of expenditure by quintile group, financial year ending 2016

UK

Source: Office for National Statistics

Source: Office for National Statistics

Notes:

1. Expenditure is calculated to be consistent with disposable income

When expressed as a percentage of expenditure[1], the proportion paid in indirect tax declines less sharply as income rises (Figure 7) compared with the level of indirect taxes paid as a proportion of household disposable income. The bottom fifth of households paid 20.0% of their expenditure in indirect taxes compared with 17.5% for the top fifth. These figures are broadly unchanged from the previous year.

Effect of benefits in kind

This publication also considers the effect on household income of certain benefits received in kind. Benefits in kind are goods and services provided by the government to households that are either free at the time of use or at subsidised prices, such as education and health services. These goods and services can be assigned a monetary value based on the cost to the government, which is then allocated as a benefit to individual households.

The poorest fifth of households received the equivalent of £7,600 per year from all benefits in kind, compared with £5,500 received by the top fifth (Effects of taxes and benefits dataset Table 2). This is partly due to households towards the bottom of the income distribution having, on average, a larger number of children in state education. At component level rail and bus travel subsidies were the only benefits in kind for which the richest households received on average more than the poorest. After benefits in kind, the richest fifth had final household incomes that were on average four times those of the poorest fifth (£63,300 compared with £17,200 per year, respectively), this ratio is the same as in fye 2015.

In fye 2016 the statistical methodology for allocating the School Meals and Healthy Start Vouchers benefit in kind has been improved to take account of free school meal policy changes. As this methodology is still under development it has not yet been adopted in the back series, therefore this improvement has caused a discontinuity for the latest period.

Notes for: Taxes and benefits lead to income being shared more equally

1. Expenditure is calculated to be consistent with disposable income.

4 . Half of households in the UK receive more in benefits than they paid in taxes

Overall, in the financial year ending (fye) 2016 (April 2015 to March 2016), there were 50.5% of all households receiving more in benefits (including in-kind benefits such as education) than they paid in taxes (direct and indirect) (Figure 8). This equates to 13.7 million households and continues the downward trend seen since fye 2011 (53.5%) but remains above the proportions seen before the economic downturn.

Looking at this figure separately for non-retired households and retired households, the trend seen for non-retired households mirrors that for all households, except that lower percentages of non-retired households receive more in benefits than they pay in taxes, 37.2% in fye 2016.

In contrast, in fye 2016, of all retired households 88.0% received more in benefits than they paid in taxes, reflecting the classification of the State Pension as a cash benefit in this analysis. A retired household is defined as a household where the income of retired household members accounts for the majority of the total household gross income. This figure is lower than its fye 2010 peak of 92.4% and the lowest since fye 2001.

Figure 8: Percentage of households receiving more in benefits than paid in taxes, financial year ending 1997 to 2016

UK

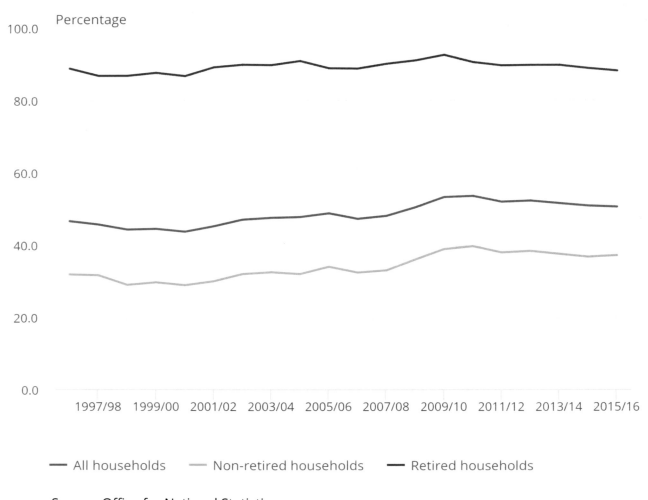

Figure 8: Percentage of households receiving more in benefits than paid in taxes, financial year ending 1997 to 2016

UK

Source: Office for National Statistics

Source: Office for National Statistics

Notes:

1. Financial year ending 1997 is the earliest year presented in this chart as changes to the underlying source data caused a break in this series at that point. Caution should therefore be taken in making comparisons with earlier years on this measure.

5 . Households with main earner between 25 and 64 paid more in taxes than they received in benefits

The effects of taxes and benefits are felt differently by households in different age groups (Figure 9). On average, in the financial year ending (fye) 2016 (April 2015 to March 2016), households with a household head aged between 25 and 64 paid more in taxes (direct and indirect) than they received in benefits (including in-kind benefits), whilst the reverse was true for those aged 65 and over, with those in their late 40s on average paying the most in taxes (£18,300). Households where the main earner was in their early 40s, whilst also paying a lot in taxes (£17,800 on average), also received the highest average amount in benefits of those below State Pension age (£15,400), due mainly to the benefit in kind received from state-provided education (£6,900).

For households with where the main earner is aged 65 and over, the State Pension and Pension Credit was the largest component of the benefits received, followed by the benefit derived from the National Health Service, which becomes increasingly important as age increases. Those households with heads under the age of 25 were the other age group who, on average, received more in benefits than they paid in taxes.

Figure 9: The effects of taxes and benefits by age of the main earner in the household, financial year ending 2016

UK

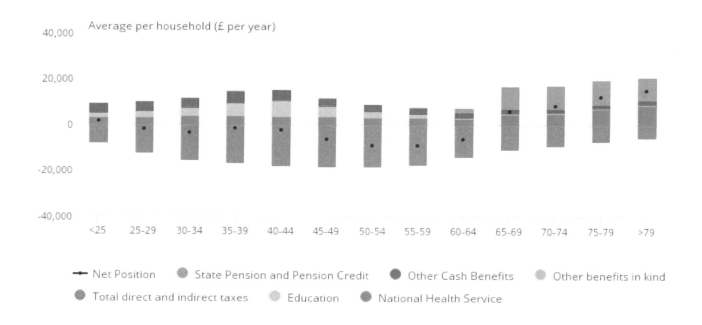

Figure 9: The effects of taxes and benefits by age of the main earner in the household, financial year ending 2016

UK

Source: Office for National Statistics

Source: Office for National Statistics

The effect of taxes and benefits on redistributing income for households in different age groups can be seen when comparing income at the different stages of redistribution for these households (Figure 10). This shows that there is much less variation across different age groups in either average disposable or final income, than there is in original income.

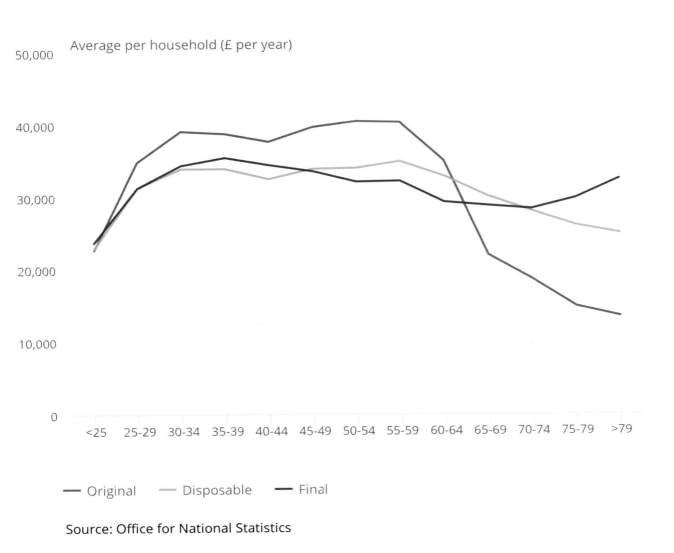

Figure 10: Household income by age of the main earner in household, financial year ending 2016

UK

Source: Office for National Statistics

Source: Office for National Statistics

In fye 2016, for households with heads aged 25 to 64, on average, their original income (before any taxes and benefits) is higher than their disposable income. However, this picture changes for those with heads over the age of 65, where average disposable income exceeds original income.

For most age groups, average final income is relatively close to disposable income. One exception is among those households with heads between the ages of 50 and 64, where average final income is lower, reflecting in part the lower in-kind education benefits received compared with younger households, due to a smaller proportion of households with school age children. The other main exception is for those households with heads aged 75 or above, for whom NHS services become increasingly valuable, increasing the average value of final income.

6 . Cash benefits have the largest effect on reducing income inequality

There are a number of different ways in which inequality of household income can be presented and summarised. Perhaps the most widely used measure internationally is the Gini coefficient. Gini coefficients can vary between 0 and 100 and the lower the value, the more equally household income is distributed.

The extent to which cash benefits, direct taxes and indirect taxes work together to affect income inequality can be seen by comparing the Gini coefficients of original, gross, disposable and post-tax incomes. Cash benefits have the largest effect on reducing income inequality, in the financial year ending (fye) 2016 (April 2015 to March 2016), reducing the Gini coefficient from 49.3% for original income to 35.0% for gross income (Figure 11). Direct taxes act to further reduce it, to 31.6%, however, indirect taxes have the opposite effect and in fye 2016 the Gini for post-tax income was 35.4%, meaning that overall, taxes have a negligible effect on income inequality.

Figure 11: Impact of cash benefits and taxes on Gini coefficient, financial year ending 2016

UK

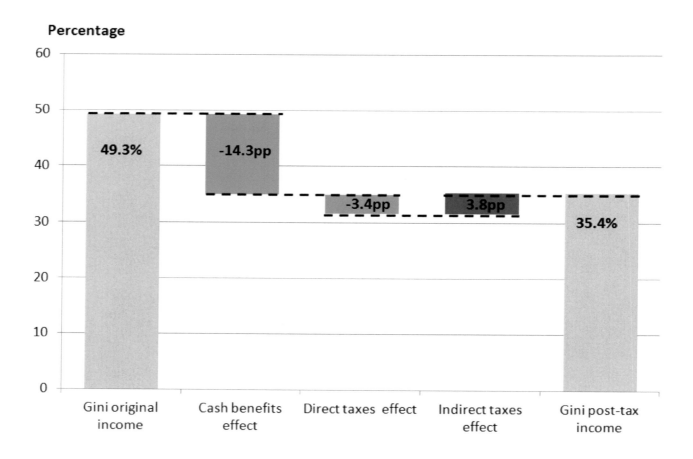

Notes:
PP=Percentage point

Analysis of Gini coefficients for all households over time (Figure 12) shows cash benefits have consistently the largest effect on reducing inequality, though there has been some variation in the size of this effect. In 1977, cash benefits reduced inequality by 13 percentage points (pp). This increased during the early 1980s and by 1984 cash benefits reduced inequality by 17pp. However, during the late 1980s, their redistributive impact weakened and by 1990 cash benefits reduced inequality by only 13pp again. More recently, there has been a slight increase in the effect of cash benefits in reducing income inequality, rising from 13.5pp in fye 2007 to 14.3 in fye 2016.

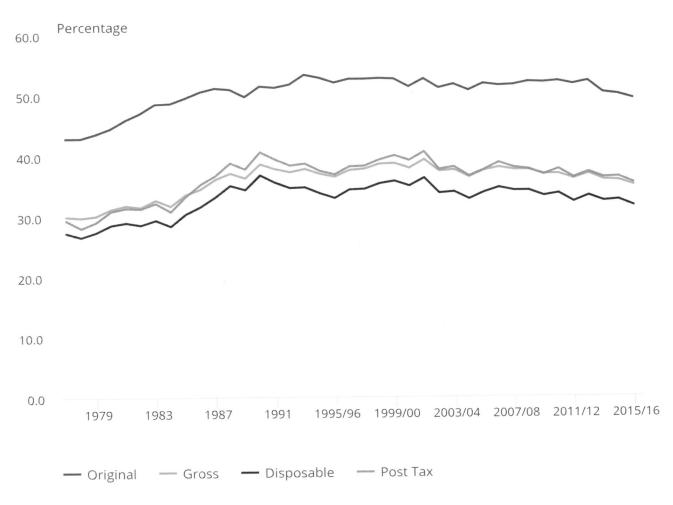

Figure 12: Gini coefficients for different income measures, 1977 to financial year ending 2016

UK

Source: Office for National Statistics

Source: Office for National Statistics

Notes:

1. Equivalised using the modified-OECD scale.

2. An improved process for calculating the Gini Coefficient has been implemented which has resulted in a change to the levels of rounding applied. Although not significant, there are minor differences to previously published Gini estimates.

7 . Housing benefit is the most progressive cash benefit, though the State Pension makes the largest contribution to the overall progressivity of cash benefits

Looking in more detail at the redistributive effect of benefits, this is dependent on two factors:

- the relative size of the benefit as a proportion of income; this can be referred to as the average benefit rate

- the progressivity of the benefit: a benefit is considered progressive when it accounts for a larger share of low-income groups' income than high-income groups – progressivity is measured through the Kakwani index (Kakwani, 1977); for benefits, a negative value indicates that the benefits are progressive and acting to reduce the level of inequality – the larger the negative value, the more progressive the benefit is

Figure 13: Progressivity and average rate of different cash benefits

UK

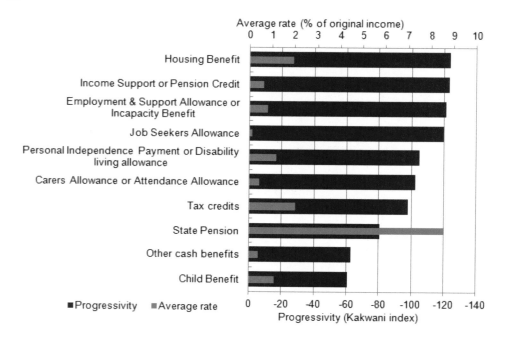

Figure 13 shows both the size and progressivity of individual cash benefits in the financial year ending (fye) 2016 (April 2015 to March 2016). This shows that whilst all the main cash benefits are progressive, the level of progressivity varies considerably. The most progressive cash benefits in fye 2016 were Pension Credit, Housing Benefit and Income Support, meaning that these were the benefits that were targeted most towards reducing inequality.

Child Benefit was the least progressive of the benefits examined, with the State Pension also less progressive than many other cash benefits.

Figure 14 shows how important individual cash benefits contribute to the overall progressivity of cash benefits and how this has changed over a 20-year period. Throughout this time, the State Pension has made the largest contribution to the overall progressivity of benefits, despite being less progressive than many of the other benefits. This is because, as shown in Figure 13, the State Pension makes up a large proportion of the total cash benefits received by households.

More detailed analysis of the impact of taxes and benefits on inequality over time using a range of measures can be found in the article The Effects of Taxes and Benefits on Income Inequality, 1977 to 2014/15 .

Figure 14: Contribution of main benefits to overall progressivity of cash benefits, financial year ending 1995 to financial year ending 2016

UK

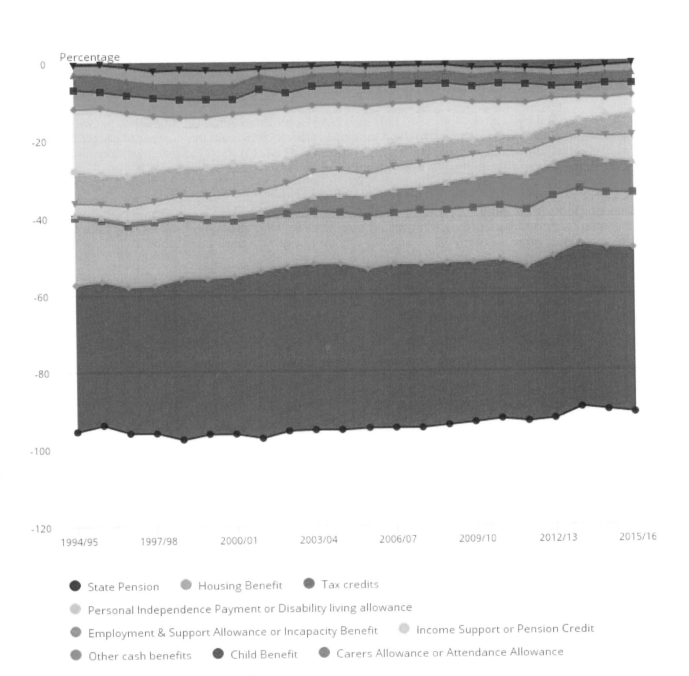

Figure 14: Contribution of main benefits to overall progressivity of cash benefits, financial year ending 1995 to financial year ending 2016

UK

Legend:
- State Pension
- Housing Benefit
- Tax credits
- Personal Independence Payment or Disability living allowance
- Employment & Support Allowance or Incapacity Benefit
- Income Support or Pension Credit
- Other cash benefits
- Child Benefit
- Carers Allowance or Attendance Allowance

Source: Office for National Statistics

Source: Office for National Statistics

197

Figure 14 highlights the effect of some of the changes to the benefits system over this period. The replacement of Family Credit with Working Families' Tax Credit in 1999, followed by the introduction of Child Tax Credit and Working Tax Credit in 2003, has lead to tax credits making an increasing contribution to the overall progressiveness of cash benefits, with tax credits making the third- largest contribution in fye 2016 (after Housing Benefit and the State Pension).

By contrast, the contribution to overall progressivity made by benefits such as Income Support, Pension Credit and Incapacity Benefit, and most recently, Employment and Support Allowance, has reduced over time. In fye 1995, these benefits together accounted for 25% of the overall progressivity of cash benefits. By fye 2016, the contribution of these benefits had reduced to 10%. This effect is the main reason why overall progressivity has generally fallen over this period, despite the increasing contribution of tax credits.

8 . Economic context

In the financial year ending (fye) 2016 (April 2015 to March 2016), outcomes in the UK labour market were likely to have directly affected household incomes. In the 3 months to March 2016, both the number of people in employment (31.6 million) and the headline employment rate (74.2%) were at their highest levels since records began. Over the same period, the unemployment rate was 5.1%, lower than a year earlier (5.6%).

Other headline indicators in the May 2016 Labour Market release suggested the labour market performed strongly in the latter months of fye 2016, which typically correlates with increasing nominal earnings growth. However, after increasing growth in early 2015, nominal regular pay growth eased and stood at 2.2% in the 3 months to March 2016.

Figure 15: Contributions to the growth of real regular pay: Consumer Price Index (CPI) inflation and the growth of average regular weekly earnings, 2008 to 2016

UK

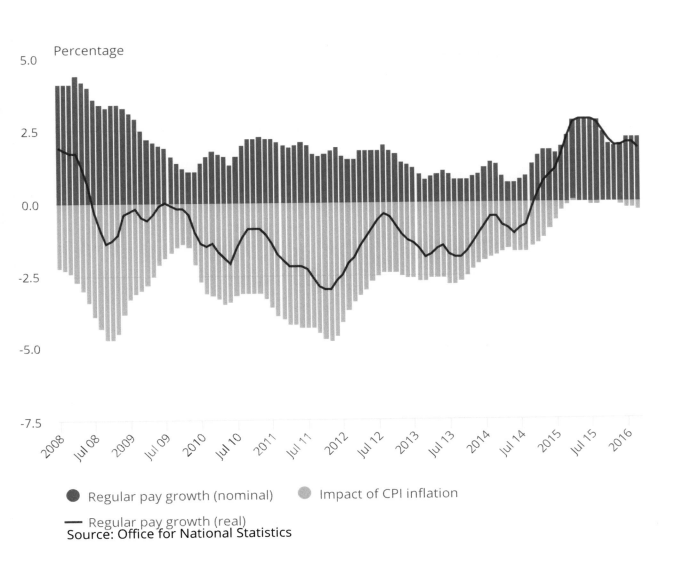

Figure 15: Contributions to the growth of real regular pay: Consumer Price Index (CPI) inflation and the growth of average regular weekly earnings, 2008 to 2016

UK

● Regular pay growth (nominal)   ● Impact of CPI inflation

— Regular pay growth (real)
Source: Office for National Statistics

Source: Office for National Statistics

Notes:

1. The data for regular pay presents the 3 months on 3 months a year ago growth rate for the month at the end of the period (the final data is for January to March 2016).

The rate of price inflation in the economy is also an important component that determines households' real income growth. There was persistent low inflation in fye 2016, driven partly by a fall in oil prices. This low inflation combined with nominal pay increases has meant that real wages continued to grow in fye 2016 as they did towards the end of the second half of the previous financial year, following several years of falling real wages after the economic downturn.

In fye 2016, real output in the UK economy increased 1.9% on the preceding 12 months, continuing a period of growth following the fye 2009 economic downturn. By the end of the period, the UK had recorded 13 quarters of consecutive economic growth. While aggregate real GDP surpassed its pre-downturn peak in Quarter 3 (July to September) 2013, GDP per head took until Quarter 4 (October to December) 2015 to overtake its pre-downturn peak.

Figure 16: Measures of economic well-being: gross domestic product per head and net national disposable Income per head, chained volume measure, Quarter 1 2005 to Quarter 1 2016

UK

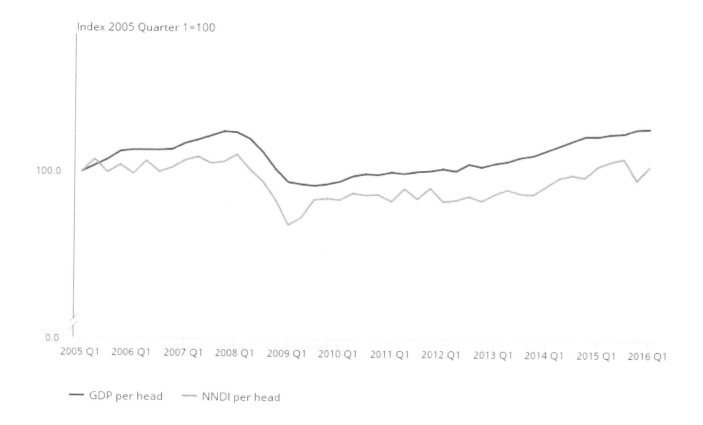

Figure 16: Measures of economic well-being: gross domestic product per head and net national disposable Income per head, chained volume measure, Quarter 1 2005 to Quarter 1 2016

UK

Source: Office for National Statistics

Source: Office for National Statistics

Figure 16 presents two alternative measures of economic well-being – gross domestic product per head and net national disposable income (NNDI) per head. NNDI per head makes two adjustments to GDP per head: firstly, subtracts the consumption of capital – the wear and tear resulting from assets being used in production – from GDP, capturing the net value of production and secondly, includes a measure of net international investment income.

Despite the indicators tracking reasonably well until 2011, NNDI per head has followed a slightly weaker growth path than GDP per head since late 2011. This continued into fye 2016. Between Quarter 1 (Jan to Mar) 2015 and Quarter 1 2016, GDP per head increased by 1.1% while NNDI per head remained unchanged.

These relatively marked differences reflect some of the more detailed developments in the UK economy. In particular, the unchanged NNDI per head over the financial year partly reflects the fall in the UK's balance on income with the rest of the world: over this period, UK earnings overseas have grown less strongly than the earnings of overseas agents in the UK. Between Quarter 1 2015 and Quarter 1 2016, the balance of earnings on foreign direct investment (FDI) (the difference between earnings from direct investment abroad and from foreign direct investment in the UK) decreased from a surplus of £2.5 billion to a deficit of £2.0 billion. This trend is largely accounted for by the fall in the relative rate of return on UK assets held overseas.

More information on the divergence of GDP per head and NNDI per head since late 2011 can be found in our Economic Well-being: Quarter 3, July to Sept 2016 bulletin.

Overall, these two measures compare relatively well with the strong growth observed in median household disposable income since fye 2014, based on the effects of taxes and benefits on household income (ETB) and nowcast estimates. More recently, growth in median household income more closely resembles GDP per head growth rather than NNDI per head growth. This possibly reflects that the fall in balance on income with the rest of the world has not impacted.

9 . What's changed in this bulletin?

From the financial year ending (fye) 2016 (April 2015 to March 2016), where income comparisons are made over time, estimates have been deflated to fye 2016 prices using the Consumer Prices Index including owner-occupiers' housing costs (CPIH) deflator. Previous publications have used the implied expenditure deflator for the household final consumption expenditure (HHFCE).

See the statement on future of consumer inflation statistics for further information.

Figure 17 shows the effect on the time series for mean equivalised disposable income between 1977 and fye 2015. The pre-downturn peak of mean household income in fye 2008 is estimated to be approximately £1,000 lower when deflated using CPIH, however, the longer-term trend since 1977 remains broadly consistent with the series deflated using HHFCE.

Figure 17: Time series of mean equivalised disposable income, 1977 to financial year ending 2015, UK (fye 2015 prices deflated by household final consumption expenditure and CPIH)

UK

Figure 17: Time series of mean equivalised disposable income, 1977 to financial year ending 2015, UK (fye 2015 prices deflated by household final consumption expenditure and CPIH)

UK

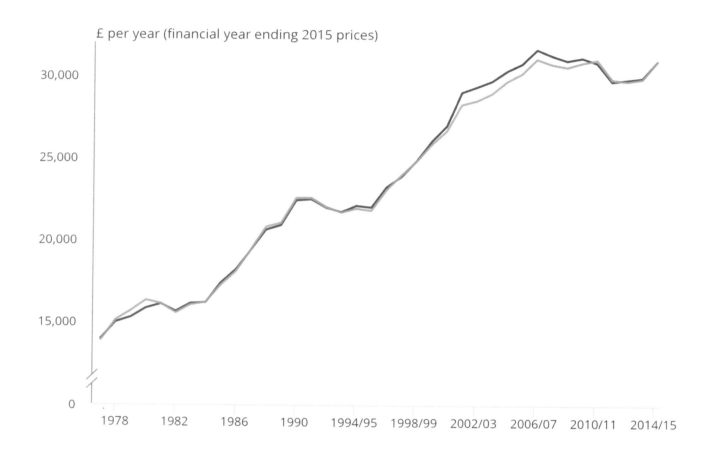

£ per year (financial year ending 2015 prices)

—— Estimates deflated by the implied expenditure deflator for household sector (HHFCE)

—— Estimates deflated by the consumer prices index including owner-occupiers' housing costs (CPI

Source: Office for National Statistics

10 . Quality and methodology

The Effects of taxes and benefits upon household income Quality and Methodology Information document contains important information on:

- the strengths and limitations of the data

- the quality of the output, including the accuracy of the data and how it compares with related data

- uses and users

- how the output was created

Analysis in this bulletin is based on our long-running effects of taxes and benefits on household income (ETB) series. The ETB series has been produced each year since the early 1960s. Historical tables, including data from 1977 onwards are also published today, along with an implied deflator for the household sector, which can be applied to adjust for the effects of inflation. Differences in the methods and concepts used mean that it is not possible to produce consistent tables for the years prior to 1977 and only relatively limited comparisons are possible for these early years. All comparisons with previous years are also affected by sampling error.

Glossary

Equivalisation: Income quintile groups are based on a ranking of households by equivalised disposable income. Equivalisation is the process of accounting for the fact that households with many members are likely to need a higher income to achieve the same standard of living as households with fewer members. Equivalisation takes into account the number of people living in the household and their ages, acknowledging that while a household with two people in it will need more money to sustain the same living standards as one with a single person, the two-person household is unlikely to need double the income.

This analysis uses the modified-OECD equivalisation scale.

Gini coefficients: The most widely used summary measure of inequality in the distribution of household income is the Gini coefficient. The lower the value of the Gini coefficient, the more equally household income is distributed. A Gini coefficient of 0 would indicate perfect equality where every member of the population has exactly the same income, while a Gini coefficient of 100 would indicate that one person would have all the income.

Income quintiles: Households are grouped into quintiles (or fifths) based on their equivalised disposable income. The richest quintile is the 20% of households with the highest equivalised disposable income. Similarly, the poorest quintile is the 20% of households with the lowest equivalised disposable income.

Household income: This analysis uses several different measures of household income. Original income (before taxes and benefits) includes income from wages and salaries, self-employment, private pensions and investments. Gross income includes all original income plus cash benefits provided by the state. Disposable income is that which is available for consumption and is equal to gross income less direct taxes.

Retired persons and households: A retired person is defined as anyone who describes themselves (in the Living Costs and Food Survey) as "retired" or anyone over minimum National Insurance pension age describing themselves as "unoccupied" or "sick or injured but not intending to seek work". A retired household is defined as one where the combined income of retired members amounts to at least half the total gross income of the household.

11 . Users and uses of these statistics

The effects of taxes and benefits on household income (ETB) statistics are of particular interest to HM Treasury (HMT), HM Revenue and Customs (HMRC) and the Department for Work and Pensions (DWP) in determining policies on taxation and benefits and in preparing budget and pre-budget reports. Analyses by HMT based on this series, as well as the underlying Living Costs and Food (LCF) dataset, are published alongside the budget and autumn statement. A dataset, based on that used to produce these statistics, is used by HMT in conjunction with the Family Resources Survey (FRS) in their Intra-Governmental Tax and Benefit Microsimulation Model (IGOTM). This is used to model possible tax and benefit changes before policy changes are decided and announced.

In addition to policy uses in government, the ETB statistics are frequently used and referenced in research work by academia, think tanks and articles in the media. These pieces often examine the effect of government policy, or are used to advance public understanding of tax and benefit matters. The data used to produce this release are made available to other researchers via the UK Data Service.

These statistics play an important role in providing an insight to the public on how material living standards and the distributional effect of government policy on taxes and benefits have changed over time for different groups of households. This new release was developed in response to strong user demand for more timely data on some of the main indicators and trends previously published in the Effects of Taxes and Benefits on Household Income statistical bulletin and associated ad hoc releases.

12 . Related statistics and analysis

A guide to official sources of income and earnings data, including the strengths and weaknesses of the different sources, is available through our website. Two other important sources of income data are the Household Disposable Income and Inequality, financial year ending 2016 release and Households Below Average Income (HBAI) release, which is produced by the Department for Work and Pensions (DWP).

Household Disposable Income and Inequality (HDII) is based on the same dataset as this release. This release provides an extension of the analysis provided in HDII, by including data on indirect taxes (such as VAT and fuel and alcohol duties) and benefits in-kind provided by the state (such as education and NHS services). All definitions and concepts are also fully consistent between the two releases.

Households Below Average Income: DWP's annual HBAI release is based on data from the Family Resources Survey (FRS) and focuses on the lower part of the income distribution. The edition of the publication for the financial year ending 2016 (April 2015 to March 2016) was released in March 2017. The methodologies and concepts used for HBAI are broadly comparable, though there are some small but important differences. For example:

- ETB includes benefits in kind provided by employers (for example, company cars) within income, but these are not included within HBAI

- HBAI includes certain benefits in kind provided by the state (such as free school meals and Healthy Start vouchers) within Before Housing Costs (BHC) income, which is otherwise equivalent to the ETB measure of disposable income; in ETB, these are included with other benefits in kind as part of final income

- HBAI makes an adjustment for "very rich" households using data from HMRC's Survey of Personal Incomes

- ETB measures inequality on a household basis, whereas HBAI measures inequality on an individual basis

Due to HBAI being based on a different survey, along with the differences described previously, HBAI and ETB estimates can differ slightly from each other. However, historical trends are broadly similar across the two sources.

This release adds to the evidence base amassed as part of the ONS Measuring National Well-being programme. The programme aims to produce accepted and trusted measures of the well-being of the nation – how the UK as a whole is doing.

Measuring National Well-being is about looking at "GDP and beyond". It includes headline indicators in areas such as health, relationships, job satisfaction, economic security, education, environmental conditions and measures of "personal well-being" (individuals' assessment of their own well-being).

Find out more on the Measuring National Well-being website pages.

Contact details for this statistical bulletin

Paola Serafino / Nathan Thomas

hie@ons.gov.uk

Telephone: +44 (0)1633 651538

Office for
National Statistics

Statistical bulletin

Social capital in the UK: May 2017

How the UK is faring in four domains of social capital: personal relationships, social support networks, civic engagement, and trust and cooperative norms.

Contact:
Katrina Morrison
QualityofLife@ons.gsi.gov.uk
+44 (0)1633 651745

Release date:
5 May 2017

Next release:
To be announced

Correction

9 May 2017

A correction has been made to the "Latest Data" of the "Percentage of people that have a spouse or partner, family member or friend to rely on..." measure in "Table 2: Indicators for social support networks". This was due to a small error when the previous 2010 to 2011 figure was stated instead of the latest 2013 to 2014 figure. You can see the original content in the superseded version. We apologise for any inconvenience.

Table of contents

1 . Main points

- The most recent data show a largely positive picture of social capital in the UK over the longer-term with over half of the indicators showing improvement over a period of 3 years; a majority of indicators showed improvement or no overall change over the shorter-term 1 year assessment.

- Most adults in the UK have at least one close friend, rising from 95% in 2011 to 2012 to 97% in 2014 to 2015. However, there has been a fall in the proportion of people saying they have someone to rely on a lot in case of a serious problem; this figure fell from 86% in 2010 to 2011 to 84% in 2013 to 2014.

- Over two-thirds of UK adults (68%) report stopping and talking to their neighbours in 2014 to 2015.

- More people are engaging in unpaid volunteering; in 2010 to 2011 the figure was 17% compared with 19% in 2014 to 2015.

2 . Things you need to know about this release

This release is part of the ONS Social Capital Project and provides an update on the 2015 publication Measuring national well-being: An analysis of social capital in the UK, which proposed 25 headline indicators of social capital selected on the basis of user consultation and feedback.

The original 25 headline indicators of social capital were proposed around a four domain framework based on earlier work by the Organisation for Economic Co-operation and Development (please see datasets for more information).

A number of these original indicators have similar counterparts included within the most recent April 2017 Measuring National Well-being (MNW) indicator set. As a result, applicable social capital headline indicators have been revised and aligned with these. This will provide a clearer picture of UK progress and implement consistent use of data sources. Two social capital headline indicators have since been removed from the original set of 25; however, two remaining headline indicators are split into two levels of measurement. This leaves 25 separate indicators for change assessment in this release. Updates since the 2015 report can be found in the datasets. Alternative sources to provide international comparability will continue to be highlighted where applicable.

We are using the latest available data, constructing time series where possible, to give an indication of change over time. This is an important part of our vision of producing timely and useful data to inform decision-making. Change is only noted as an improvement or deterioration when statistically significant using 95% confidence intervals (with the exception of Voter turnout).

3 . Introduction and background

Social capital represents the connections and collective attitudes between people that result in a well-functioning and close-knit society. We measure social capital because the connections between increasing rates of social capital and positively functioning well-being, economic growth and sustainability are extensively noted. For example, social capital is recognised as a driver for economic growth and as a facilitator for a variety of improvements for individual and wider community well-being. This makes social capital valuable not only as a snapshot of the UK's general community involvement and cohesiveness levels but also as a valuable source of information and insight for policy makers in terms of resource allocation and others looking to help strengthen and facilitate individual well-being, community well-being and societal cohesion.

We seek to monitor measures of social capital when new data become available in order to help inform policy initiatives that can improve people's lives within our communities.

4 . Assessments of change

This release includes assessments showing the direction of change for each of the indicators, whether they have improved, deteriorated or shown no overall change (see Figure 1). Comparisons have been made with the previous year's data, or the previously published figure where year-on-year data are not available, as well as an assessment of change over a 3-year period. For more information on how we assess change, please see the " Quality and methodology" section.

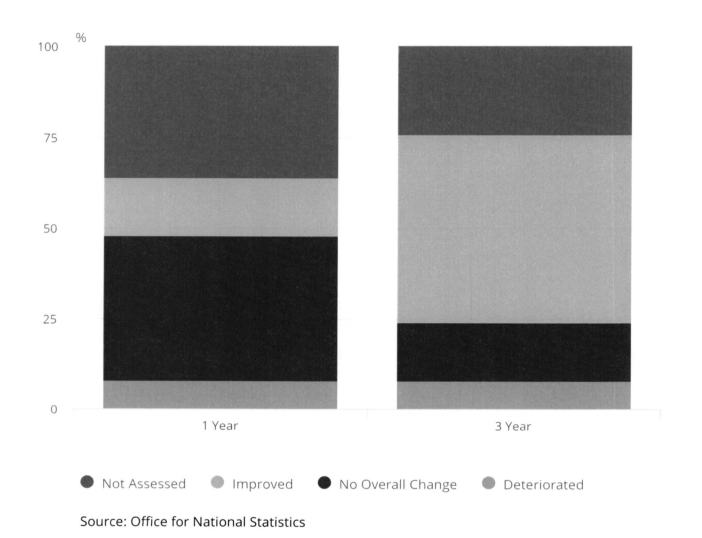

Figure 1: Assessment of change – social capital indicators

UK, May 2017

● Not Assessed　　● Improved　　● No Overall Change　　● Deteriorated

Source: Office for National Statistics

Source: Office for National Statistics

Notes:

1.Although there are 23 headline indicators of social capital, measures of reciprocal help between parents and adult children is assessed separately as giving and receiving. Feeling safe walking alone after dark is also presented for both men and women, so as a result there are 25 measures to be assessed.

1. Figures may not add to 100% due to rounding.

The most recent data show a largely positive picture of social capital in the UK over the longer-term with over half of the indicators showing improvement over a period of 3 years; a majority of indicators showed improvement or no overall change over the shorter-term 1 year assessment.

5 . Personal relationships

Table 1: Indicators for personal relationships

Measure	Geographical coverage	Current Source	Latest Year	Latest Data
Proportion of people who have at least one close friend	UK	Understanding Society: UK Household Longitudinal Study	2014 to 2015	97%
Proportion of people who meet socially with friends, relatives or work colleagues at least once a week	UK	European Social Survey	2014	61%
Feelings of loneliness often/always	England	Community Life Survey, Cabinet Office	2015 to 2016	4%
Proportion of people who have used the internet for social networking in the last 3 months	UK	Internet access - Opinions and Lifestyle Survey (OPN), Office for National Statistics	2016	63%
Proportion of people who regularly stop and talk with people in the neighbourhood	UK	Understanding Society: UK Household Longitudinal Study	2014 to 2015	68%

Source: Office for National Statistics

Our personal relationships can be a source of enjoyment and happiness in our lives and provide a sense of comfort and stability. Research shows that healthy personal relationships can be a protective factor against stress and other health issues (Kreitzer, 2016).

The percentage of people saying they feel lonely often or always has not changed significantly between 2014 to 2015 and 2015 to 2016, with the figure staying around 4% on average. However, the proportion of people meeting socially with friends, relatives or work colleagues at least once a week has decreased from 69% to 61% between 2010 and 2014 (see Figure 2).

Figure 2: Proportion of people who meet socially with friends, relatives or work colleagues at least once a week

UK, 2002 to 2014

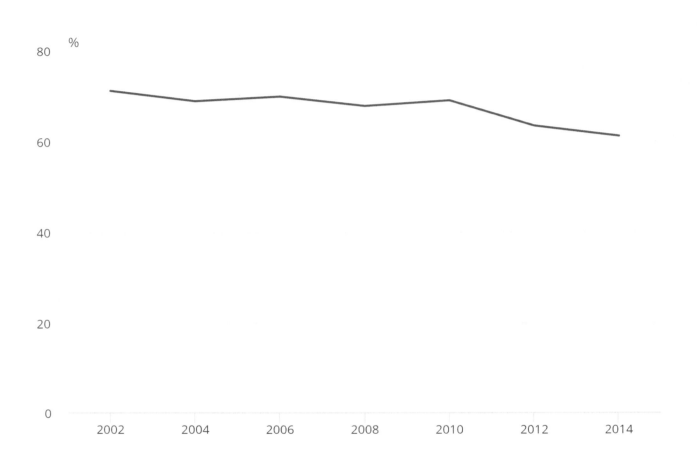

Figure 2: Proportion of people who meet socially with friends, relatives or work colleagues at least once a week

UK, 2002 to 2014

Source: European Social Survey

Source: European Social Survey

Although the percentage of people meeting socially has dropped, there has been growth in the percentage of people reporting having at least one close friend and this figure improved between 2011 to 2012 and 2014 to 2015, rising from 95% to 97%. This disparity could be due to the rise in the use of the internet for social networking over the past 3 years. In 2016, there were 63% of us who reported using the internet for this purpose in the last 3 months compared with 53% in 2013. Research into the relationship between social networking and social capital is still in its early stages but early research suggests that social networking may help bolster social capital in the form of helping people strengthen relationships and aiding integration within communities (Utz and Muscanell, 2015). We have therefore interpreted the increase in social networking as an improvement. The proportion of people who regularly stop and talk to their neighbours has also improved over a 3-year period, rising from 66% in 2011 to 2012 to 68% in 2014 to 2015.

6 . Social support networks

Table 2: Indicators for social support networks

Measure	Geographical coverage	Current Source	Latest Year	Latest Data
Percentage of people that have a spouse or partner, family member or friend to rely on a lot if they have a serious problem	UK	Understanding Society: UK Household Longitudinal Study	2013 to 2014	84%
Proportion of people who give special help to at least one sick, disabled or elderly person living or not living with them	UK	Understanding Society: UK Household Longitudinal Study	2014 to 2015	20%
Proportion of parents who regularly receive or give practical or financial help from/to a child aged 16 or over not living with them	UK	Understanding Society: UK Household Longitudinal Study	2013 to 2014	Receive: 38% _____ Give: 58%
Proportion of people who borrow things and exchange favours with their neighbours	UK	Understanding Society: UK Household Longitudinal Study	2014 to 2015	42%

Source: Office for National Statistics

Our personal relationships form the foundations of our social support networks and are important for individuals as well as for community well-being. Social support can be particularly important in helping people and communities recover from periods of difficulty or times where we need reassurance, practical or financial help. We monitor a variety of measures focusing on how connected we are to others around us and the extent to which we can rely on them for support or provide support to others.

Having someone to rely on in times of adversity can help us cope better and be resilient in the knowledge that we have someone to help. However, between 2010 to 2011 and 2013 to 2014, there has been a deterioration in the proportion of people saying that they had a spouse, family member or friend to rely on "a lot" in case of a serious problem. This fell from 86% in 2010 to 2011 to 84% in 2013 to 2014. Furthermore, reciprocal support between parents and their adult children has decreased. The proportion of parents who regularly receive practical or financial help from a child aged 16 or over not living with them decreased from 42% in 2011 to 2012 to 38% in 2013 to 2014. Furthermore, the proportion of parents saying that they were giving help has also decreased between 2011 to 2012 and 2013 to 2014 (63% and 58% respectively). We have considered these measures from the perspective of the receivers of help and as a result assess this as deterioration.

Despite this, the proportion of people who give special help to at least one sick, disabled or elderly person living or not living with them has risen from 19% to 20% between 2013 to 2014 and 2014 to 2015 (see Figure 3). For the purpose of evaluation, we have assessed this change as an improvement from the perspective of those who are receiving the care or help. However, this measure doesn't give an indication of the frequency or nature of the help and the impact this caring has on the caregiver may be something that needs to be considered in the future. A further improvement is noted in that more of us borrowed or exchanged things with our neighbours in 2014 to 2015 where the figure is reported at 42% compared with 41% in 2011 to 2012.

Figure 3: Proportion of people who give special help to at least one sick, disabled or elderly person living or not living with them

UK, between 2009 to 2010 and 2014 to 2015

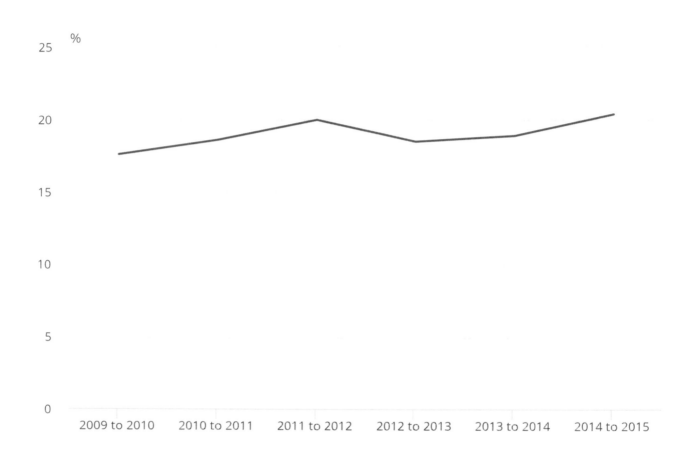

Figure 3: Proportion of people who give special help to at least one sick, disabled or elderly person living or not living with them

UK, between 2009 to 2010 and 2014 to 2015

Source: Understanding Society: UK Household Longitudinal Study

Source: Understanding Society: UK Household Longitudinal Study

7 . Civic engagement

Table 3: Indicators for civic engagement

Measure	Geographical coverage	Current Source	Latest Year	Latest Data
Percentage who volunteered more than once in the last 12 months	UK	Understanding Society: UK Household Longitudinal Study	2014 to 2015	19%
Proportion of people who are members of organisations, whether political, voluntary, professional or recreational	UK	Understanding Society: UK Household Longitudinal Study	2014 to 2015	53%
Proportion of people who have been involved in at least one social action project in their local area in the previous 12 months	England	Community Life Survey, Cabinet Office	2015 to 2016	18%
Proportion of people who definitely agree or tend to agree that they can influence decisions affecting their local area	England	Community Life Survey, Cabinet Office	2015 to 2016	36%
Voter turnout in UK General Elections	UK	Electoral Commission	2015	66%
Proportion of people who have been involved in at least one political action in the previous 12 months	UK	Eurofound, European Quality of Life Survey	2011 to 2012	34%
Proportion of people who are very or quite interested in politics	UK	European Social Survey	2014	56%

Source: Office for National Statistics

Civic engagement is about making a positive contribution to the collective life of a community or society overall. For example, this could involve volunteering for a local or national cause, taking action on a social issue or belonging to an organisation outside of work like a sports club or neighbourhood watch. Strong civic engagement networks may help to foster greater trust within communities and as a result more people willing to work together to help the community as a whole.

The proportion of people who participated in unpaid voluntary work has increased between 2010 to 2011 and 2014 to 2015. In 2010 to 2011, there were 17% of people who had volunteered several times a year or more, whereas in 2014 to 2015, this figure had risen to 19% (see Figure 4).

Figure 4: Percentage who volunteered more than once in the last 12 months

UK, between 2010 to 2011 and 2014 to 2015

Source: Understanding Society: UK Household Longitudinal Study

Source: Understanding Society: UK Household Longitudinal Study

The percentage of people who took part in a social action between 2014 to 2015 and 2015 to 2016 remained unchanged. Similarly, the percentage of people in the UK who reported membership of organisations whether political, voluntary, professional or recreational also remained unchanged between 2011 to 2012 and 2014 to 2015 (52% and 53% respectively). Being a member of an organisation can create bonds between people who have common interests and who come from different backgrounds, therefore, being a member of a political, voluntary, professional or recreational organisation alongside others could contribute to improved social integration within communities.

While the percentages of people in the UK taking part in these social activities showed no overall change, the percentage of people who were engaged with political actions has increased from 17% in 2006 to 2007 to 34% in 2011 to 2012.

Free and fair elections give people a chance to make decisions on how their country is run. Voter turnout in UK general elections shows an increase from 65.1% in 2010 to 66.2% in 2015. The percentage of people who say they are interested in politics also rose from 48% in 2012 to 56% in 2014.

8 . Trust and cooperative norms

Table 4: Indicators for trust and cooperative norms

Measure	Geographical coverage	Current Source	Latest Year	Latest Data
Percentage of those who have trust in national Government	UK	Eurobarometer	Autumn 2016	35%
Proportion of people who would say that most people can be trusted	UK	European Social Survey	2014	35%
Proportion of people who would say that most people in their neighbourhood can be trusted	UK	Understanding Society: UK Household Longitudinal Study	2014 to 2015	70%
Proportion of people who definitely agree or tend to agree that their local area is a place where people from different backgrounds get on well together	England	Community Life Survey, Cabinet Office	2015 to 2016	89%
Felt fairly/very safe walking alone after dark (men/women)	England and Wales	The Crime Survey for England and Wales (CSEW), Office for National Statistics	2015 to 2016	M: 88% / F: 62%
Proportion of people who agree or strongly agree that people around where they live are willing to help their neighbours	UK	Understanding Society: UK Household Longitudinal Study	2014 to 2015	74%
Proportion of people who agreed or strongly agreed that they feel they belong to their neighbourhood	UK	Understanding Society: UK Household Longitudinal Study	2014 to 2015	69%

Source: Office for National Statistics

Trust provides glue that holds society together; it enables relationships to flourish and people to feel safe in their neighbourhoods. Less trust within a community can mean less sense of community solidarity and cohesion.

To assess generalised trust, the European Social Survey asks, "Generally speaking would you say that most people can be trusted, or that you can't be too careful in dealing with people?" Respondents are then asked to score their ratings on a scale, from 0 to 10, where 0 means you can't be too careful and 10 means that most people can be trusted. In 2010, there were 35% of people who rated their general trust as high (7 to 10) and this remained unchanged in 2014. Another source assessing trust in national government however, over a 3-year period, noted the proportion of people who said they "tend to trust" the national government rose from 24% in the autumn (September to November) of 2013 to 35% in the autumn of 2016 (see Figure 5).

Figure 5: Percentage of those who have trust in national government

UK, between Sept to Nov 2004 and Sept to Nov 2016

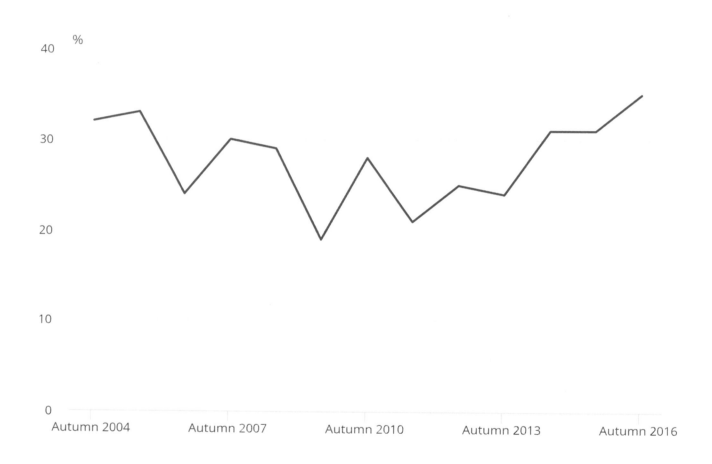

Figure 5: Percentage of those who have trust in national government

UK, between Sept to Nov 2004 and Sept to Nov 2016

Source: Eurofound: European Quality of Life Survey

Source: Eurofound: European Quality of Life Survey

Further improvements include the proportion of people who agree or strongly agree that they feel they belong to their neighbourhood rose from 63% in 2011 to 2012 to 69% in 2014 to 2015. In addition to this, the proportion of women who felt "fairly" or "very" safe walking alone after dark rose from 57% in 2012 to 2013 to 62% in 2015 to 2016.

9 . Related links

Measuring National Well-being: Life in the UK, Apr 2017

Understanding Society

Community Life Survey

European Social Survey

Eurofound: European Quality of Life Survey

The Electoral Commission

Crime Survey for England and Wales

Internet access: households and individuals

10 . Harmonisation

Unlike the 23 social capital headline indicators, five domains are currently referenced as a framework for the ONS harmonised recommended social capital question set, which was last revised in 2003 (civic participation, social participation, social networks and social support, reciprocity and trust, views about the local area).

This is the set of recommended questions we put forward for use on surveys that seek to measure social capital. The aim of the harmonisation project is to make it easier for users to draw better comparisons between data sources.

We plan to review the use of the 2003 harmonised question set in current surveys and assess which questions are still in use in present-day surveys. We will seek further user feedback and discussion around the current uses or proposed uses of social capital indicators to ensure the harmonised questions are relevant to their users.

Please contact nationalwell-being@ons.gsi.gov.uk for more information or if you wish to contribute to this project.

11 . Quality and methodology

The ONS Social Capital Project set out to establish measures that would help people to understand social capital and also help monitor it as part of the Measuring National Well-being (MNW) Programme. This report includes assessments showing the direction of change for each of the social capital indicators.

Broadly speaking, indicators have only been assessed as having improved or deteriorated if the difference between the comparison periods is statistically significant using 95% confidence intervals. If a difference is said to be statistically significant, it is unlikely that it could have occurred by chance.

Confidence intervals give a measure of the statistical precision of an estimate and show the range of uncertainty around the estimate. As a general rule, if the confidence intervals around the estimate overlap with the intervals around another estimate, there is no statistically significant difference between the estimates.

Voter turnout has been assessed using the actual increase or decrease as this is not an estimation. Other indicators have not been assessed because there are not enough data points to provide a comparison.

Contact details for this statistical bulletin

Katrina Morrison

QualityOfLife@ons.gsi.gov.uk

Telephone: +44 (0)1633 651745